Science Education Unlimited

Tanja Tajmel, Klaus Starl (Eds.)

Science Education Unlimited

Approaches to Equal Opportunities in Learning Science

Waxmann 2009
Münster / New York / München / Berlin

Bibliographic information published by die Deutsche Nationalbibliothek
Die Deutsche Nationalbibliothek lists this publication in the Deutsche Nationalbibliografie; detailed bibliographic data are available in the internet at http://dnb.d-nb.de.

ISBN 978-3-8309-1889-9

www.waxmann.com
info@waxmann.com

Cover Design: Tanja Tajmel und Anne Wegerich, Berlin
Cover Picture: Tanja Tajmel, March 2006, Club Lise at Humboldt-Universität zu Berlin
Setting: Simone Philipp, Graz

Print: Hubert und Co., Göttingen
Printed on age-resistant paper, acid-free as per ISO 9706

Table of Contents

Foreword
by Svein Sjøberg

This book definitely deserves its title! It was written by a team of scholars from different cultures and countries. They represent a wide variety of academic disciplines and in this book they consider a set of problems and challenges that are broad, nearly unlimited, in scope. Such cooperation is in itself an accomplishment, indeed too rare in academic and public life, which is often characterized by narrow specialization and with actors who are not able to communicate across invisible borders. But real challenges in our complicated world do not often follow academic, let alone national, borders. Capital, products and ideas travel without borders these days, and so do people – often simply labeled as "labor force."

People migrate to other countries, a process driven by a number of reasons and concerns. Some people travel because they seek new challenges and want to experience other, possibly exciting new environments, often also because they have found a life partner in another country. For others, the reasons are less romantic, they travel out of necessity. They search for better living conditions, a better labor market or higher salaries. For others, the reasons are not at all desirable; their relocation is simply driven by the sheer need to survive; they travel as political, religious or cultural refugees to places they hope may offer them a safer and more secure life.

The present world, in private life as well as on the labor market, is to a large extent defined by science and technology (S&T). Scientific knowledge, as well as practical technological skills are in many ways the keys that may open doors to a better life in modern societies. Conversely, the lack of such knowledge and skills provide barriers and hindrances in personal life as well as on the labor market. Hence, equal access to S&T, regardless of gender, ethnicity, language and culture are of paramount importance to personal progress, as well as to integration and participation in another country or culture. Variations on these themes are the key concerns of the authors of this important book.

Science is manifold, and science as part of education may be justified in many different ways. Science is not just instrumental to achieving personal, economical and practical goals; science is also part of culture. The world-view of modern societies is in many ways a science-based world-view. The debate over the universality of science is a hot topic in the philosophy as well as in the sociology of science. Many scholars argue that scientific knowledge is colored by the culture in which it has been developed or constructed. They provide many examples of how scientific concepts and ideas carry with them not only the language and metaphors of the culture where they were developed, but also deeply embedded cultural values and priorities. In a moderate version, it is easy to embrace the idea that scientific knowledge (and, of course, its applications!) is a cultural product, colored by the dominant ideas in the societies where it was developed. But in its extreme form, a constructivist view on the nature of science implies that the ideas in science merely reflect the prevailing power structure in the culture of its origin. Labels like "Western science" and "male science" are used by some critics. As a contrast, these critics often embrace "alternative" sciences, be they feminist science or the many forms of ethno-sciences (like "African science" or "Hindu science") that are claimed to exist in different cultures.

Such an extreme view is, however, rejected by most scholars, and many also argue that embracing this view is a recipe for leaving behind the societies and cultures where scientific culture is still not part of an everyday culture. The present book seems to support this view; the authors seem to share a view that science has contents, possibilities and values that transcend borders, and which are, indeed "unlimited," and I certainly share this view. Based on such a common platform, they explore the challenges that "outsiders" – migrants or minorities – face when meeting a society and a labor market that is based on scientific literacy in a broad meaning.

The underlying tone of the contributions is based on a shared view that not only is the right to education a basic human right, but that the same can be said about science education. There are several constraints that hinder the right to education, and these are well-addressed in a lot of literature. The virtue of this particular book is that it focuses on the particular challenges that are unique to education in the sciences. The authors come from many countries which are involved in a common project. Special focuses in the book are the challenges related to migration between countries with different languages, and, at least in part, different cultures. These challenges are addressed by experts from two "receiving" countries (Germany and Austria) and from two countries of "origin" of migrants (Turkey and Bosnia-Herzegovina).

This migration raises a series of challenges, some of which are particular to science, i.e. related to the teaching and learning of science in a second language. The problems related to science and gender are issues in most countries, although there are interesting differences between how large the problem is in different countries. It is also interesting to note that the gender issue is officially considered or perceived to be an issue in some countries, while it is more or less neglected, ignored or explained as "natural" in some other countries. In particular, the low participation of women in the "hard" sciences, like physics, is well-addressed in this book.

I am fascinated by the common adherence to basic human values and democracy that seem to underpin the writings of the authors of the book. It is most revealing to see how they, from widely different backgrounds, manage to address common important issues. These are challenges that face Europe as a whole, as well as each country in particular. I hope this book will reach its intended audience, in particular educators, policy-makers and politicians.

Oslo, July 21, 2008
Svein Sjøberg

An Introduction to Science Education Unlimited

Tanja Tajmel and Klaus Starl

As the title suggests this book is a call for unlimited science education. But why this call? Is science education limited? And if so, why and how, by whom and for whom and what exactly is it limited? And finally, if these questions can be answered, what can be done about it? *Science Education Unlimited* aims at both answering these questions, as well as making very concrete proposals for the realization of an unlimited science education.

1 The Challenge: Equal Opportunities in Science within a Diverse Society

Since World War II Europe has become an immigration continent, which is quite a new experience in the continent's history. Displaced persons, refugees, post-colonial movements marked the beginning. Migrant workers in large numbers were hired to cover the enormous need for a labor force in times of accelerating economic growth. Waves of refugees due to several conflicts all over the world, technological progress in transportation and economic globalization were attracted by the stable and wealthy post-war democracies of Western Europe. The fall of the "iron curtain" made it possible to move within the whole continent and the European Union's constant efforts for a free movement of persons together with the Union's enlargement promoted migration within the European states. The wars on the Balkans and family reunification for members of migrant workers' families caused another wave of migration in the 1990s. Although different countries show different patterns of immigration, both in motivations of people to immigrate and countries of origin, immigration had one common impact on the host countries, namely making their populations culturally, ethnically, as well as linguistically more diverse than ever before. This diversity is the paramount challenge for today's Europe, its citizens and its politicians.

Europe needs to learn – the sooner the better – to cope with this diversity and become an inclusive and open society. This requires a lot. But one major issue is undisputed: the field of education. And consequently, when it comes to education we find ourselves in the middle of a human rights topic. Those who work in the field of human rights acknowledge education as a key for the individual to find a recognized position in society. However, no matter whether intended or as a consequence, European societies functioned in an exclusionary way towards most immigrant communities, as well as towards minorities in general. This resulted in remarkable deficiencies in the education sector. Europe's societies changed profoundly, but most of the educational systems did not respond to the challenge for too a long period. Indeed, they have started only recently and they give a helpless impression too often. Direct and indirect discrimination based on gender, ethnicity, language, legal status and other factors led to underperformance, low achievement, to unequal opportunities in general, and in science education and careers in particular. Educational research revealed these shortcomings. It was the merit of the European Union to call for action and to underline the economic damage of societal exclusiveness, particularly when also demonstrating the detrimental effect on the entire community.

2 New Grounds: The Response

When the editors started to work on the topic in 2004 they were convinced that the problems can only be tackled by a multidisciplinary approach. Neither science and science didactics nor the humanities alone will find appropriate solutions, but perhaps a joint effort could. *Science Education Unlimited* puts the focus on equal opportunities in science learning and addresses the fuzzy boundaries of gender and migrant background, as well as their intersectional appearances. "Unlimited" shall be understood in many ways and at many levels: no limits in substance, no social limits and no limits in achievement, no limited careers, no gender limits and no ethnic limits, no borders and no boundaries, no vertical and no horizontal limits, but limits should be removed.

For this reason some new ground was broken. Firstly, the deficit-oriented approach was given up in order to lift up barriers and to promote existing, but wasted competencies. Secondly, broad cooperation of experts from different fields – educational sciences, law, physics, sociology, economics, linguistics, political science – was established in order to grasp the topic from all necessary points of view. Thirdly, the cooperation included experts from countries of origin (Turkey, Bosnia and Herzegovina) and countries of residence of migrants, as well as experts from different residence-countries with similar immigration patterns (Germany, Austria). Fourthly, cooperation of scientists, decision-makers and practitioners (teachers) was maintained. Fifthly, an effort was made to involve continuous mentoring. There was cooperation between high-school and university students, between students and teachers, Ph.D.-students and well-known scientists and professors, all in order to reflect the assumption that role models are of utmost importance for personal and professional development. This manifold diversity proved to be very successful and productive – the very rich results of new findings, new models and approaches, new methods, all developed for theoretical research and practical use give impressive proof that diversity pays.

Science Education Unlimited tries to cover the most relevant approaches to guarantee fair access to science education and science careers. As a precondition and a starting point we look for a strong normative basis within the human rights system in the contributions of Starl, Gilardi, Bauer and Kumar. Starl derives a human right to science education from international human rights law. Closely related to this is the discussion of barriers in the access to education, the question of fulfillment of the right to education in regard to vulnerability to discrimination. While Gilardi, Bauer, Kumar and Starl follow an individual rights-based approach, Herzog-Punzenberger and Erden discuss the societal boundary-drawing mechanisms in their contributions. Bauer and Starl examine EU strategies to overcome the crucial shortcomings and conclude that, although engaged, the programs are "economized" but not sufficiently equipped with financial resources to be successful.

Gender, migrant background and intersectionality is of course the mainstreaming topic of *Science Education Unlimited*, explicitly reflected by Baer, Tajmel, Starl, Neuhäuser-Metternich and Krummacher, Herzog-Punzenberger as well as Erden. The reasons for the manifold difficulties for women in science careers, as well as suggestions and recommendations for success are analyzed by Tajmel, Baer, Neuhäuser-Metternich and Krummacher. Baer, Neuhäuser-Metternich and Krummacher focus particularly on gender biases and call for excellence through diversity.

Tajmel, Starl and Schön build the bridge from challenges to responses with their discussion of the PROMISE-project, which was the initial step of the work we introduce with *Science Education Unlimited.*

Science education in diversity classrooms is discussed by Tajmel, Gogolin, Fer, Rösch, as well as by Wodzinski and Wodzinski. Gogolin, Rösch and Tajmel focus on language in science education. Rösch and Tajmel give very concrete advice and practical examples for practitioners in their contributions. Fer argues for social constructivist curricula in order to promote individual competencies best and gives ten recommendations for their implementation. Wodzinski and Wodzinski follow a similar track when they state that differentiation in teaching is most effective in respect to learning achievement. They give concrete instructions for various situations to promote both very gifted students, as well as students with learning difficulties.

So, starting from human rights and societal considerations, continuing with educational recommendations, *Science Education Unlimited* finally comes to teaching materials to implement science education promoting equal opportunities in the last chapter, as well as on the attached CD-ROM. The following table gives an overview of topics covered and issues addressed:

	TOPICS					INSTITUTIONS		
	Human Rights	**Migration**	**Natural Sciences**	**Gender**	**Language**	**School- Classroom**	**University**	**Educational Politics**
1. The Basis – Human Rights Aspects of Education	**X**	**X**		**X**				**X**
The Human Rights Approach to Science Education (Starl)	X	X		X				X
Special Protection for Migrants in Education? (Gilardi, Bauer, Kumar, Starl)	X	X		X				
Learning while Transgressing Boundaries – Understanding Societal Processes Impacting Students with a Migration Background (Herzog-Punzenberger)	X	X		X				X
2. The Challenge – Unlimited Access to Scientific Careers	**X**	**X**	**X**	**X**	**X**	**X**	**X**	**X**
Detect the Barriers and Leave Them Behind – Science Education in Culturally and Linguistically Diverse Classrooms (Tajmel, Starl, Schön)	X		X	X	X	X		
The Claim and the Reality of the "Knowledge Society" (Starl, Bauer)								X
"Bildungssprache" – The Importance of Teaching Language in Every School Subject (Gogolin)		X			X	X		X
Equal Opportunities and Gender in Research: Germany's Science Needs a Promotion of Quality (Baer)				X			X	X
What About the Gender Gap? The Aspirations of Female High School Students to Study Physics (Tajmel, Hadžibegović)		X	X	X		X	X	
Education in Turkey: In View of Children's Right to Education and Equal Opportunity in Education (Erden)	X					X		X
3. The Response – Science Education in Diversity Classroom		**X**	**X**	**X**	**X**	**X**	**X**	**X**
Differences Between Students – Differences in Instruction? How to Make Physics Instruction Effective for All Students (Wodzinski, Wodzinski)			X			X		
German as a Second Language – Linguistic and Didactic Foundations (Rösch)			X		X	X		
Ada Lovelace Mentoring – Engaging Girls and Women with Science and Technology (Neuhäuser-Metternich, Krummacher)			X	X		X	X	
Social Constructivism and Social Constructivist Curricula in Turkey to Meet the Needs of Young People Learning Science (Fer)						X		X
Does Migration Background Matter? Preparing Teachers for Cultural and Linguistic Diversity in the Science Classroom (Tajmel)		X	X		X	X		
4. The Outlook – Conclusion and Recommendations	**X**	**X**	**X**	**X**	**X**	**X**	**X**	**X**
5. The Practice – Teaching and Teacher Training Material on CD-ROM			**X**	**X**	**X**	**X**		

The CD-ROM contains teaching units and worksheets for science lessons in linguistically and culturally diverse science classes, videos for the purpose of teacher training and examples of the promotion of female role models in the natural sciences.

3 Acknowledgements

Certainly, many helpful hands are needed to bring a project like *Science Education Unlimited* to a successful end. Therefore we would like to express our thanks to all those who supported us in any way. First of all we would like to thank the authors for their excellent contributions and for the fruitful discussions we have had.

For the financial help to realize this book we are most grateful to the European Commission, DG Research and to the German Arbeitgeberverband Gesamtmetall, Nachwuchssicherung / THINK ING., particularly to Wolfgang Gollub who not only supported the printing, but also made available his huge network of contacts, facilitated mentoring activities and helped with sponsoring travel costs for necessary meetings.

Science Education Unlimited deals with the difficulties of learning and working in a language different from one's own mother-tongue. Most of us are not native English speakers. Even though more or less experienced, it is always difficult to express complex thoughts in a sound academic language and so we were dependant on the great job Stephanie Gilardi, Sara Moore and Ben Auger did in proof-reading, correcting, and commenting with patiently noted lines like "what do you want to say with this…," and reformulating our sometimes awkward texts. Simone Phillip at the ETC office and Melanie Völker at the Waxmann Verlag acted as patiently as the lecturers when bringing the layout to perfection. Anne Wegerich did the programming of the CD-ROM user interface. Our sincere thanks to all of them!

Finally, we would like to dedicate this work to Katerina Tomaševski who was the first UN Special Rapporteur on Education, a distinguished scientist, an engaged lawyer and a brave fighter for human rights and against injustice whose strongest arm was a fierce argument, and, who unfortunately died much too young in 2006.

We hope that the readers may enjoy what we present in the following.

Tanja Tajmel,
Klaus Starl,
September 2008

1. The Basis – Human Rights Aspects of Education

The Human Rights Approach to Science Education

Klaus Starl

The substance of the right to education aims firstly at the development of the human personality, at the consciousness of human dignity and at the fostering of respect for human rights. Secondly, it aims at enabling individuals to play an active and useful role in society; there must be no discrimination on any ground.

Austria, Bosnia & Herzegovina, Germany and Turkey are eager to provide education for all, free of charge, fully available and highly accessible; however, upon closer examination of the countries' situations and recognition of recent criticism by experts and international monitoring bodies, we find that structural racism, sexism and class prejudices reveal several weaknesses and shortcomings concerning the *access to*, the *availability of*, the *adaptability of* and, last but not least, the *acceptability of education.*

This introductory chapter aims at presenting the meaning and requirements of the right to education without discrimination in general (sections 1-3). With regard to the four considered countries, the major deficiencies will be discussed (section 4) to identify barriers in the access to education (section 5). The chapter concludes with the statement that the *right to* ***science*** *education* is derived from international human rights law.

1 The Right to Education

Human rights are rights of self-determination under the terms of equality of rights for all. Human dignity, in the framework of human rights, is an end in itself. As rights of equal freedom, human rights are the opposite of privileges. Human rights are not contingent on specific characteristics or qualifications. One is equally entitled to all the same human rights on the sole basis of being human. This is what is meant by the universality of human rights, which implicitly and logically excludes any form of discrimination. Individuals are bearers of human rights, which are obligations of the state(s). States have a threefold obligation for every human right: the obligation to respect, to protect and to fulfill the right of everyone without any distinction. The fulfillment obligation in turn has two important components: firstly, to promote and facilitate the *de facto* enjoyment of human rights and secondly, to provide the means and opportunities to enjoy those rights.

Education is both a human right in itself and an indispensable means of realizing other human rights. It is enshrined in Art. 26 of the Universal Declaration of

Human Rights (UDHR 1948). In the following, we will concentrate on Art. 13 of the International Covenant on Economic, Social and Cultural Rights (ICESCR 1966), as this is the most extensive provision on education in all human rights texts, is legally binding and is ratified by most states, particularly by those considered in our context. The right to education has a solid basis in international and regional human rights law in general.[1]

The Committee on Economic, Social and Cultural Rights (CESCR) introduces its 13th General Comment on the right to education as stipulated in Art. 13 ICESCR 1966 by explaining the essence and underlining the importance of the right to education "[*A*]*s an empowerment right, education is the primary vehicle by which economically and socially marginalized adults and children can lift themselves out of poverty and obtain the means to participate fully in their communities.*" The right to education facilitates the relationship between the individual and the society in which he or she lives. Education should empower the individual to participate fully in his or her society. "*Increasingly, education is recognized as one of the best financial investments States can make.*" The CESCR underlines that the right to education is economically rational for the society, the state and its economy and government. And further, that "*... the importance of education is not just practical: a well-educated, enlightened and active mind, able to wander freely and widely, is one of the joys and rewards of human existence.*" (CESCR 1999, para 1). Thus education is acknowledged as an end in itself.

The rationale behind the right to education can be seen from the standpoint of the individual, of the society and of the normative system. Education aims at the development of the personality and enables a person to participate fully in the society to her or his benefit and is a prerequisite to "*liv[ing] the life one values*" and a "*means to achiev[ing] well-being*" (Sen 1999). Every society or state needs an educated labor force and an informed electorate. Without education, a society cannot ensure its future. Furthermore, education functions as a multiplier by enhancing all

1 Besides the Universal Declaration of Human Rights 1948 (Art. 26), the Convention against Discrimination in Education (CADE 1960) and the ICESCR 1966 (Art. 13), it is laid down in Art. 7 of the Convention on the Elimination of all Forms of Racial Discrimination (CERD 1965), Art. 10 of the Convention on the Elimination of all Forms of Discrimination against Women (CEDAW 1979), Art. 28 of the Convention on the Rights of the Child (CRC 1989), a wide range of other international declarations and resolutions (particularly the UNESCO Convention on Technical and Vocational Education 1989 and the UNESCO Recommendation concerning the Status of Teachers 1966) as well as in the additional protocol (Art. 2) to the European Convention for the Protection of Human Rights and Fundamental Freedoms (ECHR 1950, Protocol 1 of 1952). A dense introductory overview is given by Benedek (Benedek 2006, 212-228).

rights and freedoms while jeopardizing them when it is violated (Tomaševski 2006, 7).

The aims and objectives of education are laid down in Art. 13 (1) ICESCR. Everyone has the right to education. Here, four goals of education are mentioned: firstly and fundamentally, "*education shall be directed to the full development of the human personality and the* ***sense of its dignity***," [emphasis added], secondly, education "*...shall strengthen the respect for human rights and fundamental freedoms*"; "*education shall enable all persons to participate effectively in a free society,*" and finally, the goal of education is to "*promote understanding, tolerance and friendship among all nations and all racial, ethnic or religious groups, and further the activities of the United Nations for the maintenance of peace.*"

The CESCR states that all explications and interpretations of the other conventions and declarations in respect to the right to education are implicitly encompassed by Art. 13 (1) and that these provisions are seen as concrete developments and elaborations of the objectives of education (CESCR 1999, para 5).

As already mentioned, the respect, the protection and the fulfillment of the right to education is the responsibility of states; however, in many countries, education was introduced and made compulsory long before the international human rights regime stipulated it. As Tomaševski points out, education is an important means to achieve collective political and economic goals (Tomaševski 2006, 7). It is also clear that states can abuse education to misguide the youth of a country; therefore it is necessary to respect the freedom to choose the kind of education as well as to protect individuals or groups from the prevention of the full enjoyment of education. Art. 13 (3) ICESCR guarantees the liberty of parents or legal guardians to choose schools other than public schools for their children. Art. 13 (4) guarantees the right to establish such institutions. Tomaševski[2] writes in a vivid and engaged voice "*Human rights safeguards are oriented towards balancing the right of the state to compel children to be educated and the right of their parents to decide where and how.*" (Tomaševski 2006, 29)[3].

This leads us to the question of the conditions that have to be satisfied for the compliance of education with the human right to education.

2 Katarina Tomaševski was the first UN Special Rapporteur on education from 1998 to 2004.

3 For the corresponding provisions in the ECHR see Gomien's contribution for the Council of Europe (Gomien 2005, 133-137).

2 The 4-A Scheme

Education in all its forms and at all levels must exhibit the interrelated and essential features of *Availability*, *Accessibility*, *Acceptability* and *Adaptability*. This so-called 4-A Scheme[4] was suggested and formulated by the CESCR in the General Comment 13 (CESCR 1999, para 6). The 4-A Scheme is both a threshold and a tool for the evaluation for the compliance of a respective education system with the right to education under the ICESCR.

2.1 Availability

Functioning educational institutions have to be available in sufficient quantity. Functionality requires, among other features, well- and appropriately trained teachers receiving domestically competitive salaries, as well as appropriate teaching materials of good quality. The provision must be in accordance with the terms of economic capacity and needs of a country. In this respect, some will also require facilities such as a library, computer facilities and information technology (CESCR 1999, para 6 (a)).

Art. 13 (2) (b) ICESCR states that secondary as well as vocational education must be "*generally available.*" This signifies that secondary education is not dependent on a student's apparent capacity or ability or merit. Further, it means that secondary education must be provided in such way that it be available on the same basis to all, i.e. without any discrimination.

2.2 Accessibility

Education in all its forms, institutions and programs must be accessible to everyone without discrimination. Accessibility has three interrelated dimensions (CESCR 1999, para 6 (b)):

(i) Non-discrimination – education must be accessible to all, especially the most vulnerable groups, in law and fact, without discrimination on any of the prohibited grounds (for details see the next section).

(ii) Physical accessibility – education has to be "*within safe physical reach, either by attendance at some reasonably convenient geographic location (e.g. a neighborhood school) or via modern technology (e.g. access to a "distance learning" program)*" (CESCR 1999, para 6 (b)).

4 For details on the concept, the office of the Special Rapporteur and Katerina Tomaševski in German language see Lohrenscheit 2007.

(iii) Economic accessibility – education has to be affordable to all. This dimension of accessibility is often underestimated or misunderstood. Firstly, economic accessibility requires that admission to school be free. In most European countries, most primary and secondary, as well as post-compulsory and vocational schools, are free. This might be misleading, however, as there are enormous costs besides school fees. Secondly, the right to education requires an effective subsidy and fellowship system (Art. 13 (2) (e) ICESCR). This makes it clear that (relative) poverty, social or economic status, or birth, cannot block an individual's access to all forms and levels of education. These conditions are not at all considered as barriers, but as disadvantages which have to be compensated for. The concept includes indirect costs and opportunity costs of education (see Tomaševski 2006, 27). However, the financial side is only one aspect of economic accessibility. Accessibility also means to have the *de facto* opportunities to access all forms and levels of education. This is not only expensive for households, but also has something to do with a person's social and cultural capital. This concept of "*capabilities and the freedom to achieve well-being*" (Sen 1986) suggests a "*pedagogy of poverty*" (Motakef 2006, 19). In respect to social class and economic standing, the considered education systems clearly fail. They tend to reproduce existing social and economic inequality, as we learn from a long list of educational research (a.o. see OECD 2005). The scientific literature proves that the lower the household's disposable economic resources, the less likely it is that the student will achieve a high degree of education. In regard to the provision that education should help individuals "... *lift themselves out of poverty and obtain the means to participate fully in their communities*" (CESCR 1999, para 1), regrettably, we can say that the education systems even exacerbates social inequality in the long-run. Limited economic access to education is not only unfair, it is also a human rights violation, as it is discriminatory on the grounds of social origin and property to omit effective compensation or affirmative action. From the viewpoint of welfare economics, it is inefficient, as it limits the collective prosperity below the potential maximum without any rational justification.

Primary education must be free and compulsory, secondary education must be accessible for all, irrespective of the capacity or ability of students. The case is different for higher education in this point only: that it must be accessible on the basis of capacity and merit.

2.3 Acceptability

"*The form and substance of education, including curricula and teaching methods, have to be acceptable (e.g. relevant, culturally appropriate and of good quality) to students and ... [their] parents ...*" (CESCR 1999, para 6 (c)).

This is particularly important in the present context. It is clear that school curricula and training programs for teaching staff vary from country to country and over time; however, the requirement of education being *relevant* indicates that ***science*** education can be deemed as included in the provision of Art. 13 (2) (b) ICESCR on secondary and vocational education.

The phrase "*every appropriate means*" reinforces the point that the state should adopt varied and innovative approaches to the delivery of secondary education in different social and cultural contexts. Taking a closer look at what is meant by "*culturally appropriate*" reveals an obligation of the state to deliver secondary and vocational education that is: firstly culturally sensitive towards the diversity of students where teaching staff, curricula and equipment are concerned, and secondly, engaged in promoting the mutual understanding of cultures, and, thirdly, committed to enabling students to acquire the necessary knowledge and skills for self-reliance, employability in the various sectors of economy and contributing to the general welfare of the respective society (see CESCR 1999, para 16).

In its General Policy Recommendation No. 10 on combating racism and racial discrimination in and through school education, the European Commission against Racism and Intolerance (ECRI) highlights the importance of well-trained teachers in reference to the international and regional conventions, who are to be recruited from minority groups, and the indispensability of teaching material free of stereotypes (ECRI 2006). To these ends, ECRI recommends recruiting teaching staff from minority populations (ECRI 2006, Rec.10, I.3.f) to ensure human rights education at all levels and across all disciplines (ECRI 2006, Rec.10, II.2.a); to monitor and update textbooks on stereotypes and prejudices (ECRI 2006, Rec.10, II.2.d) and finally to train the entire teaching staff to work in a multicultural environment (ECRI 2006, Rec.10, III.1-6).

However, "*cultural appropriateness*" indicates that this is not an absolute claim. Education has to take into account the cultural background of students, providing equal opportunities instead of putting pressure to assimilate. The benchmark for appropriateness remains the definition of the objectives of the right to education in Art. 13 (1), which are the development of the personality; the strengthening of the respect for human rights; the facilitation of participation in society and promotion of understanding, tolerance and friendship among all national, ethnic or religious groups.

2.4 Adaptability

The principle of adaptability requires that education be flexible in the sense that it can adapt to the needs of changing societies and respond to the needs of students within their diverse social and cultural settings. The ways and methods will differ;

however, the states are not only obliged to make all possible efforts, but also are responsible for the results and the outcome.

The principle of adaptability applies to the educational system as a whole, but also to all forms and levels as well as to all of its components as equipment of schools or universities, teaching material, curricula and the knowledge and skills of the teaching staff (see on this also ECRI's policy recommendation 10, ECRI 2006). Wodzinski gives an excellent guideline when calling for differentiation of physics lessons (Wodzinski 2007, 5, 9).

Neglecting diversity in the supply and maintenance of education disadvantages certain groups, particularly minorities or women, by limiting access and acceptance. This results in privilege being granted to others, often members of the majority population. This is, therefore, incompatible with the concept of human rights.

"When considering the appropriate application of these 'interrelated and essential features' [the 4-A Scheme, remark of the author] the best interests of the student shall be a primary consideration" (CESCR 1999, para 7).

3 Non-Discrimination

Non-discrimination is a fundamental principle of human rights by definition. Everyone is entitled to the same rights without any distinction because everyone is human. In addition to this logical principle, all human rights treaties and norms stipulate explicit provisions to prohibit discrimination. These provisions differ in their scope, their range of prohibited grounds and in the possibilities of legal enforcement. Art. 2 UDHR limits the scope to the rights set forth in the declaration itself (accessoriness). It mentions prohibited grounds exemplarily (among others: race, color, sex, language, religion, social origin, birth or other status). By stating "*such as,*" an open list of grounds is indicated; the rights in the UDHR are not legally enforceable before courts. The same wording is found in Art. 2 (2) ICESCR. This treaty is binding for the states parties, however the remedy, or the possibility of enforcement of rights, is rather weak. The most extensive provision on non-discrimination is Art. 26 of the Convention on Civil and Political Rights (ICCPR 1966). Although this remedy is weak as well, this provision is not limited to particular rights or grounds of discrimination. Of particular interest are the non-discrimination provisions of CEDAW in respect to women (Art. 1), those of CRC concerning children and of CERD concerning people of different ethnic origin (Art. 1).

At the European level, Art. 14 of the European Convention for the Protection of Human Rights and Fundamental Freedoms (ECHR 1950) prohibits discrimination as well on "*such*" grounds as race, gender, language, national or social origin, membership of a national minority, property, birth and others. Protocol 12 to the ECHR removes the accessoriness of Art. 14, which means that discrimination is prohibited in any case irrespective of an alleged violation of any right of the convention (including the right to education); however, among the states considered in our context only Bosnia and Herzegovina ratified Protocol 12 as of August 2008. Violations of the ECHR can be claimed at the European Court of Human Rights (ECtHR). The ECHR so provides the most effective remedy of all international human rights law. The European Union introduced a non binding non-discrimination clause in the Charter of fundamental rights of the European Union in 2000 (Charter of Nice 2000) and, with the "Race directive" (43/2000 EC), discrimination on the basis of ethnic origin is also prohibited within and in the access to (all forms of) education. The directive is transposed into national laws of the EU member states and cases can be brought before national civil courts.

Human rights jurisprudence, and recently legislation, developed the concepts of direct and indirect discrimination. Direct discrimination occurs when someone is treated differently from another in the same or in a similar and comparable situation on a prohibited ground, e.g. admission to a school is denied to a black child. Indirect discrimination, on the other hand, occurs when a neutral provision or rule affects people from one group less favorably than another. The discriminatory outcome may be expected, e.g. a test for admission to good quality education is highly dependant on German language skills (applies to all, but disadvantages students with another first language); or may be observed as a result, e.g. a statistically observed underperformance of immigrant children.

Discrimination is always relative, i.e. it needs a comparator to show the less favorable treatment or privileged status. This fact sometimes makes it difficult to prove discrimination, if a comparator cannot be found or named, or particularly in cases of indirect discrimination. The proof has to be given by statistical means, which are often missing. Discrimination, especially indirect discrimination, often remains invisible due to the lack of appropriate data. However, invisibility is not absence. It is again Katarina Tomaševski who excellently makes the point: "*Race has been obliterated from national statistics in the hope that it would not count if no longer counted. Hopes that making race statistically irrelevant would also make it socially and politically irrelevant have not materialized.*" (Tomaševski 2005, 39). CESCR interprets relevant data collection and monitoring as a duty resulting from Art. 13 ICESCR: "*States parties must closely monitor education – including all relevant policies, institutions, programmes, spending patterns and other practices – so as to identify and take measures to redress any de facto discrimination. Educational data should be disaggregated by the prohibited grounds of discrimination.*" (CESCR 1999, para 37).

This leads us to the next important question: The right to education requires equality, but equality of what?[5] The call for strict formal equality, building only on consistency of equal treatment, was rejected by the CESCR as it "*reflects inequality*" (Tomaševski 2006, 45), but favors the concept of equal opportunities in education. This includes, in addition to compensation for past disadvantages or less favorable initial conditions, e.g. relative poverty, so-called ***affirmative action***. The committee states that "*[T]he adoption of temporary special measures intended to bring about de facto equality for men and women and for disadvantaged groups is not a violation of the right to non-discrimination with regard to education*" (CESCR 1999, para 32). The condition under which affirmative action is legal is that these measures must not lead to unequal or separate standards for different groups, and that they will be discontinued after the objectives for which they were undertaken have been achieved.

As listed above, the various legal texts recognize different prohibited grounds for discrimination. This shall be considered in the context of access to science education. Relevant grounds of distinction are: gender or sex; race, color or ethnic origin (depending on the terms used in the respective legislation); language; national or social origin; birth; property (all relating to social class, which is not used as a term) and to some extent religion. The ICESCR covers these grounds in Art. 2. The ECHR covers them as well in Art. 14. The law of the European Union covers only those related to "race, color or ethnic origin"; however, the significance has to be judged by the court from case to case.

With regard to Art. 13 (2) (a) and (b), the CESCR clarifies additionally that "the principle of non-discrimination extends to all persons of school age residing in the territory of a State party, including non-nationals, and irrespective of their legal status" (CESCR 1999, para 34) with reference to the CRC and CADE. It has to be mentioned that in many countries (in Austria and some German states ["Länder"] as well) there exists a right to attend education for asylum-seekers or students lacking a legal residence title, but school is not compulsory. This is not in accordance with the convention, as the duty to protect the right to education is not guaranteed because the state has no power to enforce attendance.

There is also a right to basic education: "*The right to fundamental education extends to all those who have not yet satisfied their 'basic learning needs'*" (CESCR 1999, para 23). No one is to be excluded from the fundamental education necessary to participate fully in society and therefore age comes into play as a prohibited ground, which may be particularly important for refugees or immigrants.

---

5 An excellent overview on the legal concepts of equality can be found in Sandra Fredman's *Anti-Discrimination Law* (Fredman 2002).

To summarize, the considered states (Austria, Bosnia-Herzegovina, Germany and Turkey) are obliged to ensure non-discrimination on any of the grounds marked as relevant to the context.

While non-discrimination is dealt with under "accessibility," unsatisfactory levels of acceptability and above all adaptability can definitely amount to discrimination as well.

4 Compliance, Deficiencies and Criticism

In relation to Art. 13 (2) IESCR, the states have the obligation to respect, protect and fulfill each of the essential features of availability, accessibility, acceptability, adaptability of the right to education. A state has to respect the availability of education, e.g. by not closing private schools; protect the accessibility of education by ensuring that third parties, including parents, do not stop certain groups, e.g. girls, from going to school; facilitate the acceptability of education by taking positive measures to ensure that education is culturally appropriate for minorities, and of good quality for all; provide the adaptability of education by designing and providing resources for curricula which reflect the contemporary needs of students in a changing world, including appropriate content and well trained teaching staff (see CESCR 1999, para 50).

It is not the right place here to judge whether the considered education systems of Turkey, Austria, Germany and Bosnia-Herzegovina as a whole comply with the human right to education. We will focus on ***science*** **education** in secondary schools and, closely related to this, on the access to **higher education**. Additionally, we will focus on the 4-A Scheme as a structure for assessment; we will consider chances and achievement in the labor market, particularly in academia, as indicators. The considered target groups are culturally or ethnically different persons (including "migrants"[6]), women and people with limited economic resources and unfavorable social recognition. In practice, these "grounds for discrimination" are often combined. Regrettably, cultural or "racial" identity (and difference) is an important category in the public discourse. Why is it so important? That human rights provisions stipulate racial (or other) distinction as prohibited indicates that racial discrimination occurs in practice. Ideally, this criterion of distinction would be totally irrelevant, but it is not. It remains negatively connoted in our societies and it remains one of the strongest reasons for stereotyping besides sex and gender.

Even though there is also much discussion on the compliance of the educational systems with human rights standards concerning the "hard" issues, all the consid-

6 For the explanation of the term "migrants" see Gilardi, Bauer et al. in this book.

ered countries formally provide non-discriminatory access to primary education; it is free and compulsory and efforts to protect and to promote the right to education are reported. Still, a couple of serious concerns in this respect may be mentioned at a glance in the four countries.

In the case of **Austria**, the over-representation of pupils with a migration background in schools for special needs is an alarming issue. This definitely limits the access to all forms of education, as well as the prospective of success in the labor market, which again affects the opportunities to participate as a valued member in the society. "*ECRI expresses concern, however, at the still extremely high representation (19.2 % in 2002/2003) of non-citizen children in special needs schools ..., which are designed for children with special educational needs resulting from mental or physical handicaps and which do not provide possibilities for further educational attainment. More generally, ECRI notes that research seems to indicate that, even when the disadvantages linked to being of non-German mother tongue and to belonging to families with modest socio-economic conditions are taken into account, the educational gap between Austrian and non-Austrian children still appears to be disproportionate*" (ECRI, Third report on Austria 2005, para 46).

Although the legislation on education in **Bosnia & Herzegovina** has been implemented in accordance with the human rights standards, reliable reports state that it is not implemented in practice. ECRI is concerned "*... that pupils in Bosnia and Herzegovina still predominantly access education in a segregated way*" (ECRI, report on Bosnia-Herzegovina 2005, para 30) and that "*... this situation entails the risk of inter-ethnic prejudice and animosity being perpetuated through the younger generations*" (para 30). And furthermore, ECRI underlines that "*[T]his is particularly the case for the so-called 'two schools under one roof', 54 of which still exist at present in three Cantons in the Federation. In these schools, pupils of different ethnic origin use the same facilities. However, these facilities host, in actual terms, two schools segregated along ethnic lines*" (para 33). Also, ECRI is concerned in respect to minorities, migrants (returnees) and refugees "*that this situation of separation in education works as a powerful deterrent for potential returnees and undermines the sustainability of minority returns*" (para 30). On the same issues the competent UN treaty body (CESCR) expresses "*its deep concern that returnees, in particular those belonging to ethnic minorities, are often denied access to ... school education for their children ..., thereby impeding their sustainable return to their communities*" (CESCR, E/C.12/BIH/CO/1 2006, para 12). The committee is concerned "*about the practice of 'two schools under one roof', ... to teach separate curricula to children belonging to different ethnic groups*" (ibid, para 28) and "*grave concerns*" are expressed about the fact that up to 80 % of Romani children do not attend school (ibid, para 29).

The most urgent issue in the **German** educational system is the underperformance and early drop-out of pupils, in particular male students with a migration background. Pupils with a Turkish background are at the greatest risk. "*ECRI encourages the German authorities in their efforts to improve the position of non-citizen children in schools. It considers that education in German as a second language from kindergarten level upwards is one of the priority areas for action. It stresses, however, that measures aimed exclusively at non-citizen children will not suffice to ensure equality of opportunities of these children in education. In this respect, it strongly recommends initiatives to strengthen the intercultural competence of the school communities through measures targeted at the majority population as well*" (ECRI, Third report on Germany 2004, para 58). ECRI expressively calls for further measures to improve the intercultural competence of teachers.

The UN Special Rapporteur on education visited Germany in 2006. In his report to the Human Rights Council,[7] he identifies the "education challenges" in chapter IV as the discrepancies between the educational systems in the different *Länder* (para 46); the selectivity at too early a stage and the lack of adequate teaching methods for pupils with a migration background (para 49); the anxiety of change and reluctance to lose privileges on the part of the majority population, as well as the lack of pedagogical training of teachers for the response to current challenges in education (para 54). He therefore states that "*[t]his has the effect of making the educational system somewhat exclusive in nature.*" (ibid., para 89).

In **Turkey** there are two interdependent issues of concern: the strict prohibition of mother-tongue education (other than Turkish) and the low rate of school attendance of girls in the Eastern-Anatolian part of the country. ECRI "*recommended that the Turkish authorities take initiatives to ensure that children of non-Turkish mother tongue can adequately follow classes taught in Turkish. ... The children concerned are both those of immigrants and children of Turkish nationality who are of non-Turkish mother tongue*" (ECRI, Third report on Turkey 2005, para 63, 64).

The second major concern for Turkey is the school attendance of girls, which is rather low, in particular within the minority communities in East-Anatolia. Even though this is related to the above mentioned criticism, it also has another dimension. The Turkish authorities have made huge efforts to improve the situation (see Erden, in this book, chapter 2); however, members of the minority groups, in particular Kurds, deny their female children access to education due to the fact that the Turkish education system is unacceptable to them as it does not offer an education in accordance with their convictions. The argument of access stands against the ar-

8 A/HRC/4/29/Add.3 from March 9, 2007.

gument of acceptability. Girls are subject to intersectional discrimination along the line of in-group discrimination (gender) and out-group discrimination (ethnicity).

Interestingly, the criticism of the international monitoring bodies of Turkey is quite similar to that of Germany: high barriers in the access to all forms of education on the basis of language and cultural difference. In Turkey, the over-emphasis of Turkish cultural nationalism was reported, for Germany, the pressure to assimilate rooted in the policy of "Leitkultur" (Mainstream-Culture) defined by the majority population were identified as problematic in regard to human rights standards (Bielefeldt 2007). However, it has to be added that in both countries policy-makers have taken these serious concerns into account as starting points for various programs and initiatives to counteract these problems.

In summary, the international monitoring bodies criticize the lack of accessibility to education on the basis of ethnicity and language in Austria; the doubtful acceptability and the lack of availability of education on the basis of ethnicity in Bosnia-Herzegovina; the lack of acceptability of education for minorities and migrants in Turkey; and the lack of adaptability on the basis of ethnicity and language in Germany. The UN Special Rapporteur on Education, Vernor Muñoz, explicitly criticized the early selectivity of the German education system after his visit to Germany in 2006. This criticism was repeatedly addressed to Austria, Germany and Switzerland (OECD 2006) as a key factor in indirect discrimination against migrants in education.

However, the education systems comply in the sense that various forms of school types are available. For instance, there are specialized schools for a wide range of studies, vocational schools and so on, but they are not equally accessible. The major reasons for the lack of accessibility are the external factors of social inequality (education, status and income of the parents). Often combined with ethnic origin and the internal factors of insufficient acceptability and especially adaptability of the education systems, both influence accessibility negatively. Secondary education, including upper secondary and vocational education, should be accessible irrespective of the pupils' abilities and capacities. This is definitely not the case in all the considered systems. Education reproduces social inequalities instead of abolishing them and equalizing opportunities.

5 Barriers in the Access to Education

Barriers are exclusion mechanisms. We do not speak about disadvantages rooted in the *identity* of the individual. Barriers may be intentionally set or constructed, but barriers can also exist as a consequence of historical developments and a lack of socially necessary adaptation. Barriers, particularly barriers in the access to education, are often not visible at first glance. Individual responsibility for underperformance, underachievement, limited access or whatever lack of opportunities are often suggested as reasons, but only serve to build a barrier itself. Barriers may either prevent a majority or a minority from the enjoyment of full access to education or from the opportunity develop personally. The former may be the case for women, the latter for ethnic minority members.

Any exclusion based on a prohibited ground as color, "race," ethnicity, religion or gender (and other) is not compliant with the fundamental principle of human rights. It violates the states' obligation to provide for the enjoyment of any human right without any distinction. This principle justifies affirmative action to guarantee equality. Individual disadvantages have to be compensated for by affirmative action to equalize opportunities if the disadvantages are rooted in identities affecting human dignity. They are tantamount to discrimination when used as grounds for distinction or exclusion, no matter whether intended or resulting from provisions or policies.

If we can clearly observe that persons with a migration background have fewer opportunities in the labor market either because of the minor qualification they receive or because of their position below their received qualification in education, then they are deprived of full participation in society and, consequently, the objective of the right to education in Art. 13 (1) ICESCR is not fulfilled without discrimination. When it is widely known and proved that certain groups, in particular women and persons with a different descent from that of the majority population face unequal opportunities, also the *omission* of taking action by the state to promote equal opportunities with a definitive and measurable effect is assumed to be a *human rights violation*.

However, barriers are hard to identify in most cases. We need indicators to identify barriers, their consequences and their impact. We need to prove the causalities between structures or procedures with results and impact on specific groups. Only in recent years has the relevant research gained wider publicity and thus the recognition by intergovernmental institutions, the EU and national and local policy-makers. Particularly, causes and indicators in respect to social exclusion have become topics of discussion. Social exclusion has a broad, deep and long-term impact on economic performance, and not least for this reason has the case of discrimination been set on top of the agenda in the EU (FRA 2007).

Recognized indicators for the existence of barriers to the access to education are: achievement rates; labor market data; the gender-ratio in education and employment; the gap between qualification and professional status; segregation in housing and in education; legal integration indicators as participation in citizenship; the matching of qualifications with labor market needs, to mention just some of the relevant qualitative and quantitative indicators. In respect to the right to education, it is important to consider whether the individual's skills, capacity and ability are used as criteria for access to all forms of education. Furthermore, it is obviously important whether language skills are considered as a valuable asset or only recognized as an integration obligation to be fulfilled by the individual concerning the official education language.

Education research has revealed some crucial barriers that can be categorized into institutional and social barriers. Under institutional barriers we subsume legal barriers and as such being inherent in the education system. Legal barriers are related to the legal status, issues of citizenship, nationality and residence or refugee status. It is considered a barrier, for instance, that school is not compulsory for refugee children in Austria.

Within the educational system we can identify barriers related to curricula, the education and recruitment of teachers, school types and selection. Early selection in the education system obviously negatively affects the opportunities of migrant children in Austria and Germany. The lack of differentiation within the curricula influences the degree of shaping and promoting migrants' skills and capacities to make pupils themselves aware of "playing a useful role in society" as the right to education suggests. There is a lack of teachers with migration experience. The corps is not culturally diverse. Teacher training is not sensitive to the cultural and linguistic diversity of the pupils.

Social barriers encompass cultural and linguistic, as well as economic and class mobility restraints. Migrants face various social barriers; social recognition and discrimination in everyday life is one of the most important socio-psychological barriers for migrants to the access to society in general and to education in particular. A lack of successful role models reveals another piece of the picture. Societal status of professions and gender roles channel expectations and the choice of professions. Social class and poverty related to social position is the most recognized barrier to the access of all forms of education.

6 Conclusion

The human rights approach can respond excellently to the challenge of an *unlimited science education* at all levels. It requires positive action and puts technical and vocational education on the agenda for all levels of education. It builds a normative basis for planning and implementation, and the 4-A Scheme gives an appropriate framework for evaluation. A right to *science* education can be derived based on the following reasons.

Education is an end in itself. Science is an integral part of the *general knowledge of the human civilization*. Every individual is entitled to participate in this cultured and intellectual community.

From the legal point of view, the *right to science education* is stipulated in the ICESCR and the Convention on Technical and Vocational Education. It is derived from the requirement that education be relevant to the individual in order to be an acceptable way to promote the individual's personal and cultural fulfillment and to enable the individual to participate fully in society.

Finally and pragmatically, science education increases the individual's opportunities for *employment and income* and enhances the freedom of choice for the life one values.

Bibliography

Official and normative documents:

Charter of Fundamental Rights of the European Union of 18 December, 2000, 2000/C 364/01.

Committee on Economic, Social and Cultural Rights (CESCR), *General Comment No. 13, The Right to Education (Art.13)*, Twenty-first session, 8 December, 1999. German translation available: Deutsches Institut für Menschenrechte (ed.), *Die "General Comments" zu den Menschenrechtsverträgen*, Nomos, Baden-Baden, 2005.

Committee on Economic, Social and Cultural Rights (CESCR), *Bosnia and Herzegovina: Concluding Observations of the Committee on Economic, Social and Cultural Rights*, E/C.12/BIH/CO/1, 26 January 2006, para. 25.

Council Directive 2000/43/EC of 29 June 2000 implementing the principle of equal treatment between persons irrespective of racial or ethnic origin.

European Commission against Racism and Intolerance (ECRI), *Third report on Germany*, adopted on 5 December 2003.

European Commission against Racism and Intolerance (ECRI), *Third report on Austria*, adopted on 25 June 2004, CRI (2005) 1.

European Commission against Racism and Intolerance (ECRI), *Report on Bosnia-Herzegovina*, adopted on 25 June 2004.

European Commission against Racism and Intolerance (ECRI), *Third report on Turkey*, adopted on 25 June 2004.

European Commission against Racism and Intolerance (ECRI), General Policy Recommendation No. 10 on *Combating Racism and Racial Discrimination in and through School Education*, adopted on 15 December 2006.

UN Special Rapporteur, *Report on Germany*, A/HRC/4/29/Add.3 from March 9, 2007.

Literature:

Benedek, Wolfgang (ed.), *Understanding Human Rights. Manual on Human Rights Education*, NWV, Wien, 2006.

Bielefeldt, Heiner, *Menschenrechte in der Einwanderungsgesellschaft. Plädoyer für einen aufgeklärten Multikulturalismus*, transcript Verlag, Bielefeld, 2007.

European Monitoring Centre on Racism and Xenophobia (ed.), *Migrants, Minorities and Education – Documenting Discrimination and Integration in 15 Member States of the European Union*, Office for Official Publications of the European Communities, Luxemburg, 2004.

Forum Politische Bildung (ed.), *Dazugehören? Fremdenfeindlichkeit, Migration, Integration*, Forum Politische Bildung, Wien, 2001.

Fredman, Sandra, *Discrimination Law*, Oxford University Press, New York, 2002.

Gomien, Donna, *Short Guide to the European Convention on Human Rights*, Council of Europe Publishing, Strasbourg, 2005.

Hossenfelder, Malte, *Der Wille zum Recht und das Streben nach Glück. Grundlegung einer Ethik des Wollens und Begründung der Menschenrechte*, Verlag C.H. Beck, München, 2000.

Lohrenscheit, Claudia, *Die UN-Sonderberichterstattung zum Recht auf Bildung und ihre Grundlegung durch Katarina Tomaševski*, in: Overwien, Bernd and Prengel, Annedore (eds.), *Recht auf Bildung. Zum Besuch des Sonderberichterstatters der Vereinten Nationen in Deutschland*, Verlag Barbara Budrich, Opladen, 2007.

Mecheril, Paul and Quehl, Thomas (eds.), *Die Macht der Sprachen – Englische Perspektiven auf die mehrsprachige Schule*, Waxmann Verlag, Münster, 2006.

Motakef, Mona, *Das Menschenrecht auf Bildung und der Schutz vor Diskriminierung – Exklusionsrisiken und Inklusionschancen*, Deutsches Institut für Menschenrechte, Berlin, 2006.

Office of the United Nations High Commissioner for Human Rights (OHCHR) and United Nations Educational, Scientific and Cultural Organization (UNESCO) (ed.), *Dimensions of Racism*, United Nations, New York, 2005.

Organisation for Economic Co-Operation and Development (OECD) (ed.), *Where Immigrant Students Succeed – A Comparative Review of Performance and Engagement in PISA 2003*, OECD, Paris, 2006.

Overwien, Bernd and Prengel, Annedore (eds.), *Recht auf Bildung. Zum Besuch des Sonderberichterstatters der Vereinten Nationen in Deutschland*, Verlag Barbara Budrich, Opladen, 2007.

Tomaševski, Katarina, *Racism and Education*, in: United Nation Educational, Scientific and Cultural Organization (UNESCO) (ed.), *Dimensions of Racism*, UNESCO, Paris, 2005.

Tomaševski, Katarina, *Human Rights Obligations in Education: The 4-A Scheme*, Wolf Legal Publishers, Nijmegen, 2006.

Sen, Amartya, *Inequality Re-examined*, Harvard University Press, Cambridge Massachusetts, 1986.

United Nation Educational, Scientific and Cultural Organization (UNESCO) (ed.), *United to Combat Racism*, UNESCO, Paris, 2001.

United Nation Educational, Scientific and Cultural Organization (UNESCO) (ed.), *Convention against Discrimination in Education (1960) and Articles 13 and 14 (Right to Education) of the International Covenant on Economic, Social and Cultural Rights: A Comparative Analysis*, UNESCO, Paris, 2006.

Volf, Patrik and Bauböck, Rainer, *Wege zur Integration – Was man gegen Diskriminierung und Fremdenfeindlichkeit tun kann*, Drava Verlag, Klagenfurt, 2001.

Weiss, Hilde (ed.), *Leben in zwei Welten – Zur sozialen Integration ausländischer Jugendlicher der zweiten Generation*, VS Verlag für Sozialwissenschaften, Wiesbaden, 2007.

Wodzinski, Rita, Wodzinski, Christoph and Hepp, Ralph (eds.), *Naturwissenschaften im Unterricht Physik – Differenzierung* (99/100), Erhard Friedrich Verlag GmbH, Seelze, 2007.

Special Protection for Migrants in Education?

Stephanie Gilardi, Veronika Bauer, Sarah Kumar, Klaus Starl

Are there reasons for special protection of migrants' right to education? How can this special protection be justified? To better understand this issue, some general thoughts on migration shall be given and the particular vulnerability of this group of persons shall be explained. To begin, the term "migrant" must be defined:

"*A person who moves to a country other than that of his or her usual residence for a period of at least a year, so that the country of destination effectively becomes his or her new country of usual residence*" (United Nations Statistical Division 1998, 18). Although this definition is quite useful, there remains much space for confusion in the given context as this definition only encompasses the so-called first generation. With regards to education, it has been suggested that this definition refers to the concept of vulnerability (Daudet and Eisemann 2005; Nowak 2001, 258-261; Tomaševski 2003; Vandenhoule 2005) in relation to such factors as nationality, legal residence status, social status, color, language, culture, religion, ethnic origin or descent, rather than to migration only. A range of difficulties exists in the factual and legal classification as the terms "migrant," "immigrant," "foreigner," "alien," "members of ethnic minorities" or even "refugee" and "asylum-seeker" are often confused, used simultaneously, or just differently received.

Migration is a complex, globally growing phenomenon. Nearly 200 million people worldwide – three percent of the global population – are considered to be migrants according to the UN (General Assembly 2006, 6). Nine million people are refugees on the run from state persecution or because their states cannot protect them from other forms of prohibited persecution (Global Commission on International Migration 2005, 83). Most of the world's migrants emigrate from China (nearly 40 million), India (about 20 million) and the Philippines (7 million; Global Commission on International Migration 2005, 84). The greatest numbers of immigrants can be found in the USA, the CIS (former Soviet Union States) and in Germany (Global Commission on International Migration 2005, 83). In the year 2005, Europe was host to about 64 million migrants (United Nations Department of Economic and Social Affairs 2006, 2). In 2004, about 25 million non-nationals were living within the EU, about 5.5% of the total population (Eurostat 2006, 1). Most of these persons entered the EU through Germany, Spain, the UK and Italy (Eurostat 2008, 70).

In the given context, the different forms of migration can be categorized either by legal classification or by the motivations and causes of migration. While the first takes a particular system as the starting point, the latter puts the individual at the center of interest. On the one side there is voluntary migration – people leaving their country of origin/usual residence of their own free will and trying to settle in another country, mostly in search of better living conditions. On the other side, forced migration is when people are forced to leave their country of origin/usual residence because of e.g. war, prosecution, trafficking etc. Furthermore, a distinction has to be drawn between legal and illegal migration, although it has to be stated that the boundaries between those two areas are first of all fluid and secondly subject to the power and will of the states that receive migrants. In recent years, legal migration to EU countries has been restricted to only a very small number of cases annually (Bendel 2005, 20-31).

To better understand the issue of migration, the so-called "push and pull factors" also have to be mentioned. Push factors are those which "lead" people out of their country of usual residence/origin. These factors might be politically, economically, culturally or environmentally based. Pull factors are those which attract people to a certain region or country to which they want to immigrate – those factors can also be economic, political, cultural or environmental.

1 Vulnerability to Structural Discrimination

Again – is there a need of special protection for migrants in education and why? Aren't the general provisions on education as described by Starl in the first chapter of this book sufficient to protect migrants in the field of education? Where is the added value of specific provisions for migrants?

Although 2008 marks the 60th anniversary of the right to education guaranteed to every individual in Article 26 of the Universal Declaration of Human Rights of 1948 (UDHR), many individuals are still unable to gain access to it. Although discrimination on the basis of any prohibited ground named in this document – those rooted in the identity of the individual, such as race, gender, place of birth and others – is strictly prohibited by the Declaration, individuals often face barriers to full or partial enjoyment of their right to education without direct discrimination ever having taken place.

The group of migrants is generally acknowledged to be a group of specific vulnerability. That means that with regards to education, migrants run a higher risk of being discriminated against than members of the "majority population."

In the words of Manfred Nowak, in his contribution on the right to education: "*Experience shows that governments tend to use the system of education as a means to systematically discriminate against ethnic, religious and linguistic minorities as well as other vulnerable groups, such as women or blacks. If governments wish to prevent certain groups from equally participating in the political, social, economic or cultural life in their countries, one of the most efficient methods is to deny them equal access to education or to maintain segregated educational facilities with different educational standards*" (Nowak 2001, 259).

When it comes to difficulties in accessing the right to education, female migrants in particular are at great risk; these individuals often must overcome multiple barriers excluding them from access to their right to education. Barriers to access often stem from a combination of forces, such as current economic, social, academic, or familial circumstances, as well as personal and migration history, and socio-psychological factors. To compensate for these forces, additional special protection must be implemented with the goal of increasing the (female) migrant student's access to education for the sake of equal treatment.

Access to, and realization of, the right to education plays a particularly crucial role for migrants and for our modern society, shaped as it is by migration. For not only does education provide the migrant individual with the means to take part in her community, it also promotes integration, understanding and tolerance among ethnic, racial and religious groups, a function of crucial importance when considering interaction within the diverse populations of many modern societies. Education in the receiving country can and should be an important tool for the integration of migrants. Due to language barriers and cultural misunderstandings, a special emphasis has to be put on the integration of immigrants in general and of immigrant children in particular. It is particularly important to consider this "generation one and a half," or children who were "taken along" by their parents to migrate to another country than their country of birth.

2 Normative Efforts

It has to be mentioned that there is no human right to residence in a specific country. States have the sovereignty to decide who enters and stays in their territory (United Nations General Assembly 2006, 17). But as soon as a person is in a specific country, all the human rights valid and ratified in this state apply to this person. That means that e.g. a migrant staying in Austria has the right to enjoy his/her right to education as laid down in the international instruments ratified by that state. Even though all the general provisions on the right to education apply to migrants, and should be guaranteed without discrimination, it still has to be stated that additional special provisions for those migrants are also in existence. The International Convention on the Protection of the Rights of All Migrant Workers (ICMW) explicitly provides guarantees for migrant workers, but does not cover refugees and other migrants who do not fall under the definition of migrant workers as put down in the Convention. Article 30 ICMW on education reads: "*Each child of a migrant worker shall have the basic right of access to education on the basis of equality of treatment with nationals of the State concerned. Access to pre-school education institutions or schools shall not be refused or limited by reason of the irregular situation with respect to stay or employment of either parent or by reason of the irregularity of the child's stay in the State of employment.*" However, the Convention has been ratified by only 37 countries, mainly by countries of migrants' origin, among them Bosnia and Herzegovina, as well as Turkey, but not by Austria or Germany.

Furthermore, the Geneva Convention on Refugees includes a specific provision for education, stating in Art. 22 that "*all refugees shall enjoy the right to education without discrimination.*" For refugee children, the CRC also includes a non-discrimination provision in Art. 22.

Several efforts have been made by UNESCO to prevent, abolish and increase protection against discrimination of vulnerable groups such as migrants in education. A wide range of normative instruments covering all aspects of education in all forms and at all levels reveals a commitment to an inclusive right to education. However, the implementation of this principle is still hampered by several problems. There are still certain groups that are hardly covered by any normative instrument. Some instruments are not specific enough regarding clear-cut measures to be taken in implementing the human right to education for vulnerable groups.

At the European level, a number of normative instruments were adopted in order to improve the human rights protection of migrant workers and in order to ensure mutual recognition of educational or academic certificates (European Social Charter 1961, European Convention on the Legal Status of Migrant Workers 1977, Convention on the Participation of Foreigners in Public Life at Local Level 1992). The EU adopted two important directives in this respect, the so-called "Race-Directive"[1] and the so-called "Residence-Directive."[2]

3 Unequal Conditions and Difficulties

As a result of diverse factors, the odds are stacked against the migrant seeking education in a host country. The migrant is particularly vulnerable to not being able to access her right to education, one that is guaranteed her in law, but must also be guaranteed in fact. Barriers to education often seem like they might be the result of a lack of dedication or ability in the individual student; perhaps they are not making

1 Council Directive 2000/43/EC of 29 June 2000 implementing the Principle of Equal Treatment between Persons Irrespective of Racial or Ethnic Origin.

2 Council Directive 2003/109/EC of 25 November 2003 concerning the Status of Third-country Nationals who are Long-term Residents

enough of an effort to adjust to a new academic environment. Lack of academic achievement, poor results, minimal understanding or lack of participation seem to reflect a failing on the part of the migrant student; however, these barriers do not originate with the individual's ability, but rather, are often the result of a complex combination of forces working together to hinder the student's access to her right to education. There are strong indicators that show the very real nature of these barriers to the access of education. They are revealed by the European Commission against Racism and Intolerance (ECRI), the Programme for International Student Assessment (PISA), The European Monitoring Centre on Racism and Xenophobia (EUMC)[3]. These include, but are not limited to, achievement rates, labor market data, gender ratio in education and employment, the gap between qualification and professional status, and segregation in housing and education.

3.1 First Accommodation

A myriad of challenges await the immigrant student entering a new school system, or the second generation migrant working to distinguish herself academically among native peers. First generation migrants, or those who have themselves relocated to a different country within their lifetime, experience the challenges of migration firsthand. They must adjust to a new culture and a new social situation; they must learn to cope with a new school system, classroom environment and teaching style. Often, these first generation students must also struggle to learn the language of their host country. Second generation immigrants, though they have grown up within the social and school systems of the host country and may be intimately familiar with the culture and language of the host country, nonetheless often must contend with some of the same obstacles that make education elusive for those students who have just arrived.

3.2 Socio-Economic Standing of the Migrant Family

For students with a migration background, one common barrier that often limits access to education is poverty. In migrant and native families alike, lower income increases the chance of poor school performance. Often, the migrant seeking a position in the labor force faces great difficulties due to lack of qualification, necessary connections, or insufficient language skills in the teaching language. Not only does this have the potential to strain relationships within the family, it often holds migrant families below the poverty line. Lack of money keeps families in low-income neighborhoods segregated from the majority population and keeps students

3 On 1 March 2007 the European Union Agency for Fundamental Rights (FRA) was established as the successor to the EUMC.

in poorly staffed, poorly equipped schools which also may be characterized by social and academic environments that may not be conducive to learning, or in the worst case, that may be hostile and violent.

For economically disadvantaged migrants, accessibility is also limited by additional costs that come along with education. For example, costly tutoring in the language of the host country is often essential for a migrant student not only to be academically competitive or successful, but sometimes simply to participate in the classroom.

3.3 Family's Capacity to Support

Along with the lack of material resources in migrant families, poverty and a parent's difficulty entering the workforce often contribute to a great deficit in family resources. When parents work in jobs that take them out of the home for long hours, sustained investment in the day-to-day events of a child's education is often difficult. Shouldering the burden of providing for a family often relegates a child's education to a lower priority level in favor of the more immediate objective of family survival. It is sometimes the case that migrant parents may not have the resources to take an active interest in a child's studies; they may not be able to offer needed support and encouragement, nor have the time to spend discussing academics or social issues surrounding a child's school experience. For migrant families who have relocated from a country where education is a luxury, the simple fact that a child attends school may be a satisfying source of pride; however, school attendance in itself does not constitute access to education.

Another critical family resource that often falls short of the mark is a parent's facility for communicating with a child's educators. Communication among parents, teachers and school administration plays an important role in the education process; it is through communication at parent-teacher association meetings and at one-on-one conferences that academic goals are set and problems resolved. When a child's parents are distanced from the school system due to unfamiliarity with the education system, a language barrier, lack of interest or time, then that child is denied an important support structure that would enrich her education. Lack of integration at the parental level, even in such things as networking with other parents and involvement in the life of the school, is a barrier to a student's full enjoyment of her right to education.

4 Institutional Barriers

4.1 Integration at School

Lack of integration at the student's level is also a barrier to equality in education. For school aged children, the social and academic spheres are often in very close contact. A school system can work to facilitate integration and be a place of inclusion, or it can be the site of routine exclusion and prejudice. It is in this context that well-trained teachers sensitive to the needs of migrant students and armed with strategies for integration are essential. In the worst case scenario, a school classroom can be a place of mistrust and exclusion, setting migrants apart from the mainstream classroom culture, creating distance between them and their native peers. Schools are often places where privilege is reproduced. Acceptance, approval, and integration are key in an environment where even the status of being a migrant in and of itself can be a barrier to success in education; social isolation not only damages an individual's sense of self, but also detracts from her overall experience of education.

4.2 Exclusive School System

Another barrier to accessing the right to education lies with the structure of a school system itself. In countries where students are separated and "tracked" into different schools at a young age based on ability (and accordant future careers) such as Austria and Germany, migrants who are just beginning to adjust to a new school environment are separated from students who have had the benefit of being schooled in their native language in a familiar academic setting. Because of those difficulties in assimilation and integration which are often coupled with the challenge of learning in a new language, migrants tend to be "late bloomers," whose confidence level and academic skill are only realized after they have already been channeled into educational tracks characterized by minimal challenge and low expectations. Immigrant children are often very hard workers who learn to use the educational opportunities of their host country to their greatest advantage; however, in the time it takes to adjust to a new education system, highly motivated migrant students often miss the opportunity to advance to a more challenging academic track.

4.3 Victims of Forced Migration

A further layer of difficulty in attaining access to education results from migrant cases where relocation is involuntary. In addition to the challenges of transition faced by voluntary migrants, victims of forced migration must also contend with the after-effects of a relocation that was carried out against their own will. Forced migration includes cases of refugees fleeing their homelands to escape state persecution. These migrants may have histories characterized by episodes of violence and trauma at an early age. Even voluntary migrations sometimes show an aspect of forced migration; children, juveniles, and women are often brought by family members to a new country without being involved in the decision, or even against their will.

In these cases, institutional barriers such as legal status, citizenship issues, nationality, residence and refugee status often arise for those without permanent residence status. Refugee children and asylum seekers, for instance, are free to attend school in Austria, but are not required by law to do so. Although this legal provision may seem beneficent, any child granted the option to exempt herself from primary education has been done a great disservice. In some cases, children may not yet be in a position to fully understand the benefits of and indeed, the necessity of early school attendance. Non-compulsory primary education constitutes a barrier to the access not only of higher levels of education, but also to the right to education itself (United Nations General Assembly 2007).

Children of undocumented migrants are also free to attend school in Austria; however, because of their residence status, they may be faced with the dilemma of whether to stay out of school and out of the public eye, or possibly jeopardize their family's stay in a host country by attending classes. When fear of deportation keeps a migrant child out of school, access to her right to education is endangered.

Victims of trafficking – individuals recruited and transported out of their countries of origin by means of deception or force for the purpose of exploitation – have also experienced forced migration. Of trafficked victims, women make up a disproportionately large segment; approximately 87% of trafficked persons are female (Ndiaye 2007; UNODC 2006, 77). 37% of the victims are children (UNODC 2006, 77).

The transitions required by migration are great, and the additional aspect of gender, traditional gender roles, and social and cultural expectations placed on the female make this transition more difficult. Migrants who relocate to Western societies from more traditional cultures may run up against a clash of interests between the family and the educational system, between the idea of the female as a caregiver who must create and maintain family unity, and the female as an individual human being with a right to education and curiosity. For the female migrant, daring to step outside a role that is acceptable to her family or her group may lead to in-group discrimination and social stigma (see Erden, in this book).

4.4 Cultural Determination of Gender Roles: In-Group Discrimination for Being a Woman

In addition to a lack of encouragement, or even downright discouragement, from family members if the female migrant happens to belong to a culture that does not place high value on the academic achievements of females, in fields such as mathematics and the hard sciences, migrant as well as native girls must contend with a history of male achievement. In these disciplines, a distinct lack of female role models also contributes to the difficulty of entering and achieving success in what is still today considered a less socially-acceptable education and career path for females.

Any girl who chooses to pursue one of these academic disciplines often has to persevere despite a resounding lack of positive reinforcement; additionally, a migrant girl must often balance a clash of interests and cultures each morning when she leaves the domestic world for that of school and learning, a transition that has the potential to create considerable amounts of stress and to serve as a barrier to the realization of her educational goals (United Nations Economic and Social Council 2006).

5 Conclusion

In conclusion, migrants do not enjoy *special* protection in the sense of a "higher" (qualitative) or "additional" (quantitative) level of protection.

The principle of equal treatment, although formally provided by law, is not realized in practice. Due to various reasons, certain vulnerable groups such as migrants face a higher risk of being discriminated against in the field of education. Migrants do not constitute a homogenous group; their only common characteristic is a particular vulnerability taking various facets.

Barriers to accessing the right to education can hinder the migrant at many levels. Aspects of legal and residential status as well as any institutional discrimination run the migrant up against the system and the majority society. Group discrimination also prevents the migrant from realizing her right to education. An individual may often be perceived and treated as inferior by society on grounds such as ethnicity or gender. Often, individuals with a migration background are situated in weaker economic or social conditions. At the level of the individual, the migrant usually suffers a lack of social connections or of a network of support. Forced migrants may often have to cope with the after-effects of trauma or stress from previous experiences. With regard to forced migration, international humanitarian law obliges the receiving state to "take over" human rights protection from the defaulting state. For many, however, the struggle of being a stranger in an unfamiliar society is enough to erect a considerable barrier to accessing education.

Although normative instruments applicable to certain groups facing a higher risk of being discriminated against exist in order to ensure their actual enjoyment of the right to education, there are still gaps in legislation. Existing inequalities between citizens and non-citizens in national legal systems justify positive measures that aim at compensating for a protection formally provided by law but not implemented in practice. In particular, strengthening participation rights as provided for in CERD, CEDAW or the EU "Race-Directive" may lead to the empowerment of vulnerable groups in realizing their human rights.

In order to *fulfill* the human right to education by law and in fact, it is necessary to provide for instruments and measures which *compensate* for the particular vulnerability migrants face. "Special" protection actually means fulfillment of the right to education for all and with this in mind, it aims at the *de facto* implementation of the *formal* principle of equal treatment.

Bibliography

Bendel, Petra, *Immigration Policy in the European Union: Still Bringing up the Walls for Fortress Europe?*, in: Migration Letters (2, 1), Migration Letters, London, 2005.

Council of Europe, *European Social Charter*, European Treaty Series No. 35 of 18 October 1961, available online at: http://conventions.coe.int/treaty/en/treaties/html/035.htm (last checked: 25 June 2008).

Council of Europe, *European Convention on the Legal Status of Migrant Workers*, European Treaty Series No. 93 of 24 November 1977, available online at: http://conventions.coe.int/Treaty/EN/Treaties/Html/093.htm (last checked: 25 June 2008).

Council of Europe, *Convention on the Participation of Foreigners in Public Life at Local Level*, European Treaty Series No. 144 of 5 February 1992, available online at: http://conventions.coe.int/Treaty/en/Treaties/Html/144.htm (last checked: 25 June 2008).

Daudet, Yves and Eisemann, Pierre Michel, *Commentary on the Convention against Discrimination in Education*, UNESCO, Paris, 2005.

European Union, *Council Directive 2000/43/EC of 29 June 2000 implementing the Principle of Equal Treatment between Persons Irrespective of Racial or Ethnic Origin.*

European Union, *Council Directive 2003/109/EC of 25 November 2003 concerning the Status of Third-country Nationals who are Long-term Residents.*

Eurostat, *Statistics in Focus, Population and Social Conditions (8/2006), Non-national populations in the EU Member States*, European Communities, Luxembourg, 2006, available online at: http://epp.eurostat.ec.europa.eu/cache/ITY_OFFPUB/KS-NK-06-008/EN/KS-NK-06-008-EN.PDF (last checked: 25 June 2008).

Eurostat, *Europe in Figures, Eurostat Yearbook 2008*, European Communities, Luxembourg, 2008, available online at:
http://epp.eurostat.ec.europa.eu/cache/ITY_OFFPUB/KS-CD-07-001/EN/KS-CD-07-001-EN.PDF (last checked: 25 June 2008).

Global Commission on International Migration (GCIM), *Migration in an Interconnected World: New Directions for Action*, GCIM, Geneva, 2005.

Ndiaye, Ndioro, *The Chain of Trafficking: Supply and Demand: Conference on the Challenge of Trafficking in Women and Girls: Meeting the Challenge together*, Speech delivered on 5 March 2007, available online at:
http://www.iom.int/jahia/Jahia/cache/offonce/pid/1336?entryId=13281 (last checked: 25 June 2008).

Nowak, Manfred, *The Right to Education*, in: Eide, Asbjorn, Krause, Catarina and Rosas, Allan (eds.), *Economic, Social and Cultural Rights*, Kluwer Law International, The Hague, 2001.

Tomaševski, Katarina, *Education Denied, Costs and Remedies*, Zed Books, London/New York, 2003.

United Nations Department of Economic and Social Affairs, *Trends in Total Migrant Stock: The 2005 Revision*, United Nations, New York, 2006.

United Nations Economic and Social Council (ECOSOC), *Report of the Special Rapporteur on the Right to Education, Vernor Muñoz, on Girls' Right to Education, E/CN.4/2006/45 of 8 February 2006*, available online at:
http://daccessdds.un.org/doc/UNDOC/GEN/G06/106/70/PDF/G0610670.pdf?OpenElement (last checked: 25 June 2008).

United Nations General Assembly, *Implementation of General Assembly Resolution 60/251 of 15 March 2006 entitled "Human Rights Council", Report of the Special Rapporteur on the Right to Education, Vernor Muñoz on his Mission to Germany,* A/HRC/4/29/Add.3 of 9 March 2007, available online at:
http://daccessdds.un.org/doc/UNDOC/GEN/G07/117/59/PDF/G0711759.pdf?OpenElement (last checked: 25 June 2008).

United Nations General Assembly, *International Migration and Development, Report of the Secretary-General,* A/60/871 of 18 May 2006, available online at: http://www.unhcr.org/protect/PROTECTION/44d711a82.pdf (last checked: 25 June 2008).

United Nations Office on Drugs and Crime (UNODC), *Trafficking in Persons – Global Patterns*, UNODC, Vienna, 2006.

United Nations Statistical Division, Department of Economic and Social Affairs, *Recommendations on Statistics of International Migration, Statistical Papers Series M, No. 58, Rev. 1*, United Nations, New York,1998, available online at:
http://unstats.un.org/unsd/publication/SeriesM/SeriesM_58rev1E.pdf (last checked: 25 June 2008).

Vandenhoule, Wouter, *Non-Discrimination and Equality in the View of the UN Human Rights Treaty Bodies*, Intersentia, Antwerpen/Oxford, 2005.

Learning while Transgressing Boundaries – Understanding Societal Processes Impacting Students with a Migration Background

Barbara Herzog-Punzenberger

1 Introduction

Boundary-drawing processes are the mechanisms through which groups are constituted and their existence enforced. While children of immigrants grow up in the society of their future, they do not face the same circumstances of living and learning as their "native" peers with whom they will build the future of their common society. Through manifold mechanisms framed in the nation-state ideology of today's societies, their access to knowledge and development is structured in particular ways. The legal framework, the national self-understanding and the educational system are among the most important institutional settings that more often enforce than transcend the boundaries stemming from migration. Schools are not only places of learning but they also fulfill different functions in modern nation-states. This idea helps to understand some of the problems students with a migration background are facing and it helps to explain differences in a country-comparative view. Practical examples are drawn from the Austrian context in particular.

Starting from the hypothesis that access to knowledge and personal development is structured in particular ways depending on the social position of an individual, students with a migration background might face quite specific obstacles to developing their full potential. The social position of an individual in the societal structure is mainly determined by categorizations such as gender (male/female), racialisation[1] (black/white/color), ethnicity (German/Turkish/Yugoslav ...), class (socio-economic background of the family) and legal status (national, non-national legal resident, unauthorized resident). Actually, the processes by which material and discursive categories shape the life and learning of the students, the way they are produced, experienced, reproduced and resisted in everyday life is far from fully understood. As James A. Banks (Banks 2004. XV) puts it, "*The issue of minority underachievement is undertheorized and requires more complex and nuanced explanations and theories than those that currently exist.*" In this article I will follow the approach of intersectionality that originated in women's studies in the beginning of the 1980s and that has spread to many disciplines since then

1 Racialisation refers to the discursive processes whereby the existence of different races as biologically distinct human groups mainly tied to visible traits is socially enacted.

(McCall 2005). Described in a very condensed way, categories as mentioned above do not only have an impact on life and learning, but the very position of an individual at a particular intersection of these differences colors the context of learning in each specific situation. Instead of showing how this works out in particular learning situations on the individual level, in this article I will describe on a more general and abstract level how we can try to understand the impact of the different categories. From an individual point of view it is pretty clear that the situation of a girl from a poor family with an insecure legal status and racialized features in a disadvantaged neighborhood school is tremendously different from the situation of a white boy from a middle class family with a secure legal status in a well-off neighborhood school[2] participating in a science class. To explain the mechanisms behind these axes of differences on the societal level I will draw on insights mainly from social and cultural anthropology, political science, history, as well as sociology to explain how the opportunities in society are structured differently for students with a minority, and more specifically migration, background compared to those who represent the majority group in a society.

2 Equal Opportunity

This book is about equal opportunity in science education. What is equal opportunity? "Equal opportunity" is a term hard to define. It has been used in various ways since the 1970s to indicate a social environment where immutable traits such as physical characteristics of a person or inherited traits such as social status does not impede the development of talents on an individual level and the principle of meritocracy on the societal level. Connected to the theoretical approach of intersectionality, it would mean that differences such as ethnicity, religion, social class and legal status ultimately should have no impact on intellectual achievement or other forms of merit as in the context of science learning. It has turned out to be very difficult, however, to arrive at a general and consistent definition of the term, the question being: What are the *relevant* opportunities and how can equality *be measured*?

3 Legal Membership

One of the most important questions when dealing with the idea of "equal opportunity" is the question of relationality. Equal in reference to what? In the context of

2 In a complex social situation, such as a school class, the positioning of the other actors (schoolmates, teachers, ...) matter just as much as the individual positioning.

im/migration, the group of reference is – seen from the most general point of view – the population without a migration background. Many inhabitants with a migration background are first and foremost not equal because the legal framework of their host country sets out how far non-citizens are allowed to be treated unequally – in the "targeted" law on strangers (*Fremdenrecht* as it is called in German) but also in other legal texts. To begin with, non-citizens are not allowed to stay without conditions; their right to residence oftentimes is limited by the availability of contracted labor (labor migrants) or otherwise financial resources (entrepreneurs or those of independent means). They are not allowed to work without restrictions – to get permission, the employer has to check with the labor-market service first if there are nationals available for that job. They are not allowed to participate in political processes – voting or being elected. They are not eligible for certain benefits (housing, education and training stipends, old age care, ...) and excluded from certain positions, professional (e.g. in the civil service) and otherwise.

3.1 Differences of Specific Legal Statuses in Different Countries

The reader might think now that this is painting the picture black and white. For one thing, non-nationals within the EU are oftentimes nationals from other EU-countries and therefore have to be treated almost equal. Also in the case of third country nationals many have been naturalized and their children have already been born as citizens of the country to which their parents migrated. Another important differentiation in a country comparison is the fact that the legal discrimination against strangers or third country nationals can be markedly different among the countries (see Migrant Integration Policy Index MIPEX). For example, in Sweden the difference in access to resources and opportunities of participation between long-term residents from non-EU-countries and nationals is rather small, while in Austria the difference is comparatively big. By considering the whole range of statuses and connected rights and obligations a wide variety has opened up and it becomes clear that it makes little sense to speak about students with migration background as one category even if only looked at under the legal lens.

3.2 Legal Status and Learning

Why do we bother with this in the context of learning? What has to be kept in mind for the following chapters is that legal discrimination is one of the most eminent and clear-cut forms of boundary-drawing between groups of people today. The consequences of exclusion through legal mechanisms might also manifest themselves in the next generation, *even* when descendants are naturalized right away as is the case in *jus soli* systems.[3] An illustrative example is the difference in school-success of student citizens whose parents are unauthorized immigrants in the USA compared to those who have had a regular legal status right from the beginning and who share all other characteristics of parents such as socio-economic background, country of origin and time of arrival (Fix et al 2008, Bean et al 2007). Regarding the cumulative effect on these migrants' children of an insecure legal situation, socio-economic hardship, little educational experience of parents and membership in a group which is perceived to be at the lower end of the social hierarchy and their self-concept, research is scarce in some countries such as Austria.[4]

4 Boundary-Drawing

As individualistic as our societies and times may be, no one is a real monad existing by him- or herself, especially not in the process of growing up. Therefore, students are not only individuals; they experience themselves and are experienced by others as members of groups or at least categories – fe/male, Catholic/Protestant/Muslim/atheist, subproletariat/proletariat/petit bourgeois/…, urban/rural and so on. Categorization is an effort by the human mind to create order in an excruciatingly complex universe. We categorize the whole of our environment and almost everything we experience. It is important to remember that the outcome of categorization in the case of human beings is that we tend to interact differently with different categories of people. Children do not only learn about their surroundings, but also about themselves and their abilities, i.e. acquiring self-concept through interaction with other people – with other children on the playground, in the kindergarten, in school, with adults in private and public spaces and with institutions. Many students with a migration background experience a special situation regarding their place in the social universe precisely because their patterns of belonging do not fit the established patterns of group membership.

The expectation oftentimes is that one be either an Austrian (or German/Swiss/Swede) or a Turk (Serb/Moroccan). It is not as comforting to belong to a new category which is in the process of establishing itself and fighting for its right

3 *Jus soli* means the "right of the soil," i.e. granting the citizenship of the country of birth independent of the citizenship of the parents as is the case in the USA.

4 As a starting point, however, Rosenthal and Jacobson explained basic mechanisms in their influential book *Pygmalion in the Classroom: Teacher expectation and pupils' intellectual development* (1968) and lately for the German speaking readership Schofield (2006) gave an overview of results concerning stereotype threat, as well as the effects stemming from the composition of the students according to achievement and from the teacher's expectations. Not to forget class reproduction through the educational system building on Bourdieu (1977) as well as Boudon (1974) and Bernstein (2000).

to normality as it is to belong to established groups, especially to the majority which is privileged in many respects. Obviously groups do not exist per se, but are constituted through interaction and discourse. This insight is just as true for ethnic or national groups as it is for any other category of groups.

4.1 Ethnicity and Culture

For a long time, ethnic groups were equated with "cultural" groups, i.e. allegedly the members of a specific ethnic group shared the same culture. Through anthropological research it became more and more clear that cultural boundaries are not clear-cut and cultural traits frequently cross group boundaries. On the other hand, it is quite obvious that members of the same ethnic or national category do differ in a lot of ways depending on their socio-economic background, their regional bases, their gender, religion, ideology and other axes of differences. For an example, taken from Austria, it is quite hard to identify the shared culture of a conservative Catholic farmer in the Tyrolean mountains, an atheist socialist worker in a steel plant in a mid-sized city such as Linz and a liberal Protestant bourgois, i.e. member of the upper middle class in metropolitan Vienna. Apart from their daily routines, value-systems and rituals, which differ enormously, even their dialects and sociolects would pose some difficulties in communication although they are members of the same "culture." In reality, however, the opportunities of interaction and communication between these representatives of a "culture" are quite limited as the people mostly stay within their "circles." Much of the common cultural understanding therefore is learned in school and fostered through administrative structures and routines as well as media and other discourses.

4.2 Difference and Sameness

Thus, the "objective" amount of difference or sameness is not decisive for the existence of an ethnic group, nor is it for the membership in an ethnic group. The existence of an ethnic group fundamentally depends on the boundary drawing mechanisms. Real or constructed differences are made to be relevant for the differentiation of two groups – a discursive process. These markers can be minute differences in physical appearance, dressing or habits, but they can also point to differences in attitudes and value-systems. The importance of particular markers, as well as group boundaries, shifts. As pointed out by anthropologists (Barth 1969), political scientists (Bauböck 1994) and sociologists (Shibutani and Kwan 1965, Alba 2003) the nature of these processes allows individuals to cross boundaries and change group memberships; however, the boundaries blur and the distinctions are seen to be not as big as previously thought. Eventually the whole boundary can move and the "normality" of the group includes either practices, values, etc. formerly seen to be signifiers of the other group, i.e. the whole group is included in a major, albeit latent, change of the collective self-understanding of another group.[5] Students with migration background, especially heirs to the "guest worker policy," experience exactly those processes. Roughly speaking, three alternative routes can be distinguished: either they (1) change group membership and decide – with or without their parent's consent – to become part of the majority (assimilation) or they (2) want or feel obliged to stick to their parent's heritage and group of origin (persistence) or they (3) rely on both sources which can either mean that they switch between the groups, including practices, allegiance and membership, according to circumstances (circumstantialism, instrumentalism) or that they create more or less consciously a new category by choosing and merging specific aspects and creating new practices etc. (constructionism). In any case, going to a public school in their parents' country of immigration, the question faced by students with a migration background very often is: Do I belong to this society? Do they want me to be a full member? And do I *want* to belong to this society at all?

Even when a young person can answer this question quite clearly with yes, this does not mean that his own allegiance is accepted by established members of the group. So, the dominating political or media discourses may signal very clearly that new members are not accepted as long as they do not assimilate fully. Even then, origin can be seen as a boundary marker, i.e. on the individual level a signifier of the membership to another group.

4.3 Religious Affiliation, Gender Relations, Language Competence

At the beginning of the article, the individual's position in a specific learning situation was described against the background of the theory of intersectionality, i.e. situations are framed by all the axes of differences significant in a society. Individuals do not experience only one category such as age, gender or migration background, but all of them at once.[6] This does also mean that they should not be understood as simply adding up, but rather as experienced intersections of differences. Answers to the question which differences are the most important ones for students in school can only be context-dependent, i.e. country-specific. At the same time,

5 Less frequent is the case of an entirely new group such as Creoles in the Caribbean emerging as a hybrid group from the indigenous population and African slaves brought to the Americas.

6 The question of which differences are the most important ones, if there are in fact only a limited number of categories that are relevant for intersectionality and if it is adequate to establish a certain hierarchy (gender, racialization or ethnicity being the most important difference) cannot be discussed here (see also Gürses et al. 2001, 33-35). This analytical and practical problem is basically not resolved.

not least because of globalization, some general patterns can be observed since the end of 1990s which are relevant for almost all European countries. Religious affiliation, gender relation and language competence have gained amplified importance in boundary-drawing between groups. This can also be interpreted as a development accompanying the decreasing importance of legal status for long-term residents and their children – as many of them have naturalized or legal discrimination is negligible as in the case of EU citizens inside the European Union, especially the "old" member-states. At the same time, legal status is still highly relevant for those not naturalized and more so for groups with an insecure or non-existent legal status (see also paragraph on legal membership).

During the last few years, students with a real or perceived affiliation with Islam, oftentimes those whose parents immigrated from Turkey or Morocco, experienced particularly obvious boundary-drawing by the mainstream society, as manifested in the media and right wing but also mainstream political parties. This process obviously was fuelled by the activities of terrorists who tried to construct a binary worldview where on the one side fundamentalist Islam was the solution for all (political) problems and the ultimate truth, and on the other side everything else was evil and to be destroyed. In this process oftentimes politicians of Western European countries and the US played the complementary role, fitting neatly into the binary pattern. The definition of friends and foes, the characterization of certain countries as axes of evil and statements like: Those who are not for us are against us are perfect examples of an equally binary worldview promoted by "the West."

4.4 We Are All Feminists Now! How Austria Became a Feminist Country

In most Western European countries the discursive differentiation between European societies and Muslim immigrants, mostly labor migrants of low social background, was highlighting the differences not only in religious affiliation but also in gender relations and language competence. Intersectionality became clearly visible in the case of Muslim women. Within a very short time, gender equality was not a feminist issue anymore but the whole (Austrian, German, Dutch, ...) society defined itself as gender equal, contrary to Muslims or Turkish immigrants who were described as anachronistically backwards (Fassmann, Reeger et al. 2007) The respective "culture" was portrayed as a manifestation of gender inequality. The factual contradictions in generalizations and idealizations of the majority society are concurrently suppressed or portrayed as comparatively unimportant: the fact is that income between men and women still differs considerably, housework is still largely distributed unequally between the sexes and caring for children or old relatives is mainly a female task.[7] Oftentimes, a connection to scientific data that show a much more complicated image of the majority society itself is omitted.[8] Even the most conservative political parties discovered in this situation their mission for gender equality when few years ago they still had built their profile on family values tied to traditional gender roles of housewives staying at home and caring for children, keeping the household and caring for the husband.[9]

4.5 Language Competence Becoming More Important in the Course of Labor-Market Transformations

A similarly marked shift has happened in the area of language competence. Close to perfect knowledge of the majority language suddenly was seen as a prerequisite for participation in society, when before language competence was mostly relevant for specific kinds of jobs. In the course of the transformation of the labor market from industry-based to a post-industrial knowledge-based economy, the role of language also changed. During the guest worker recruitment period, most societies simply did not care if unskilled workers were able to communicate.[10] They just had to learn the few words they needed to "function" in the way expected by their employers. Communication with "guest workers" was of no great interest for most locals; they would not mix anyways. The co-workers oftentimes also were non-natives with another mother-tongue. In this way, it is no wonder that language competence did not improve dramatically over time. There was little incentive or opportunity to improve the language skills for many foreign workers, even more so for family members who reunited later and were mostly working at home, such as housewives with several children.

On the other hand, the reduced literacy skills of the natives were not of great interest either. Secondary analphabetism of mother-tongue speakers was completely denied for a long time and research on this topic is scarce in many countries. Only when PISA showed that in fact the majority of 15-year old students at risk (low reading and writing skills) were natives e.g. in the case of Austria, it was clear that

7 For a detailed analyses of racism, orientalism, exotism, sexism and antisemitism in Austrian school books see Markom and Weinhäupl 2007.

8 In a recent study on youth in Austria it was shown that more than half of the 16 to 25 year old population without a migration background does not believe in gender-equality (Polak, Kromer and Friesl 2008).

9 The same dynamic could be observed regarding homosexuality especially in the Netherlands where a photo showing two men kissing each other was part of the citizenship test.

10 This is true for different European countries to different degrees. One of the early examples of a different approach was Sweden. As a result of negotiations between the employers' federation and the unions, in the 1960s immigrants had a right to language instruction.

problems with language were not the exclusive "privilege" of students with a migration background.

5 National Identity

Whereas in the past section on boundary drawing, anthropological insights were discussed, in the next section the historical setting of the nation-state, its role as a homogenizing force and its link to education and schooling will be introduced. National (or ethnic)[11] identity is often perceived as one of the main axes of difference. National identity is constructed so that collectivities that imagine themselves as nations – i.e. politically self-governing territorially bound entities with a particular set of culture(s), language(s), religion(s) – oftentimes try to trace their roots back from time immemorial. The effort to condemn to oblivion all the changes and battles over which culture, language, and religion could gain hegemony and therefore be forced upon subjects is an effort to increase the legitimacy of the present set of culture, language, religion.[12] Because the constructed character of collective identities is latent, i.e. not conscious, it is even possible to naturalize national or ethnic identity. In history this has led to a connection between culture/language and body/blood/genes and the idea that certain groups of people cannot be assimilated.

5.1 The Nation-State and Cultural Homogenization

Migration is frequently portrayed as the overwhelming force diversifying today's societies. Today's societies, in turn, have been imagined each as a rather homogenous entity called "the nation." Some were designated as nations earlier, like the French nation at the end of the 18th century, and others only later, like the Austrian nation only after WWI and finally as an attitude shared by the majority of the population only after WWII. While institutional memory tends to highlight only those aspects which fit into the dominant framework, factual history tells a different story. Linguistic, religious and cultural heterogeneity was rather impressive in many urban spaces, not least in Vienna at the turn of the 19th/20th century. After WWII, however, Austria was constructed as the German-speaking, Catholic coun-

11 Since nations can be multi-ethnic or states can be multinational the boundary between nation and ethnic group is not as clear as it might seem at first sight. Whereas the term "nation" always implies the will to political self-government, i.e. a state-structure (but there are also nations without a state like the Kurds or Palestinians), ethnic groups are usually those who share all the other features with nations except for the power-position.

12 A good example from Austria is the fact that large parts of Austria were protestant, in some provinces even the majority of the population, right before the counter-reformation, was buried under the myth that Austria is THE catholic country from the first Christianisation on.

try with little reflection upon the homogenizing processes that had been going on during its history, starting with the counter-reformation in the 16th century up to the National Socialist eradication of all groups and minorities that did not fit the imagined Germanic ideal in the 20th century. Although processes of homogenization were particularly violent in some phases of history, in many instances they are more subtle, and unnoticeable in instances when a monistic normality has simply been created through everyday practices and routines, mass media and education. One of the most important institutions of homogenization is school.

6 The School-System

Schooling has several functions in a modern society. Ernest Gellner (Gellner 1983) in his theory on nationalism described why nation-states simply would not work without schools. Contrary to agrarian societies, the modern industrial economy rests on a division of labor where people have to be able to communicate with anonymous others about complex matters. This is one of the reasons why a basic training or compulsory education is necessary for a state with a modern economy. Adding to this idea, I would claim that schooling in today's societies has four different functions:

- Liberal function: pertains to the development of the abilities and talents of the individual student, i.e. cognitive, emotional, social and physical.
- Economic function: prepares individuals for their working-life and tries to match the population to the economy, i.e. labor-market of a society.
- Political function: safeguards the stability of the political system, in our case the democratic nation-state, i.e. citizens' self-understanding and their understanding of rights and duties.
- Cultural function: reproduces a specific (often more regionalized) variation of the national high-culture, i.e. recognizing, memorizing and expressing in the fields of language, music, movement, architecture, sculpture, painting, etc.

Contrary to other learning environments, schooling, during the phase when it is compulsory for children, not only has a liberal and economic function,[13] but also a clear political function which is strongly connected to the cultural function, namely reproducing the nation-state with its specific collective identity. There are, however, two dimensions to this: the first is that of the school as an institution that tries to make sure that the individual will identify with the political community, the country, the nation-state where the school is situated or to which it belongs. Apart

13 This is also the case for most formal and informal education not connected to school.

from identification, which is the emotional dimension of the political function, there is also a cognitive dimension. To make sure that citizens can communicate with one another and with the state, not only literally but also symbolically, they have to learn the language and to decipher the "signs."

Each national identity materializes in a vast multiplicity of ways, spatially, through signs, names, symbols, monuments and other buildings especially in the public space, as well as maps,[14] temporally through the timing of the day, the week (free Sundays), the year, holidays (e.g. Christian calendar), administratively through data-gatherings like censuses, registers, and, last but not least, through professional memorizing such as museums and historical writings.

6.1 Primary and Secondary Socialization

All these practices and the particular knowledge get transmitted in school. Depending on the resources and the orientation of the family, and not least their class background, children might be familiar with a lot of practices and knowledge experienced in school or they might not. Especially at the point of entry, many things may seem more or less alien to the child who does not come from a typical middle class family. In the family, children experience primary socialization. These experiences and abilities get transformed through secondary socialization in public institutions like kindergartens and especially compulsory schooling. Children do not only learn mathematics and science, reading and writing, as well as artistic and physical articulation, but they also learn to what extent they belong to a certain community, the nation, or a particular social class. They also learn what it means to be a good citizen and what it is to be "normal" in this society. This is why school is a crucial place for children to build their self-concept and get a feeling for their place in the social universe.

Depending on the teacher and the composition of the class, as well as the attitude of the parents, children can experience the challenges school confronts them with as a natural way to grow in society, or they can experience them as a series of smaller and bigger provocations that finally can result in a need for self-denial related to their family background and in the end in a deep uncertainty. A feeling of alienation can result from differences in social class, language (including sociolect or dialect), religious orientation, or cultural background, as well as sexual orientation.

14 E.g., the national weather forecast of the Austrian public TV channels ORF1 and ORF2 include South Tyrol which belongs to Italy but is seen as inhabited by descendants of Austrians.

6.2 Socio-Economic Background

So far we have touched upon differences regarding gender, nation/ethnicity, language, religion, legal status – but the most important of all differences still is the socio-economic background.

Although there is still much to find out about the exact mechanisms of intergenerational processes, we do know about the strength of "social inheritance." What is important at the level of society and policy-making, is that different school-systems are able to counteract the intergenerational inheritance of educational disadvantage to different degrees. Especially through PISA, the Program for International Student Assessment (OECD 2004, OECD 2005), as well as PIRLS, the Progress in International Reading Literacy Study, it has been possible to compare student populations in different countries and find out about the importance of parents' education, profession, social and cultural capital, as well as migration background and language spoken at home, in order to explain outcomes in science, mathematical and reading literacy of 15 and 10 year old students respectively.

Looking at the countries that performed above OECD-average in PISA 2003, all except Belgium showed a lower impact of socio-economic background on students' performance in mathematics than the OECD-average. These countries manage comparatively well to balance differences in socio-economic background of the students, at least better than others. Most interestingly, above average performance and low impact of socio-economic background is not a privilege of countries which have a very low share of students with migration background – an argument which is often used to explain Finland's success in PISA. Canada, for example, together with Australia is one of the countries with the highest shares of students with a migration background, as well as students who do not speak the language of instruction at home. Nevertheless, students in Canada do profit from an educational system that is able to counter-balance the socio-economic background of the families comparatively well. Canada produces only a small share of at-risk students while ranking among the top countries in all the PISA tests and all the fields of literacy.

With respect to schooling and differences in learning processes and outcomes, the socio-economic background of the student explains a bigger share of difference than any cultural, religious or linguistic background. In some countries it was even shown that after accounting for socio-economic background no difference in performance was left between different groups of origin, especially concerning 2nd generation (UK, Sweden). Still there are several countries were differences in performance cannot be explained by the characteristics available so far, so that the difference left unexplained is called "ethnic penalty" – a difference in learning achievements connected to country of origin and language spoken at home among the 1st and 2nd generation. Austria and Germany are among the countries with the highest ethnic penalty concerning performance of 10-year-old as well as 15-year-old students. However, in all countries the impact of the socio-economic background is higher than the impact of what is connected to migration.

7 Conclusion

In this article I tried to describe how different societal structures impact students and their learning. Following the constructivist understanding of students' learning, each individual constructs his/her own knowledge in an active process. This process is colored by the position the individual student occupies in the societal universe, and each of the learning processes, i.e. societal structures, the composition of the classroom, the expectancy of the teacher play an eminent role. The intersectional approach stresses the importance social categories play in the self-understanding and development of the student's learning capacities, depending on his/her position in the social universe. To better understand the position can be imagined as being located at the intersections of axes of difference, of which the most important are class (socio-economic background), gender, racialisation (visibility), ethnicity, religion, language and legal status. In describing these axes of difference I wanted to highlight their performative power in the boundary-drawing processes of groups, stressing legal status as one which was not getting much attention so far. The individual student as the locus where ascriptive categories manifest themselves and are possibly transformed into group membership is one perspective on the preconditions of the learning processes. The other is the structure of the educational system through which the students have to navigate. This becomes especially plausible in a country-comparative view.

In terms of educational processes, schools still are one of the main spaces of learning and more specifically of earning credentials. Concerning the impact of school systems on students with a migration background we already got valuable information from the large scale students' assessment studies. I wanted to add another explanatory level to the existing analyses in this article. Understanding schooling in terms of different the functions it has to perform in modern nation-states can help in being able to grasp why increasing heterogeneity poses problems to the existing school systems. Therefore I proposed to distinguish analytically between four different functions of schooling (liberal, economic, political, cultural) which are given different weight and importance in different societies. In my understanding this expresses itself at all levels of schooling – from the structural to the didactical level. At the same time it is expressive of different societal self-understandings in a very general and comprehensive way. To prove these ideas and scrutinize the empirical details is a task for upcoming research.

Bibliography

Alba, Richard and Nee, Victor, *Remaking the American Mainstream. Assimilation and Contemporary Immigration*, First Harvard University Press, Cambridge, 2003.

Banks, James A., *Foreword. Migration, Education and Change*, in: Luchtenberg, Sigrid, *Migration, Education and Change*, Routledge, London and New York, XIII-XVI.

Barth, Fredrik, *Introduction*, in: Barth, Fredrik, *Ethnic Groups and Boundaries. The Social Organization of Culture Difference*, Universitetsforlaget, Oslo, 1969, 9-38.

Bauböck, Rainer, *The Integration of Immigrants*, Council of Europe, Strasbourg, 1994.

Bean, Frank, Brown, Susan, Leach, Mark and Bachmeier, James, *Becoming Stakeholders: The Structure, Nature and Pace of U.S. Integration Among Mesican Immigrants and Their Descendants*, Report to the Merage Foundation for the American Dream Symposium on Immigrant National Leaders, University of Irvine, May 2007.

Bernstein, Basil, *Pedagogy, Symbolic Control and Identity, Theory, Research, Critique*, Revised Edition, Rowham & Littlefield, Lanham et al., 2000.

Boudon, Raymond, *Education, opportunity and social inequality. Changing Perspectives in Western Society*, John Wiley and Sons, New York, 1974.

Bourdieu, Pierre, *Reproduction in Education, Society and Culture*, Sage Publications, London, 1977.

Fassmann, Heinz, Reeger, Ursula and Sari, Sonja, *migrantinnen bericht 2007*, Bundeskanzleramt, Wien, 2007.

Fix, Michael, McHugh, Margie, Terrazas, Aaron, Matteo and Laglagaron, Laureen, *Los Angeles on the Leading Edge. Immigrant Integration Indicators and Their Policy Implications*, Migration Policy Institute, Washington, 2008.

Gellner, Ernest, *Nations and Nationalism*, Blackwell, Oxford, 1983.

Gürses, Hakan, Herzog-Punzenberger, Barbara, Reiser, Karl, Strasser, Sabine and Cinar, Dilek, *The Necessary Impossibility: Dynamics of Identity among Youth of Different Backgrounds*, in: Journal of International Migration and Integration (2, 1) 2001, 27-54.

Markom, Christa and Weinhäupl, Heide, *Die Anderen im Schulbuch. Rassismen, Exotismen, Sexismen und Antisemitismus in österreichischen Schulbüchern*, Braumüller, Wien, 2006.

McCall, Leslie, *The Complexity of Intersectionality*, in: Signs Journal of Women in Culture and Society (30, 3), 2005, 1771-1800.

Migration Policy Group and British Council, *Migrant Integration Policy Index MIPEX*, Brussels 2007, available online at: www.integrationindex.eu (last checked: 30 October 2008).

OECD, *School Factors Related to Quality and Equity. Results from PISA 2000*, OECD Publishing, Paris, 2004.

OECD, *Where Immigrant Students Succeed. A comparative review of performance and engagement in PISA 2003*, OECD Publishing, Paris, 2005.

Polak, Regina, Kromer, Ingrid and Friesl, Christian, *Lieben. Leisten. Hoffen. Die Wertewelt junger Menschen in Österreich*, Österreichisches Jugendinstitut, Wien 2008.

Schofield, Janet Ward, *Migrationshintergrund, Minderheitenzugehörigkeit und Bildungserfolg. Forschungsergebnisse der pädagogischen, Entwicklungs- und Sozialpsychologie*, AKI-Forschungsbilanz, Wissenschaftszentrum Berlin, 2006.
Shibutani, Tamotsu, Kwan, Kian M. and Billigmeier, Robert H., *Ethnic Stratification: A Comparative Approach,* MacMillan, New York, 1965.

2. The Challenge – Unlimited Access to Scientific Careers

Detect the Barriers and Leave Them Behind – Science Education in Culturally and Linguistically Diverse Classrooms

Tanja Tajmel, Klaus Starl, Lutz-Helmut Schön

1 Introduction

The guarantee of equal access to education for all students has been declared one of the utmost concerns of modern and open school systems. However, empirical studies outline the differences in performances of migrants and non-migrants, girls and boys and people of different socio-economic backgrounds. International studies of school achievement such as the *Program for International Students Assessment* (PISA), show that students with a migrant background are behind those of their peers without a migrant background (OECD 2004, 2005). Referencing the PISA-results of 2006, Manfred Prenzel said, "*Even in the field of natural sciences, you can find in many states (furthermore) huge differences in achievement between youth with and without a migrant background. These differences are particularly pronounced in Germany and Belgium*" (PISA-Konsortium Deutschland 2007, translation by Sara Moore). As long as the percentage of migrants and women in various fields and job positions of science is unequal to their percentage of the total population, we can consider them as *underrepresented*. We have to assume a situation of persistent inequality with social barriers in the access to positions that are suitable to the qualifications of the aspirants. The existence of whole groups of people doing comparatively worse in the field of the natural sciences exhibits an important challenge for educational research in order to identify the causation of the present situation.

In this article we present a model of quality improvement for science education in a linguistically and culturally diverse society. The first step of this process is the identification of barriers and limitations in science education which hamper migrants especially. In the next step objectives and approaches to solutions are defined. In a third step the objectives are put into practice; in our case, in the form of an international project, which provides a framework for interdisciplinary and intercultural collaboration.

2 Basic Questions

Prior to the process of barrier-analysis and goal-setting, profound questions have to be clarified in order to identify the threads for further investigations. Let's start provocatively: What *is* the problem exactly? Why is it a problem at all, when certain groups are underrepresented and perform worse than others in the natural sciences? Is this the case everywhere or do examples exist where this underrepresentation does not occur? And finally, do we have to change science education or should we leave well enough alone?

More scientifically formulated, we define three distinct areas of research:

- Human Right to Education
  Can the Human Right to a natural science education be derived from the Human Right to Education?
- Underrepresentation of certain groups
  Can reasons be found why certain groups are underrepresented in the field of physics, by international comparison?
- Linguistically and culturally diverse science classes
  What kind of new challenges are brought to science classes of cultural and linguistic diversity?

Can the human right to a natural science education be derived from the Human Right to Education?

The human rights approach is appropriate in order to handle all those different challenges that occur in connection with an infinite access to natural science education. This attempt requires positive measures in order to support disadvantaged groups, and puts job training as well as technical education on the agenda. The right to education represents a normative principle for its conception and implementation. Education is an aim in and of itself. The natural sciences are an integral part of general education in human civilization. Therefore, every human being has a right to take part in cultural and intellectual society. Legally, the right to a natural science education can be derived from the Convention on Social, Economic and Cultural Rights, and from the Convention on Technical and Vocational Education (Starl in this book, chapter 1). Education has to be relevant and acceptable in order to guarantee the personal and cultural development of every human being. Pragmatically speaking, the natural sciences increase individual possibilities for employment and economic profit, and therefore the chance to lead the life that one has always wanted and wished to have.

Can reasons be found why certain groups are underrepresented in the field of physics, by international comparison?

International comparisons prove that not all countries suffer from an underrepresentation of women in the field of physics. In Bosnia and Herzegovina and also in Turkey at least 50% of all professorships are held by women. In contrast, in the natural scientific departments in Germany this ratio is only 10% (Willand 2007).

After 30 years of research on girls' needs with regard to physics education, and research on the gender gaps in the natural sciences the following question must be raised: *Will the underrepresentation of women in industrialized and high income countries change in the next generation?* The international comparative research project *The Relevance of Science Education* (ROSE) (Schreiner and Sjøberg 2004) investigated young people's orientations towards science and technology in about 40 countries. The study revealed that the relevance of science and technology, as perceived by students, is linked to the level of development of a country. "*The more developed a country is, the less positive young people are towards the role of S&T in society.*" (Sjøberg and Schreiner 2005). An explorative study among female high school students in Germany as a high-income country and Bosnia-Herzegovina as a low-income country (Tajmel and Hadžibegović in this book, chapter 2) indicates that in Germany the underrepresentation of women in the field of physics will not change in the next generation. Moreover, it has been shown that more female students in Germany *with* a migrant background desire to study natural sciences at a university than those without a migrant background. Taking into account the university statistics on employed researchers (professors and PhD-students) it can be stated that in Bosnia-Herzegovina, where more women are employed in the field of physics, more female students choose physics as a subject. Thus, we assume that the existence of female role models and the cultural association of the image of women with the profession of a physicist might positively impact the female students' decision of whether to study physics.

What kind of new challenges are brought to science classes of cultural and linguistic diversity?

The increasing linguistic heterogeneity in society, marked by migration, constitutes new challenges to the field of science education. The neglect of this factor by teachers, teacher trainers and science-education policy makers leads to the status of unequal opportunities for students. Although many teachers see very clearly that the diversity of their students requires differences in instruction in order to meet the individual needs of the students, many creative teaching intentions are dropped due to insufficient time and the pressure to fulfill the curriculum. But, when is the curriculum regarded as fulfilled? When the teacher has taught the content or when the content was successfully communicated to the students? The reference to educational standards which must be reached, raises another question: Does the standard-based education policy promote or impede diversity-sensitive instruction? As educational standards are measured by standardized tests, they probably promote the one-size-fits-all teaching concept indirectly due to time limits and time management efficiency reasons. Thus, the challenge to science education policy is to develop curricula and to define standards in a way that promotes the consideration of culture and language in the science classroom. The challenge to the science classes is, firstly, to put diversity mainstreaming and culture-sensitive pedagogy into practice and secondly, to integrate language learning methods [Rösch and Tajmel in this book, chapter 3].

3 Analysis of Barriers for Migrants in Science Education

In order to identify what kinds of discrimination are specifically impeding the access to science education for migrants, we use the *logical framework for analysis and goal-setting* (AusAID 2005). Starting with the undesirable state of affairs, a cause is hypothesized. From this, other outcomes are derived, i.e., outcomes with their own further impacts. This logical cause-effect connection is followed, until the undesirable state of affairs is elucidated.

Figure 1 describes the deduction of a negative state of affairs out of a hypothetical cause over several partial causes.

In this case the negative state of affairs is that migrants demonstrate comparably less scholastic achievement in the subjects of natural science, and that they are underrepresented in the career fields of natural science. The hypothetical cause we assumed is the lack of consideration of linguistic and cultural diversity within natural science classes and the lack of mutuality between science teacher training and the target group of the science lessons.

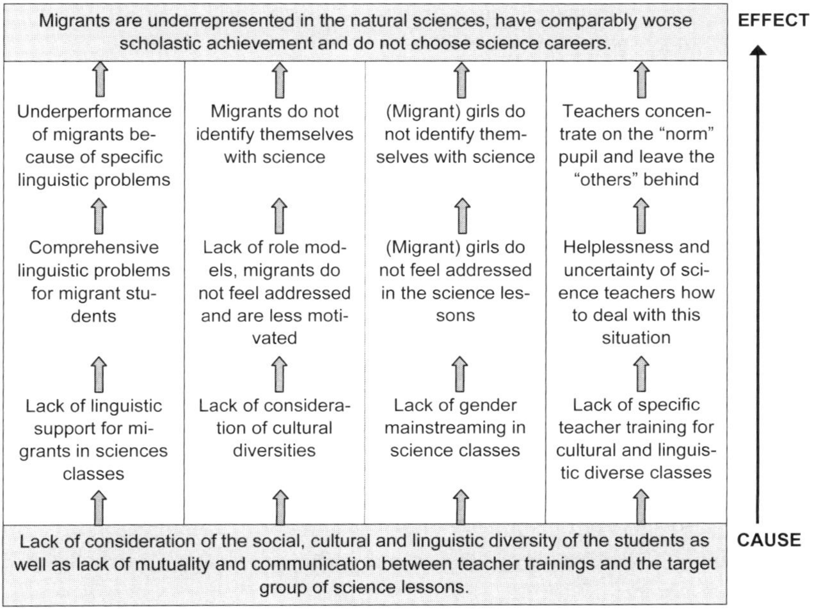

Lack of role models, migrants do not feel addressed and are less motivated

Helplessness and uncertainty of science teachers how to deal with this situation

Figure 1: The Problem Tree

3.1 Conceptual Delineation of "Barrier"

On the basis of the problem analysis, we can identify three types of barriers that impede access to education: (A) linguistic, (B) cultural, and (C) institutional barriers. We chose an approach that does not focus on the deficits of migrants (i.e. lack of German language skills). In our analysis, if we address *deficits* in the following, we address *deficits of science classes and of the educational system.*

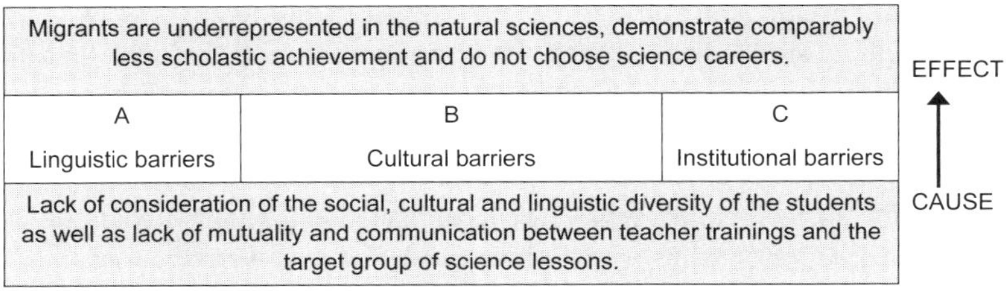

Migrants are underrepresented in the natural sciences, demonstrate comparably less scholastic achievement and do not choose science careers.
EFFECT
Teachers concentrate on the "norm" pupil and leave the "others" behind
A
Linguistic barriers
B
Cultural barriers
C
Institutional barriers
Lack of consideration of the social, cultural and linguistic diversity of the students as well as lack of mutuality and communication between teacher trainings and the target group of science lessons.
CAUSE

Figure 2: The three categories of barriers for migrants in science education.

In our model the socio-economic background of students is not considered as a barrier. Socio-economic differences are facts in every society and open school systems make – or at least try to make – accessibility to primary and secondary education independent of one's economic status.

We defined barriers that are changeable by school authorities, by teachers and by teacher trainers. But neither school authorities nor teachers or teacher trainers can influence or reduce the economic differences between the students' families. In contrast, the fact that the school system represents a certain social class and culture and, thus, predominantly addresses students with a certain *cultural capital*, which includes a certain social and economic background, is considered a cultural barrier which can be changed.

3.2 Linguistic Barriers

Linguistic barriers are considered as deficits of the science classes and not of the students or their families. Students who are not native speakers are generally disadvantaged in classes taught in their second language, since they have to communicate in a language which is neither their first nor best. Students who are native speakers have an advantage. A linguistic barrier should be understood as a barrier caused by insufficient consideration of linguistic abilities, which might impede the success of migrants in education in the natural sciences to such an extent that they do not receive a proper education in natural science.

It is a very common argument in this context that the insufficient second language knowledge of the students' parents and the lack of second language acquisition within their family and at pre-school age were the exclusive reasons for students' language problems. In other words, if students with a migrant background acquired the second language within their families, there would not be any need for linguistic support or consideration of language in science classes at all. This presumption is hypothetical and its empirical verification is impossible. First of all, the usage of the term "migrants" suggests homogeneity of a certain group of people. In fact, this term subsumes profoundly diverse persons with diverse biographies. They migrated from different countries at different ages due to different reasons with a different length of stay, have differently educated parents and different first languages. The only common attribute is that the person or the parents of the person were not born in the country they are actually living in. Of course, it is supportive for a child's education to have educated parents who are interested in and take care of the education of their child. However, educational systems cannot count on this positive influence from parents, simply because the parents were themselves also born into a more or into a less educated family with more or less support. Some women who grew up in rural areas in newly industrialized countries like Turkey did not attend school for longer than two years (Erden in this book, chapter 2). Who would blame these women for not teaching their children a foreign or second language? The second language acquisition at pre-school age is definitely an important factor and the lack of second language acquisition at pre-school age might be one reason for the poor performance of students in science, but it is one inequality among others (*e.g.* the socio-economic status of the family, the education of the parents, etc.). All educational policies in countries with open school systems declare that the compensation for these inequalities is the task and responsibility of the school system. Consequently, the conception of the open school system includes and hence should be prepared for heterogeneity among students. If, nevertheless, a certain group of students does not succeed in school, due, for example, to the lack of second language acquisition at pre-school age, it can be assumed that the school system is not fulfilling its defined task. So far, the language ability of students in natural science classes has either not or not sufficiently been taken into account.

3.3 Cultural Barriers

The German school system represents a *monocultural and monolingual habitus* (Gogolin 1994). It is a principle of (German) society, that monolinguality of the society and its members is *normal*. The cultural habitus of school is indicated by the cultural and social ancestry of teachers and by the *cultural capital* (Bourdieu 1992) which the system demands from the students. The monocultural habitus is reflected by depiction of subject specific contents in schoolbooks and also the depictions of persons and objects in textbooks. They do not reflect the multicultural diversity of society but reflect a certain social class, language and culture. Ethnic and gender differences are being constructed within schools, and deficits are attributed to migrant students and the terms "typical (Turkish, Arab, Muslim, boy, girl)" and "atypical" are being used (Weber 2003). Consciousness-raising and preparedness for change is very difficult, particularly in the area of natural sciences, because the widespread assumption exists that natural sciences are objective and value-neutral. However, natural sciences are not only associated with maleness but also with white and Western culture (Aikenhead and Jegede 1999).

Gender constructions are a cultural phenomenon and empirical data has been gathered on the field of gender studies in natural sciences during the last 30 years. The discussion of the consideration of gender differences in physics classes started in the 1970s and 1980s. Studies showing tremendous differences between boys' and girls' interest and school achievement in subjects like physics and mathematics were the trigger for this increased research interest (Hoffmann 1985; Enders-Dragässer and Fuchs 1989). In search of causal factors, it was concluded that the deficits could not be ascribed to the girls, but to the way physics classes were taught (Muckenfuß 1995; Hoffmann, Häußler and Lehrke 1998). It was shown that the examples in physics classes concentrated much more on the interests of boys than on those of girls. It is concluded that first, classes can only be successful when prepared such that different experiences of both sexes are taken into consideration and, second, when the classes are based on interactive instead of competitive structures (Lorenzo, Crouch and Mazur 2005). In a Swiss co-education study (Herzog et al. 1998) a checklist of girls' needs was developed for teachers. Further studies showed that the more the criteria were fulfilled, the more satisfied students (both male and female) were with the lessons. Moreover, it was observed that the motivation of both boys and girls was increasing (Häußler and Hoffmann 1998). From this it can be concluded that classes designed to fulfill girls' needs appeal to all students and can therefore be seen as "better classes."

Many recommendations exist regarding criteria for quality improvement of science classes (Duit and Wodzinski 2006; Wodzinski and Wodzinski in this book, chapter 3) and for an improved arrangement of physics classes for gender inclusion (Lorenzo, Crouch and Mazur 2005), though they have not been sufficiently fulfilled. However, awareness of problems regarding the educational needs of migrants is still nascent. We assume that similar deficits in classes (seen in gender studies) are also responsible for the comparably worse achievements of migrants: lacking opportunities for identification, as well as lacking connection to lifestyle and to areas of interest.

Like linguistic barriers, cultural barriers are not deficits of the migrants, but deficits of the classes; they are deficits of education, in the form of insufficient differentiation and insufficient consideration of the migrants' diverse lifestyles.

3.4 Institutional Barriers

Institutional barriers are understood as barriers on which a single qualified teacher or teacher student does not have notable influence. Examples of institutional barriers are, for instance, teacher training sessions which insufficiently educate teachers in handling new challenges brought by a linguistically and culturally heterogeneous society. The lack of diversity education among teachers leads to insufficient skills and to an inadequate integration of language advancement which does not meet the actual language skills of the students.

In the following we focus on the institutional barrier of inadequate science teacher training. Besides the teacher training, other institutional barriers to be addressed in further analyses are:

- the curricula, where linguistic supportive activities and the required additional time remain unconsidered;

- the standards of testing and grading: The background of the students is not taken into account; students are downgraded by directive because of linguistic mistakes in science classes;
- the decision-making processes regarding the allocation of students to different kinds of schools;
- infrastructural parameters like the determination of class sizes or the time for teachers' cooperation such as interdisciplinary teaching;
- the social construction of ethnic minorities within the school as an institution.

Bukow suggests a differentiated analysis of the following 5 fields to identify processes of ethnicization within the school system (Bukow 1996, translation by Tanja Tajmel):

- Is the equal treatment of students during school enrollment undermined by ethnicization (*e.g.* by the only one-sided German definition of linguistic competence)? For instance, as German is the language of school, students whose first language is not German and thus have less competence in German are said to have "insufficient linguistic competencies," whereas the competencies in their language of origin remain unconsidered.
- Is it taken for granted that family support at home compliments the learning at school, and are students who do not have these prerequisites therefore disadvantaged?
- Are students discriminated against as members of minorities by peer-groups and thus negatively affected in their motivation to learn?
- Are ethnic indications in the school-culture of relevance?
- Do ethnic indicators play a role in fundamental decisions like allocation of students to different types of schools?

4 Defining goals and measurable objectives

The next step is to deduce objectives and needs of action to address the deficiencies which are identified in the Problem Tree (fig. 1). Their logical sequence is shown in the Objective Tree (fig. 3).

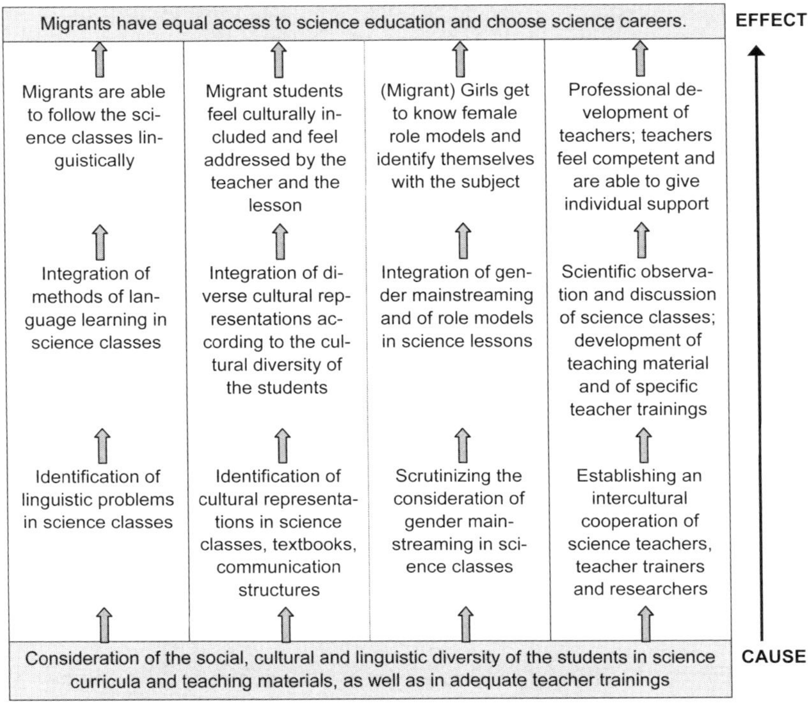
Migrants have equal access to science education and choose science careers.
EFFECT
Migrants are able to follow the science classes linguistically
Migrant students feel culturally included and feel addressed by the teacher and the lesson
(Migrant) Girls get to know female role models and identify themselves with the subject
Professional development of teachers; teachers feel competent and are able to give individual support
Integration of methods of language learning in science classes
Integration of diverse cultural representations according to the cultural diversity of the students
Integration of gender mainstreaming and of role models in science lessons
Scientific observation and discussion of science classes; development of teaching material and of specific teacher trainings
Identification of linguistic problems in science classes
Identification of cultural representations in science classes, textbooks, communication structures
Scrutinizing the consideration of gender mainstreaming in science classes
Establishing an intercultural cooperation of science teachers, teacher trainers and researchers
Consideration of the social, cultural and linguistic diversity of the students in science curricula and teaching materials, as well as in adequate teacher trainings
CAUSE
Figure 3: The Objective Tree.

According to this analysis the quality development of culturally and linguistically diverse science classes requires improvements in the following fields:

• Integration of language learning in science classes	⟹ to reduce barrier A
• Diversity mainstreaming and multicultural education in science classes • Gender mainstreaming and female role models	⟹ to reduce barrier B
• Framework for teachers' professional development	⟹ to reduce barrier C

– The overall objective and goal is: Promoting migrants in science education and in choosing science careers. The following are *measurable component objectives* and *actions to be set* in order to put theory into praxis: to sensitize teachers to the needs of second language learners and to the linguistic and cultural barriers in science classes;

- to identify good practices of science teaching in linguistic and culturally diverse classrooms;
- to develop "barrier-free" teaching material for science classes and teaching methods to encourage and promote those students with migrant backgrounds in the field of natural sciences;
- to develop teacher training for linguistically and culturally diverse classrooms;
- to foster female role models, especially for migrant students;
- to develop recommendations for school authorities;
- to collaborate with countries of residence and countries of origin.

5 The PROMISE Project

To establish a framework for activities in order to achieve the defined objectives and to explore the specific field we developed the PROMISE Project (Promotion of Migrants in Science Education) (Tajmel and Starl 2005). PROMISE was carried out as a project within the 6th Framework Program of the European Union in Germany, Austria, Bosnia-Herzegovina and Turkey between 2005 and 2007. The fundamental idea of the project was that access to science education should be equal for all students, independent of their social, cultural and linguistic background.

Right from the start it was clear to us that the project must be a cooperative effort of both *countries of origin and countries of residence*. It is inevitable in the consideration of cultural diversity that experts from different cultures should be equally involved. By the same token we considered it necessary to integrate different disciplines like science education, language education, social sciences and human rights. One might be an expert in physics education, but in order to discover all the difficulties of language that migrants meet in physics lessons, the cooperation with language education experts is necessary.

In order to do justice to multidisciplinary and international relevance, the project was conceptually designed as an international collaboration between institutions in countries with migrant ancestry like Turkey and Bosnia-Herzegovina, and which are migrant destination countries like Germany and Austria. In addition, linguistic, social and educational sciences were to be represented in the project, besides the central subjects of science and science education.

Figure 4: The PROMISE Project partners: (*clockwise from the left*) Humboldt Universität zu Berlin, Germany; the European Training and Research Centre for Human Rights (ETC), Graz, Austria; Yildiz Technical University Istanbul, Turkey; the Deutsche Gesamtmetall Arbeitgebervereinigung; University of Sarajevo, Bosnia and Herzegovina; University of Vienna, Austria; (*in the center*) ETC-Graz, coordinator Klaus Starl; HU-Berlin, scientific co-ordinators Tanja Tajmel, Lutz-Helmut Schön.

6 Professional Development for Teachers in Culturally and Linguistically Diverse Science Classes – The PROMISE-Teams

To increase the professional development for teachers, so called PROMISE-Teams (Tajmel and Starl 2005, 39-40) were established at each partner university. The key task of the PROMISE-Teams was to develop and modify science lessons and science teaching methods in order to make them accessible and acceptable for migrants. The components of the conceptual design of the PROMISE-Teams are as follows.

6.1 Interdisciplinary Collaboration of Natural Sciences and Languages at University and School

Professional development requires structures and frameworks to give teachers the opportunity to become knowledge creators instead of information receivers. Teacher-networks and partnerships between university and school are regarded as adequate structures for this purpose. To improve the quality of science teaching, various projects on interdisciplinary instruction and interdisciplinary networking were carried out in the 1990s, like the Anglo-American STS (Science-Technology-Society) – and STSE (including environment) – approach (Aikenhead 1994; Tal, Dori, Keiny and Zoller 2001), the German project PING (Praxis Integrierte Naturwissenschaftliche Grundbildung) (Lauterbach 1992), and the Austrian project IMST (Innovations in Mathematics and Science Teaching) (Krainer et al. 2002). The represented disciplines have been mostly mathematics, physics, chemistry, biology and informatics.

The professional development for science teachers in culturally and linguistically diverse schools affords specific competencies and knowledge that is relevant for instructing second language learners which are not sufficiently established at the present. These teachers need to gain a profound knowledge about language-learning processes and about the specific problems of second language learners differentiated from those of foreign language learners. Consequently, there is one further discipline which we propose to be necessarily included in the interdisciplinary teamwork in order to improve the quality of science education in culturally and linguistically diverse classes: *the languages*. Therefore, the PROMISE-Teams consisted of science teachers, language teachers, science education researchers *and* researchers in second language acquisition.

6.2 Quality Improvement by Action Research

Action research is a process of problem solving, which is led by individuals who are working with others on a team. The aim is to improve the method of problem solving by a reflective circle of planning, actions, and fact-finding about the result (Lewin 1946). In science education, action research has been used as a way to improve the quality of teaching and learning, in teacher training and professional development (Altrichter, Posch and Somekh 1993), in research on science learning, and in curriculum development.

Within the PROMISE Teams, action research was used to sensitize teachers to linguistic barriers, to identify good practices and to develop science lessons, which have been videotaped in parts and discussed within the team.

6.3 PROMISE-Conferences and Scientific Input

Part of the reflection process of the PROMISE-Teams was to provide regular scientific input from external experts. For this purpose annual PROMISE-Conferences were organized (Tajmel and Starl, 2005, 43). The feedback from the different PROMISE-Teams from Germany, Austria, Bosnia-Herzegovina and Turkey was of high relevance, especially in reflecting the cultural representations and the cultural sensitivity of the developed science lessons.

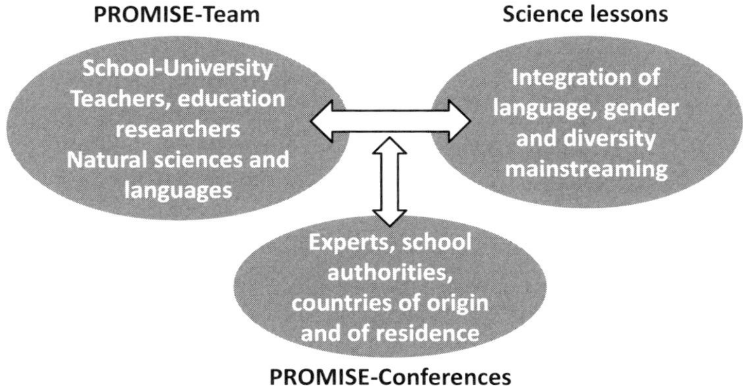

Figure 5: Professional development of science teachers and quality improvement of science classes in the framework of the PROMISE project.

7 Promoting female students with migrant background – "Club Lise"

To foster the role of female students in the science education process, activities on different levels have been set up.

7.1 Gender-mainstreaming in Science Classes

Gender-mainstreaming was an inherent part of the PROMISE-Teamwork. It was applied to the development of science classes, to the elaboration of teaching material, as well as to the process of self-reflection on the teachers' professional acting in science classes. Gender-mainstreaming is implemented when the following criteria are applied:

- considering the different experiences of girls and boys with technology and science;
- using language which addresses both girls and boys;
- bringing the scientific content into a context with the students' everyday life;
- considering the different learning style of girls and boys;
- fostering communication within the science lessons;
- avoiding attributions, such as the idea that girls or boys are less talented in something;
- avoiding the impression that physics is male.
  (Herzog et al. 1998, translation by Tanja Tajmel).

7.2 Mentoring of Female High-School Students

In order to promote female students in the natural sciences, we established a team named *Club Lise* (after the female physicist Lise Meitner) at all partner universities (Tajmel and Starl, 2005, 41-42). Members of the *Club Lise* were high school students who were interested in sciences and who probably would enroll in science studies at a university within the next year, female university students and female researchers. The university students and researchers acted as mentors, the high school students were mentees. The *Clubs Lise* from Austria, Germany, Turkey and Bosnia-Herzegovina met once a year for a meeting called *Club Lise International*. The objectives of *Club Lise* are:

- to encourage migrant female high school students on the cusp between school and university by familiarizing them with universities through organizing meetings with scientists and scientific working groups;
- to foster the students' self-consciousness through the possibility of presenting their own scientific work at international meetings and PROMISE-conferences (see also *The Club Lise Show* on the CD-ROM);
- to support the specific individual scientific interest of each single student.

7.3 Female Role-Models in Natural Sciences

As the gender gap in physics in the two project partner countries Turkey and Bosnia-Herzegovina is remarkably smaller than in Germany and Austria, role models in the sciences were easy to find in the project partner institutions. Thus, one of the main purposes of the annual international *Club Lise* meetings was to build an international network of female high-school students and female scientists in order to make it clear to the students, that sciences and especially physics is a *normal* profession for women.

A remarkable project on female role models was carried out by the *Club Lise Istanbul*: Club Lise students interviewed Ayse Erzan, a renowned Turkish scientist, about her scientific career. The talk was videotaped and transcribed so that it might be implemented in science classes and teacher training sessions. (The video of the interview can be found on the CD-ROM).

8 Conclusion and Outlook

In this article we presented a model to improve the quality of science education for a society of linguistic and cultural diversity. Within the framework of the PROMISE project discriminating and limiting factors of science education were taken up and taken into consideration. Professional development of science teachers and quality improvement of science lessons were initiated and female high school students in particular were promoted within the Club Lise mentoring. On the basis of the project, research and activities became lively at partner universities and in international cooperation. Club Lise has continued as a mentoring measure for female students. In Austria and Germany the issue of linguistic promotion in science classes has been implemented in several teacher training programs. Finally, an overview of the characteristics of PROMISE is as follows:

- The **solution-oriented approach** instead of the deficit-oriented one.
- The focus on the **human right to science education.**
- The cooperation of **countries of origin and countries of residence** in issues of science education, the first one of this kind in Europe.
- The quality improvement of science education and professional development for teachers by **interdisciplinary team work**, conceptually designed as **PROMISE-Teams**: teachers and education researchers in the disciplines of mathematics and natural sciences, languages, human rights and social sciences, which is also the first one of this kind to address this issue.
- The **mentoring of migrant female students** from secondary schools by university students, conceptually designed as **Club Lise.**

Bibliography

Aikenhead, Glen S., *What is STS Science Teaching?*, in: Solomon, Joan and Aikenhead, Glen S. (eds.), *STS Education: International Perspectives on Reform*, John Wiley & Sons, Toronto, New York, 1994.

Aikenhead, Glen S. and Jegede, Olugbemiro J., *Cross-cultural Science Education: A Cognitive Explanation of a Cultural Phenomenon,* in: Journal of Research in Science Teaching (36, 3), 269-287, 1999.

Altrichter, Herbert, Posch, Peter and Somekh, Bridget, *Teachers Investigate Their Own Work: An Introduction to the Methods of Action Research*, Routledge, New York 1993

Australian Agency for International Development (AusAID), *The Logical Framework Approach. AusGuideline,* Australian Government, 2005.

Bourdieu, Pierre, *Ökonomisches Kapital – Kulturelles Kapital – Soziales Kapital*, in: Bourdieu, Pierre (ed.), *Die verborgenen Mechanismen der Macht*, VSA, Hamburg, 1992, 49-79.

Bukow, Wolf-Dietrich, *Feindbild: Minderheit. Zur Funktion von Ethnizität*, Leske + Budrich, Opladen, 1996.

Duit, Reinders and Wodzinski Rita, *Guten Unterricht planen*, in: *Naturwissenschaften im Unterricht Physik* (2/06); Erhard FriedrichVerlag GmbH, Seelze/Velber, 2006.

Enders-Dragässer, Uta and Fuchs, Claudia, *Interaktionen der Geschlechter*, Juventa, Weinheim, 1989.

Gogolin, Ingrid, *Der monolinguale Habitus der multilingualen Schule*, Waxmann, Münster, 1994.

Häußler, Peter and Hoffmann, Lore, *Chancengleichheit für Mädchen im Physikunterricht – Ergebnisse eines erweiterten BLK Modellversuch,* Zeitschrift für Didaktik der Naturwissenschaften (4), 1998, 51-67.

Herzog, Walter, Gerber, Charlotte, Labbude, Peter, Mauderli, Donatina, Neuenschwander, Markus P. und Violi, Enrico, *Physik geht uns alle an. Ergebnisse aus der Nationalfondsstudie „Koedukation im Physikunterricht"*, Universität Bern, Bern, 1998.

Hoffmann, Lore, *Differences in the Subjective Conditions of Interests in Physics and Technology for Boys and Girls*, in: *Girls and Science and Technology. The Third International GASAT Conference. Supplementary Contributions.* Chelsea College, London, 1985, 70-78.

Hoffmann, Lore, Häußler, Peter and Lehrke, Manfred, *Die IPN Interessensstudie Physik,* Institut für Pädagogik der Naturwissenschaften (IPN), Kiel 1998.

Krainer, Konrad, Dörfler, Willibald, Jungwirth, Helga, Kühnelt, Helmut, Rauch, Franz und Stern, Thomas (eds.), *Lernen im Aufbruch: Mathematik und Naturwissenschaften. Pilotprojekt IMST^2*, Studienverlag, Innsbruck, 2002.

Lauterbach, Roland, *Praxis Integrierter Naturwissenschaftlicher Grundbildung (PING)*, in: Häußler, Peter (ed.), *Physikunterricht und Menschenbildung*, Institut für Pädagogik der Naturwissenschaften (IPN), Kiel, 1992.

Lewin, Kurt, *Action Research and Minority Problems*, in: Journal of Social Issues 2(4), 1946, 34-46.

Lorenzo, Mercedes, Crouch, Catherine H. and Mazur, Eric, *Reducing the Gender Gap in the Physics Classroom*, in: Am. J. Phys. 74, 2006, 118-122.

Muckenfuß, Heinz, *Lernen im sinnstiftenden Kontext*, Cornelsen Verlag, Berlin, 1995.

OECD, *School Factors Related to Quality and Equity. Results from PISA 2000*, OECD Publishing, Paris, 2004.

OECD, *Where Immigrant Students Succeed. A Comparative Review of Performance and Engagement in PISA 2003*, OECD Publishing, Paris, 2005.

PISA-Konsortium Deutschland (ed.), *PISA 2006. Die Ergebnisse der dritten internationalen Vergleichsstudie*, Waxmann, Münster, 2007.

Schreiner, Camilla and Sjøberg, Svein, *Sowing the Seeds of ROSE. Background, Rationnale, Questionnaire Development and Data Collection for ROSE (The Relevance of Science Education) – a Comparative Study of Students' Views of Science and Science Education (Acta didactica 4/2004)*, Department of Teacher Education and School Development, University of Oslo, 2004, available online at: http://www.ils.uio.no/forskning/publikasjoner/actadidactica/index.html (last checked: 13 August 2008).

Sjøberg, Svein and Schreiner, Camilla, *How Do Learners in Different Cultures Relate to Science and Technology? Results and Perspectives from the Project ROSE (the Rele-*

vance of Science Education), in: Asia-Pacific Forum on Science Learning and Teaching (6, 2), Forword p. 1, 2006.

Tajmel, Tanja and Hadzibegovic, Zalkida, *Would You Like to Study Physics? A Comparative Study on the Intentions of Female Students in Germany and Bosnia-Herzegovina to Study Science*, Conference proceeding GIREP-EPEC Conference Opatija 2007, University of Zagreb, 2008.

Tajmel, Tanja and Starl, Klaus, *PROMISE – Promotion of Migrants in Science Education*, European Training and Research Centre for Human Rights and Democracy (ETC Graz), Occasional paper No. 18, 2005, available online at: http://www.etc-graz.at/typo3/index.php?id=74 (last checked: 15 August 2008).

Tal, Revital T., Dori, Yehudit J., Keiny, Shoshana and Zoller, Uri, *Assessing Conceptual Change of Teachers Involved in STES Education and Curriculum Development – the STEMS Projekt Approach*, in: International Journal of Science Education, 23(3), 2001, 247-262.

Weber, Martina, *Heterogenität im Schulalltag. Konstruktion ethnischer und geschlechtlicher Unterschiede*, Leske + Budrich, Opladen, 2003.

Willand, Ilka, *Hochschulen auf einen Blick. Ausgabe 2007*, Statistisches Bundesamt, Wiesbaden 2007, 26-27.

The Claim and the Reality of the "Knowledge Society"

Klaus Starl and Veronika Bauer

The European Union is often called a "peace project." This might be true to some extent, and it was certainly one of Schuman's major motivations in creating a co-operative regional association for the coal and steel industries, as well as to transnationalize the control over the main resources for conventional wars. However, the European Communities were always clearly focused on an economic cooperation in order to ensure growth and economic wealth, and they still are. However, it was an important step in the European history of civilization to institutionalize the idea that economic wealth can be better achieved by peaceful economic cooperation rather than by war and conquest. Besides the commitment to security and the rule of law and democracy, the commitment to human rights is one of the fundamental principles of the European Communities and also the European Union. But, neither the EC nor the EU were ever seriously considered to be "human rights institutions" as such, nor did the EU consider human rights as an end in itself. However, human rights were always seen as a necessary – but not sufficient – condition for economic wealth. Still – under the pressure of some of the Member States – the EC over time developed a human rights policy, closely linked to the common constitutional tradition of the Member States, and also to the European Convention on Human Rights and the jurisprudence of the ECtHR.

The efforts by the EU started in the late 1990's to counter discrimination and promote equal opportunities are not to be misunderstood as a discovery of a lack in the fulfillment of human rights or as a common social policy. These efforts concern to a greater degree the need to equalize income distribution and economic opportunities. The EU recognizes the economic externality of discrimination (i.e. the state pays through the social insurance system for the consequences of discrimination in the private economic sector), as well as the opportunity costs of lacking well-trained labor force and a list of other *economic* issues. In short: social inclusion pays because it is deemed to increase productivity and thus induces economic growth and the well-being of the nation. Although the reasons brought forward were human rights arguments, the so-called anti-discrimination directives, the action program to fight discrimination, the science and society programs, the years of Equal Opportunities for All and Intercultural Dialogue all focus on the workplace and on the access to goods and services and, in contrast to the human rights approach, they limit the prohibition of discrimination to an exhaustive list of grounds. The human rights system, represented by the UN or the Council of Europe, goes far beyond this economic approach by the EU because it places the individual rights of persons in the center as a goal and not mainly as a means to pursue other goals, i.e. economic ones. However, the notion of equality in a cohesive society as established with the Amsterdam Treaty calls for structural change and compensation for past damage caused by discrimination, which has to be acknowledged as an extremely important step in the right direction (see for example: Poiares Maduro 2005; De Schutter 2005; Starl 2006).

1 The Claim

The so-called "Knowledge Society," a program of the European Commission, has set its goals, called the "Lisbon Goals," very high: the European Union's economy is to become the most competitive in the world, and by doing so ensure growth, employment and increased welfare. Furthermore, the "Knowledge Society" sets out that people of all ages within the EU should have access to lifelong learning. All this may be achieved not primarily by *industrial* production, but by enhancing and further developing (natural or technical scientific) *knowledge*. A growth of the scientific labor force capacity of 15% from 2000 to 2010 was initially planned, which would comprise an additional number of 700,000 scientists. Social cohesion, the catch phrase fashionable in this context, was the instrument of achievement and the guarantee of sustainability and stability, but it was also necessary to "invite" women and socially disadvantaged persons, migrants and members of minorities to take pro-active part in this development in order to achieve the economic goals rather than just the social ones in terms of the operative figures. This was made clear in the Presidency Conclusions Lisbon European Council 2000: "*The shift to a digital, knowledge based economy, prompted by new goods and services, will be a powerful engine for growth, competitiveness and jobs.* ***In addition*** *it will be capable of improving citizens' quality of life and the environment.*"(Emphasis added)[1] This was then corroborated in 2003 by the European Council stating the "*importance of investment in human capital and lifelong learning as a prerequisite for the promotion of European competitiveness, for achieving high rates in growth and employment and for moving to a knowledge-based economy.*"[2]

In 2005, a plan to re-start the Lisbon Strategy was formulated, as the initial plan did not meet the expectations. The Commission issued the paper *Working Together for Growth and Jobs – A new start for the Lisbon Strategy* stating that "*The Commission proposes a new start for the Lisbon Strategy, focusing our efforts around*

1 Council, Detailed work program on the follow-up of the objectives of Education and training systems in Europe, 2002/C 142/01, 3.

2 Social and human capital, Council Resolution, 9688/03m 24.

two principal tasks – delivering stronger, lasting growth and creating more and better jobs."[3] Again here the focus is clearly on economy rather than on the rights of the individual or the advancement of women or migrants to careers with good reputations.

In 2006, the Parliament, together with the Council, issued Decision No 1720/2006/EC establishing an action program in the field of lifelong learning. Among other things, it stated that "*a Lifelong Learning Programme should therefore be established to contribute through lifelong learning to the development of the EU as an advanced knowledge society, with sustainable economic development, more and better jobs and greater social cohesion.*"[4] This Decision reiterates the goals of the Lisbon Strategy and frames a detailed plan on how to set up the lifelong learning program within the EU, comprising four strands, again looking for sustainable economic development, more jobs and social cohesion. In 2007, the Working Party on Social Questions introduced the term of "*flexicurity*" in the EU knowledge society discourse. "*Flexicurity involves the deliberate combination of flexible and reliable contractual arrangements, comprehensive lifelong learning strategies, effective active labor market policies, and modern, adequate and sustainable social protection systems.*"[5] Flexicurity should allow framing individual strategies within the Member States so as to guarantee the highest possible achievement of the Lisbon Goals. Flexicurity demonstrates that the Lisbon strategy is not about changing discriminatory structures for the sake of the fulfillment of human rights, but for economic reasons.

2 Reality check: The Case of Austria

Women and migrants are clearly underrepresented in the Austrian academic science landscape. Although the performance of women and girls in the Austrian education system has improved vastly since the 1970's, this is not reflected in their achievement in science careers and their actual positions. But still, the Austrian legislature did not react accordingly. The Committee on the Elimination of Discrimination against Women (CEDAW) expressed its concerns on the implementation of the EC equal treatment directives in its recent Concluding Comments on the Austrian CEDAW state report. It concludes that the scope of the Austrian Equal Treatment Law limits discrimination to the workplace (CEDAW 2007, para 11). Al-

3 Commission of the European Communities: Working together for growth and jobs – A new start for the Lisbon Strategy Brussels, 02.02.2005 COM (2005) 24.

4 Decision No 1720/2006/EC of the European Parliament and of the Council of 15 November 2006 establishing an action programme in the field of lifelong learning.

5 The Working Party on social questions, 15497/07, 4.

though an amendment which extends the scope to the access to goods and services is in preparation, it regrettably excludes the area of education.

While the enrolment ratio in primary education shows a proportion of 48.1% girls and 11.7% foreign pupils and slightly changes in secondary I to a proportion of 50.3% girls and 9.1% foreign pupils, mainly due to demographic changes, it shows a clearly different picture in the ratio at the end of secondary II which marks the admission to higher education. 56.4% are young women, but only 5.6% are foreign pupils who finish school with permission to access higher education (BMBWK 2005). While the expectations of achievement are better for young women than those for young men, the foreign background reduces the likelihood of advancement to higher education dramatically. However, there are no official data on female migrants, as well as no data by which to compare migrants' and non-migrants' achievement in terms of their socio-economic status. It can be observed that migrants tend to attend vocational schools and that they are underrepresented among those who go on to higher education.

The picture changes in higher education. The enrolment ratio for women is about 20% higher than for men, both for Austrians and foreign students. Almost the same applies for graduates. 14% of all students graduate in science fields. It has to be mentioned that nationality and migration background overlap in different ways, and so the picture is distorted a bit. On the one hand foreigners – mostly Italian and German – come to study, and on the other hand the category "foreigner" does not count naturalized persons with migration background.

While chemistry and biology are female dominated, physics remains a male subject. When it comes to careers and positions in the academic science field, it seems there has been no progress: the high female educational achievement seems not to impact the likelihood of professional achievement. Only 29% of research assistants, 16% of habilitated[6] staff and 13% of professors are women. There is only one female professor of physics in Austria. While many say that this will change over time with the higher proportion of female graduates, this has not been evident so far as the proportion of female research assistants is cut to half at the transition point from graduation (56%) to university employment (29%) (Statistic Austria 2006).

There are many structural deficiencies to complain about, such as the increasing ethnic segregation in schools, the bad reputation of ethnically diverse schools, the missing support for learning in a second language, the absence of female migrant role models, the limited access to higher education for socially disadvantaged groups, the learning with "white male-dominated" curricula, the less encouraging

6 "facultas docendi" or: postdoctoral lecture qualification.

labor market perspectives for the target group, the lower income for highly qualified female graduates, both in fact and in terms of expectations, and last but not least, the obstacles for women in entering top careers.

Austria is not necessarily representative for all EU Member States, but it is an important case study because it is representative of the German-speaking area and it shows some of the structural problems, which might occur in most of the European countries with similar immigration patterns.

3 Conclusion

Despite several inconsistencies in data definitions and the lack of data concerning women with a migration background, it can be observed that migrants do not evidence the same success in overall achievement expressed in terms of educational achievement and the advancement to academic science careers. While female students tend to perform better than male students in school and in higher education, and are overrepresented in the teaching profession at schools, they are strongly underrepresented in the scientific community, particularly when it comes to positions with a high reputation and higher income.

The European Union attempts to counteract these facts with the concept of the "Knowledge Society" and calls for a strengthened social cohesion. What in principle would have been a promising development path in Europe had to acknowledge that 0.5%[7] of the overall program's budget is just not enough to break up long lasting structural barriers that prevent minorities, migrants and women from easy access to higher education and equal opportunities in science careers and income. In summary, the "Knowledge Society" is rather a policy to support economic competitiveness and to a certain extent more of a welfare-economic than a human rights-centered approach. But, this drop in the ocean in terms of financial support does not really give the Lisbon Strategy a high level of credibility.

A human rights-centered approach to education would clearly contribute to positive structural change in scientific academia. Such an approach would emphasize commensurate compensation and equality of opportunities rather than the current approach, which only emphasizes increased "social cohesion." While the former focuses on the development of the individual, the latter focuses on economic goals, in which the development of the individual is a means to achieve these goals. However, the "Knowledge Society" program should not be criticized, but the pretensions to breaking barriers to enhance individual opportunities. The inadequate

7 See: http://cordis.europa.eu/fp6/budget.htm: 88 million euros compared to a total budget of almost 18,000 million for the research framework program.

budgeting could easily rather corroborate existing structures than change existing discriminatory patterns.

Bibliography

Bundesministerium für Bildung, Wissenschaft und Kunst (BMBWK), *Statistisches Taschenbuch 2005*.

Committee on the Elimination of Discrimination against Women (CEDAW), *Concluding comments for Austria*, CEDAW/C/AUT/CO/6, 02.02.2007.

De Schutter, Olivier, *The Prohibition of Discrimination under European Human Rights Law – Relevance for EU Racial and Employment Equality Directives*, European Commission Unit D.3, Brussels, 2005.

Jaichand, Vinodh, Sembacher, Anke and Starl, Klaus, *Anti-Discrimination for the Judiciary*, NWV, Vienna-Graz, 2006.

Poiares Maduro, Miguel, *The European Court of Justice and Anti-Discrimination Law*, in: European Anti-Discrimination Law Review (2/Oct 2005), European Network of Legal Experts, European Commission, Brussels and Utrecht, 2005.

Starl, Klaus, *The Theoretical Background of Discrimination*, in: Jaichand, Vinodh, Sembacher, Anke and Starl, Klaus, *Anti-Discrimination for the Judiciary*, NWV, Vienna-Graz, 2006.

Statistic Austria, *Hochschulstatistik 2005/06*.

"Bildungssprache" – The Importance of Teaching Language in Every School Subject

Ingrid Gogolin

1 Preliminary Remarks

Equality of opportunity is an illusion. However, the continuous creation of unequal educational opportunities is not unavoidable. Instead, it is a result of insufficient use of the room for maneuvering within any given educational system to overcome the constraints set by unfavorable living conditions of children, or by other factors with an influence on school success. The recent international comparative evaluations of academic achievement, e.g. the PIRLS- and PISA-Studies, brought this fact to light once again. International comparison makes it clear that some educational systems succeed better than others in loosening the interdependence between children's academic achievement and their social, linguistic, or cultural backgrounds. In this respect, the German educational system can learn a lot from other systems.

In this paper I will first of all look back at political efforts which were made by the Federal Republic of Germany – at least in the Western part of it – since the 1960s, to promote academic achievement among immigrant minority children. These efforts were not as successful as had been intended. I will present some research results which indicate reasons for the unwanted inequality of educational opportunities for immigrant minority children. One of these reasons is the "Bildungssprache" – the specific linguistic register which has to be mastered as a prerequisite for academic achievement and success in school. In the last section of my contribution I will explain the term "Bildungssprache" and try to show its importance for teaching and learning – everyday, and everywhere.

2 Political Efforts toward Integration: A Retrospect

To loosen the ties between social, linguistic or cultural background and the chances of better educational achievement is the ultimate promise of any modern public educational system; indeed, this is the initial justification for their creation since the 18th century in Europe. Since the European nation-states face immigration, this promise also applies to children with an immigrant background. The majority of these children grow up and live in more than one language (Extra and Yağmur 2004). Germany, among other European immigration countries, has made a number of efforts to integrate minority children into its educational system. In retrospect it becomes clear that since the 1960s numerous endeavors have been undertaken to reduce the disadvantages to these children. The commitment to achieve equal opportunities for them can be found in every preamble to relevant rules and regulations, e.g. the directives for schools of the federal German states. It was included in guidelines and curricula; the Conference of German Ministers of Education – a joint institution for the harmonization of the federal states' education policies – ratified several notable recommendations in this respect, including a recommendation for intercultural education, to give one example. The abundance of suggestions, instructions and experiments aiming at equal chances for immigrant minority children in German schools is documented in Gogolin, Neumann and Reuter 2001. A forward projection of this survey up to now would reveal a continuing creation of regulations, explanations and practical initiatives all aimed at supporting immigrant students. One of the practical initiatives is a project called "Support for Immigrant Minority Children and Youth (FÖRMIG)" which is being run in ten federal states from 2004 to 2009.[1]

We can therefore speak of manifold efforts towards integration of migrants since the 1960s. Indeed the educational success of this group has largely improved since then. Just to give some examples: in 1977-78, only three of four immigrant minority children or adolescents of school age in Germany actually attended a school; only every second adolescent of the respective age attended a vocational training school; only a third of the foreign children of school age achieved a secondary school-qualification, and only a sixth of the adolescents were granted admittance to vocational training (cf. Klemm 1979). Today, this situation has been overcome. But the creation of unequal chances has not been overcome yet – neither in the secondary system nor in vocational training.

3 Unequal Chances Remain

Recent research has continuously shown that vast disparities between children with and children without an immigration background still exist today. A glance at the findings of studies such as PIRLS or PISA clearly shows this; here are just some examples:

The recent PIRLS- and PISA-studies (cf. Bos et al. 2007; PISA-Konsortium Deutschland 2007) have repeatedly provided evidence for the underachievement in reading, mathematics and science tasks/tests of fourth graders or 15-year-olds with an immigrant background to that of the respective non-immigrant groups. Indeed, a

1 The program is monitored and evaluated by the Institute of International and Multicultural Comparative Education of the University of Hamburg; the spokeswoman is the author of this article. A description of the program can be found on www.blk-foermig.uni-hamburg.de.

backlog in proficiency has been discovered in nearly all of the participating countries. Migration seems to carry a risk to school success and achievement that is difficult to neutralize in any educational system – except in cases where the migrants came from a specially favored social group (cf. Stanat and Christensen 2006, 69).

Yet at the same time it is obvious that school systems dealing with similar tasks of integration utilize the leeway they possess quite differently. The German school system performs poorly; the discrepancy in achievement between immigrant and non-immigrant children is exceedingly large. The PIRLS-Study of 2006 for example shows an average gap of 48 points between immigrant and non-migrant children, i.e. half a standard deviation (cf. Schwippert et al. 2007). A more detailed look at reading competence shows that about 70% of the children from immigrant families, but only 40% of the children with no immigrant background score below sound reading competence (competence level III). The highest competence level is reached by almost 15% of the non-immigrant children, but not even by 4% of the immigrant minority children (cf. loc. cit., 253). The difference between immigrant and non-immigrant children has remained almost unchanged between PIRLS 2000 und 2006.

Looking at the age group of 15-year-olds, previous PISA studies had discovered a significantly larger gap in achievement than was observed in primary schools. The achievement difference of some migration groups averaged approximately 100 test scores in PISA 2000, 2003 and 2006; i.e. the academic achievement of about two school years. Particularly embarrassing was the fact that first generation immigrants showed higher competences than those of the second generation, i.e. the students who had presumably never lived or attended a school anywhere else but in Germany. This result contradicts the expectations and experiences of other immigration countries: attending the education system of the new country of residence as long as possible, ideally from the first day of school, has usually proven to be beneficial for immigrants and not turned out to be a disadvantage. In Germany however, this is not the case. Here, the measured competences of first generation adolescents are higher than those of the second generation throughout all domains which were tested in PISA (for an international comparison of PISA 2006-results in this respect, see Christensen and Segeritz 2008).

Obviously, the efforts made in the German educational system have not loosened the tight interdependence of educational success and the social, linguistic and cultural background of (immigrant minority and other) children and youth. This leads to the question: what are the reasons for this unpleasant and unexpected phenomenon?

4 Explanatory Attempts: Contextual Factors

The difference in achievement between migrant and non-migrant children in the German school system can partially be explained by the unfortunate socio-economical situation of immigrant families and, consequently, their possession of relatively little cultural capital in comparison to that of parents born in the host country (cf. Schwippert et al. 2007, 259; Walter and Taskinen 2007, 350). Previous research attempting to explain more of the differences followed various hypotheses, which were so far primarily based on characteristics and attributes of the migrants themselves or of their living conditions. A number of research projects were constructed along such hypotheses, e.g. the assumption that the national background would serve as a possible explanation for greater or lesser school success. This was strongly called into question as early as the 1980s; it was argued that superficial phenomena – such as nationality and the features attached to it – could not ultimately be responsible for the differential distribution of educational success in groups of pupils. In her survey of the relevant studies, Heike Diefenbach concludes: "*It has not been empirically verified that the disadvantages of children and youth from migrant families can be explained mainly by the fact that their cultural predispositions would not match the expectations of German schools or by the comparatively poor socio-economic situation of their families*" (Diefenbach 2007, 153 [translated by Ingrid Gogolin.]; cf. also Müller and Stanat 2006).

Another complex of responsible features for the differences in achievement was the assumption of low educational aspiration on the part of immigrant families and low motivation of the learners. But in the end, there is again little evidence supporting these suppositions. Older as well as more recent studies (Stanat and Christensen 2006) indicate essentially the opposite observation: they discover high aspirations on the part of immigrant families as well as preparedness to invest in the education of their children. In some interpretations, in fact, particularly these attitudes and behavior were held against the immigrant families, as it was considered that they had too high – "unrealistic" – expectations of their children's educational opportunities and their potential careers, which would in the end be harmful to their children.

As a matter of fact, the migrant families' great interest in the educational success of their children can be explained by many research-based arguments, culminating in the conclusion that a successful school career for their descendents would fulfill the desire for a better future that is usually connected with a migration project. The immigrant children themselves share these aspirations: in related studies, they regularly turn out to be highly motivated and interested in their success in school (cf. e.g. Stanat and Christensen 2006; Müller and Stanat 2006).

According to these results, migrant families can be considered as the "natural allies" to official authorities that want to improve their integration. Nevertheless, it is necessary to learn more about the ways in which the obviously existing readiness and potential of these families and their children can be transferred into activities which actually promote their scholastic success. Some practical approaches to this task are being implemented to the satisfaction of the participants (e.g. in the context of the program FÖRMIG, see www.blk-foermig.uni-hamburg.de). But we still dispose of too little reliable knowledge about the best possible interactions and cooperation between families and educational institutions, as well as too few safe assumptions about educational measures which would actually have strong positive effects.

5 A Closer Look into Schools: The Relevance of "Bildungssprache"

The assumption that immigrants have a "wrong" linguistic living condition has also been vehemently pursued in a number of studies. The mastering of the language of school and teaching – in our case German, the mastery of which being determined mainly by evaluation of the reading competence in this language – was identified as decisive for minor academic success. In various surveys comparing academic performance, a large proportion of the measured differences in achievement are resolved by the answers to the question: which language is spoken at home? In PISA 2006, for instance, the statistical control for social background and the language spoken by the family lower the test scores of second generation immigrant minority children approximately by a third. Looking at adolescents of the first generation, the differences almost disappear (Walter and Taskinen 2007, 350). As an interpretation of such findings, the praxis of using a language at home different from the school language is considered to be the main reason for disadvantages among immigrant minority children.

Indeed, the interdependence between academic performance and proficiency in the language used to measure this performance is plausible and convincing. The assumption, however, that the language used outside of school is the main reason for achievement disparities will have to undergo a more precise inspection. At least some research shows that the achievement of pupils coming from a family which utilizes a language other than the school language does not necessarily suffer from any detrimental effects. There is some evidence that the preferred spoken language in the family *as such* is not of relevant influence to the academic performance of children but, more precisely, the reading and writing practices which are customary in a family. According to these studies, children from families which are generally acquainted with and make frequent use of reading and writing skills similar to those used in school and within the educational system hold a lasting advantage with respect to their academic performance, as compared to children who do not experience this kind of preparatory socialization. The advantage seems to be independent of the specific language used to introduce these practices (cf. overview in Leseman et al. 2007).

Observations like these invite us to take a closer look into the practices of schools and teaching, and their potential difference from language practice outside school, in order to discover reasons for the fact that obviously relevant linguistic abilities as prerequisite for high performance are not acquired by a considerable proportion of children.

The work group at Hamburg University that I am part of is investigating this problem. We are following two traces:

On one hand, in cases where children and adolescents who are growing up with two languages and only one of these languages is developed and taught at school (see Gogolin and Neumann 2008), we are interested in the effects this has on their educational opportunities. On the other hand, we are also busy with ongoing research projects that address the question of whether the divergence between "academic language" and everyday, colloquial language is responsible for the perpetuation of inequalities in educational opportunity. Here, we are picking up the hypothesis that the reading and writing practices in the family is decisive for the difference in performances rather than the language which is being used outside school.

The distinction between "academic language" and everyday or colloquial language is based on M.A.K. Halliday's *Functional Grammar* which provided an instrument to describe the differences between structural features in language usage dependent on its context (cf. Halliday and Matthiessen 2004). For the English language the attributes of the various registers have already been described with respect to their relevance to the educational context (cf. Schleppegrell 2004; Lesemann et al. 2007). For German, the study of relevant characteristics has only just begun (see for instance Gogolin and Roth 2007). For the German research context, we developed the term "Bildungssprache" as equivalent to the English term "academic language" (see Gogolin 2006).

According to our reading, "academic language" or "Bildungssprache" involves a formal register of speech. This may also be relevant outside the educational context, in formal language usage; thus it is as such not exclusive to the area of education. It does, however, carry exceptional importance and weight in the context of education:

- because it is used in tasks and texts, in textbooks and other teaching materials on the one hand, and

– because it is the register of evaluation processes and examinations.

The importance of this register increases correspondingly to the development of the learner's biography, and complementary to his/her state in his/her school career. Whereas at the beginning of a school education contents can more or less be conveyed in everyday language, the more the contents differentiate and develop into "subjects," the more specific the appropriate language register will be. On the normative level "Bildungssprache" denotes the register which is expected to be mastered by the "successful pupil."

The register of "Bildungssprache" differs from other registers on the lexico-semantic, morpho-syntactical and textual level. The differences can briefly be indicated as follows: "Bildungssprache" is composed in the written mode of language, even if the actual discourse itself is oral; it shows characteristics of formal, monological and textual communication, whereas everyday language shows characteristics of oral, informal, dialogical language usage (cf. Gogolin and Roth 2007).[2]

From American, English and Australian research we have adopted the theses that the acquisition of competence in "Bildungssprache" is not a simple and quasi-natural addition to the command of oral speech. Instead, it is essential to introduce the learners explicitly to the special features of the various registers; and it is necessary to do so in a systematic and continuous manner over an extended period of time. According to this research, it is not only necessary to practice thoroughly the difference between the different registers of "Bildungssprache" and everyday language, but – especially for learners having to master a second language as the language of schooling – to introduce the learners explicitly and continuously to the different sets of rules which refer to the different registers (cf. the overview of respective research results in Bourne 2008; Gibbons 2006).

In order to verify these hypotheses, we started a number of research projects, which focus on how teachers in linguistically heterogeneous classrooms in German schools actually organize their lessons in linguistic terms on one hand, and on the other hand on the question of how students with different linguistic backgrounds master elements of "Bildungssprache" in different contexts. Up to the present, we have received a number of indications that the relevance of "Bildungssprache" and the close interdependence between "learning a topic" and "learning the language relevant to it" is not a matter of teachers' attentiveness – in particular if they are not specialized language teachers.

2 It is not necessarily the language which is actually used in the classroom; cf. for this observation, see Schütte 2008.

As language development and related issues have up to now not been considered fundamental assets of teacher education in the German tradition, nor in the self-concept of being a teacher, the absence of teachers' awareness of the importance of language is not surprising. It goes along with a strong belief which is deeply anchored in the German educational system, i.e. the habitual assumption that the language abilities which are sufficient for educational success will more or less "naturally" develop in the course of the development of the "mother tongue." These ideas about the natural maturation of a "mother tongue" were developed in the 19th century, together with the ideologies of a "natural" connection between an individual and his/her nation-state and national language (cf. the genesis of this common sense in Gogolin 1994; see also Gogolin and Krüger-Potratz 2006, chapter 2). It is an element of this common sense that language education is the task of a specialized language teacher, whereas all other teachers can rely on a sound basis of language abilities for the contents they teach – with one exception: the specific terminology which is more or less distinct from the terminology of other subjects or of everyday language. Indeed, as research shows, the terminology as such creates far fewer (language) learning problems than the structural features of "Bildungssprache" do (cf. Gibbons 2006).

Finally, in order to illustrate this observation, I will present an example of "Bildungssprache" which is taken from mathematics teaching. The example derives from one of our research projects.[3] The project dealt with the question of whether children without and children with an immigrant background – the latter usually living in bilingual conditions – perceive mathematical tasks in similar or in different ways. The example presented here was taken from a math textbook for grade 6; the students which were observed in our study attended grade 7.

Among other tasks we asked our interviewees to paraphrase the following mathematical task:

> Im Salzbergwerk Bad Friedrichshall wird Steinsalz abgebaut. Das Salz lagert 40 m unter Meereshöhe, während Bad Friedrichshall 155 m über Meereshöhe liegt. Welche Strecke legt der Förderkorb zurück?
>
> (In the salt mine at Bad Friedrichshall rock salt is being mined. The salt deposit is 40m below sea level, while Bad Friedrichshall is situated 155m above sea level. What is the distance of the skip?)

According to experienced mathematics instructors, this is a mathematical problem presented to the students in a prototypical text. Looking at the problem through the eyes of the linguist, a number of linguistic subtleties appear. In order to solve the

3 Gogolin et al., *Learning Mathematics in the Context of Linguistic and Cultural Diversity*. A Research Report for the German Research Foundation (DFG).

problem students have to be acquainted with some mathematical terminology, and also with terminology stemming from other subjects (e.g. salt mine, skip) or which is being used in mathematics as well as in other subjects, but with a meaning that is not necessarily identical (e.g. distance). If we look deeper into the linguistic task which is presented in this example we discover that the mastery of the specialist vocabulary is not the clue to mastering the mathematical problem – it is not even necessary to understand terms such as "salt mine" or "skip," as these are irrelevant for the calculation which has to be carried out. Most relevant for the modeling of the mathematical problem are indeed the structural words which as such and standing alone are more or less meaningless, but rule the sense of the mathematical operation which is required: such as the prepositions "below" and "above." If a learner misunderstands these, or does not discover their importance, s/he will not be able to see which kind of – in the end rather simple – calculation s/he has to carry out.

In the context of language support for children and youth who are living with more than one language (and, incidentally, for quite a few monolingual students as well) this example shows the challenge of extracting meaning from "Bildungssprache"-texts. The structural aspects of texts, as indicated in such examples as conjunctions, prepositions, or in other features of text composition, carry the messages which are essential for the understanding of a given problem. Very often – as is the case in the above example for the word "while" – the students have to disregard a denotation which they are used to; in the given case they have to ignore the temporal denotation of this term which is usually used in everyday language, whereas here it functions as establishing a relation. The mastering of "Bildungssprache" goes along with subtle, nondescript messages, the decoding of which is sometimes hindered rather than supported by everyday language comprehension. One example from our research project illustrates this: see Edda's paraphrase of the mathematical problem; she said:

> Edda: es steht also hm – die wollen Steinsalz abbauen – Bad Frieshalle oder wie das hier steht
> Interviewerin: hm Bad Friedrichshall
> Edda: hm – Bad Friedrichshall ja – hm – und das liegt aber vier/vierzig Millimeter unter des Meeres vierzig Meter – ne – und jetzt wissen sie nicht – welche Strecke sie nehmen sollen.
> (Edda: it says well hm – they want to mine rock salt – Bad Frieshalle or what it says here
> Interviewer: hm Bad Friedrichshall
> Edda: hm – Bad Friedrichshall yes – hm – and that lies four/forty millimetres below sea level forty metres – isn't it – and now they don't know which route to take.)

This solution, by the way, comes from a "German" girl who grew up and lives monolingual in German. The fact that this girl does not have an immigrant background points to the aspect mentioned before: the chances for learners to master "Bildungssprache" are influenced by the practices of reading and writing in their families – regardless of whether they live mono- or bilingual and regardless of which language is actually spoken at home and at school. And it points to another conclusion as well: in cases where the family is not familiar with and supportive of their children's acquisition of "Bildungssprache," the children will have no other chance to acquire this register than by the support of teachers and their teaching, which systematically reflects and accounts for language education, in any given subject matter.

Bibliography

Bos, Wilfried et al., *IGLU 2006, Lesekompetenzen von Grundschulkindern in Deutschland im internationalen Vergleich*, Waxmann, Münster, 2007.

Bourne, Jill, *Making the Difference: Teaching and learning strategies in multiethnic schools*, in: Gogolin, Ingrid and Lange, Imke (eds.), *Durchgängige Sprachbildung – das Konzept des Modellprogramms FÖRMIG*, Waxmann (Reihe FÖRMIG EDITION, in preparation), Münster/New York, 2008.

Christensen, G. and Segeritz, M., *Immigrant Student Achievement in an International Perspective*, in: *Carl-Bertelsmann-Preis 2008*, Bertelsmann-Stiftung, Gütersloh, 2008, in preparation.

Diefenbach, Heike, *Kinder und Jugendliche aus Migrantenfamilien im deutschen Bildungssystem. Erklärungen und empirische Befunde*, VS-Verlag, Wiesbaden, 2007.

Esser, Hartmut and Steindl, Michael, *Modellversuche zur Förderung und Eingliederung ausländischer Kinder und Jugendlicher in das Bildungssystem. Bericht über eine Auswertung im Auftrag der Bund-Länder-Kommission für Bildungsplanung und Forschungsförderung*, Köllen, Bonn, 1987.

Gibbons, Pauline, *Unterrichtsgespräche und das Erlernen neuer Register in der Zweitsprache*, in: Mecheril, Paul and Quehl, Thomas (eds.), *Die Macht der Sprachen. Englische Perspektiven auf die mehrsprachige Schule*, Waxmann, Münster/New York, 2006, 269-290.

Gogolin, Ingrid, *Der monolinguale Habitus der multilingualen Schule*, Waxmann, Münster/New York, 1994.

Gogolin, Ingrid, Neumann Ursula and Reuter, Lutz, *Schulbildung für Kinder von Minderheiten in Deutschland 1989-1999. Schulrecht, Schulorganisation, curriculare Fragen, sprachliche Bildung*, Waxmann, Münster/New York, 2001.

Gogolin, Ingrid, Kaiser, Gabriele and Roth, Hans-Joachim, *Learning Mathematics in the Context of Linguistic and Cultural Diversity. A Research Report for the German Research Foundation (DFG)* (Mathematiklernen im Kontext sprachlich-kultureller Diversität. Forschungsbericht an die DFG.), Hamburg, 2004.

Gogolin, Ingrid, *Bilingualität und die Bildungssprache der Schule*, in: Mecheril, Paul and Quehl, Thomas (eds.), *Die Macht der Sprachen. Englische Perspektiven auf die mehrsprachige Schule*, Waxmann, Münster/New York, 2006, 79-85.

Gogolin, Ingrid and Krüger-Potratz, Marianne, *Einführung in die Interkulturelle Pädagogik*, Barbara Budrich/ UTB, Opladen, 2006.

Gogolin, Ingrid, *Institutionelle Übergänge als Schlüsselsituationen für mehrsprachige Kinder. Expertise für das Bundesministerium für Familie, Frauen und Jugend*, erstellt im Auftrage des Deutschen Jugendinstituts, 2007, available online at: http://www.dji.de/bibs/384_8312_Expertise%20Gogolin_Uebergaenge.pdf (last checked: August 1st, 2008).

Halliday, Michael A.K. and Matthiessen, Christian, *An Introduction to Functional Grammar (3rd Edition)*, Arnold, London, 2004.

Klemm, Klaus, *Ausländerkinder in deutschen Schulen – Zahlen und Prognosen*, in: Hansen, Georg and Klemm, Klaus (eds.), *Kinder ausländischer Arbeiter*, Neue Deutsche Schule Verlagsgesellschaft, Essen, 1979, 31-44.

Neumann, Marko et al., *Schulformen als differenzielle Lernmilieus. Institutionelle und kompositionelle Effekte auf die Leistungsentwicklung im Fach Französisch*, in: Zeitschrift für Erziehungswissenschaft (ZfE), 10. Jg. (2007), Heft 3, 399-418.

Leseman, Paul et al., *Home Literacy as a Special Language Environment to Prepare Children for School*, in: Zeitschrift für Erziehungswissenschaft (ZfE), 10. Jg. (2007), Heft 3, 334-355.

PISA-Konsortium Deutschland (eds.), *PISA 2006. Die Ergebnisse der dritten internationalen Vergleichsstudie*, Waxmann, Münster/New York, 2007.

Schleppegrell, Mary, *The Language of Schooling*, Lawrence Erlbaum Mahwah, New Jersey, 2004.

Schütte, Marcus, *Grundschulmathematikunterricht unter Berücksichtigung sprachlich-kultureller Diversität in der Schülerschaft*, Inaugural Dissertation, Universität Hamburg, 2008, Publication in preparation.

Schütte, Marcus, Gogolin, Ingrid and Kaiser, Gabriele, *Mathematiklernen und sprachliche Bildung. Eine interaktionistische Perspektive auf dialogisch strukturierte Lernprozesse im Grundschulunterricht unter Berücksichtigung der sprachlich-kulturellen Diversität der Lernenden*, in: Schenk, Barbara (ed.), *Bausteine einer Bildungsgangtheorie*, VS-Verlag, Wiesbaden, 2005, 179-195.

Schwippert, Knut et al., *Lesekompetenzen von Kindern mit Migrationshintergrund im internationalen Vergleich*, in: Bos, Wilfried, et al., *IGLU 2006. Lesekompetenzen von Grundschulkindern in Deutschland im internationalen Vergleich*, Waxmann, Münster/New York, 2007, 249-269.

Stanat, Petra and Christensen, Gayle, *Schulerfolg von Jugendlichen mit Migrationshintergrund im internationalen Vergleich*, BMBF, Bildungsforschung Bd. 19, Bonn/Berlin, 2006.

Stanat, Petra and Müller, Andrea G., *Schulischer Erfolg von Schülerinnen und Schülern mit Migrationshintergrund*, in: Baumert, Jürgen, Stanat, Petra and Watermann, Rainer (eds.), *Herkunftsbedingte Disparitäten im Bildungswesen. Vertiefende Analysen im Rahmen von PISA 2000*, VS-Verlag, Wiesbaden, 2006, 241-255.

Walter, Oliver and Taskinen, Päivi, *Kompetenzen und bildungsrelevante Einstellungen von Jugendlichen mit Migrationshintergrund in Deutschland: Ein Vergleich mit ausgewählten OECD-Staaten*, in: PISA-Konsortium Deutschland (eds.), *PISA 2006. Die Ergebnisse der dritten internationalen Vergleichsstudie*, Waxmann, Münster/New York, 2007, 337-366.

Equal Opportunities and Gender in Research: Germany's Science Needs a Promotion of Quality

Susanne Baer

1 There is a Snag which has to come Loose

The issues of equality and gender, as well as larger visions of diversity in science, are nowadays well known and all relevant actors are aware of them. Everything about these issues has been said and everybody seems to agree. There are findings and assessments of the status quo, as well as of numerous strategies and instruments related to equality in personnel recruitment and to equality in the shape of concepts and content in science (e.g. European Commission 2004, 2006). In some instances, there are still calls for more research and for more data. In fact, it would be favorable if the *three relevant levels* as identified by the US-American science historian Londa Schiebinger (Schiebinger 2004) would be better understood: women in science, the gender of science and the gender of knowledge. In this respect, the evaluation of measures and more data on gender in research as a fundamental research question and as an impulse for all disciplines and academic fields are definitely needed. There is no time to waste; and we have reached a moment for taking action. However, although everything seems clear and agreed upon, apparently there is a snag somewhere.

If there is consent on equality *in theory*, why is it so difficult implementing it in practice? The Question was highlighted by the German Federal Minister for Science Annette Schavan in 2007? Why is it not a "winner," not a nice issue for politics, not a dashing phrase in science policy, such as "excellence" and "innovation" (Baer 2007)? And why does the call for *gender* often evoke rather strange reactions – stranger, even, than the call for diversity, which is however not heard as often in German-speaking scientific contexts yet?

This paper shall focus on the snag which this issue is hung up on, with the goal of motivating those in leadership positions, but also all others active in the community of science to loosen this snag, the fishing hook in the flesh of science, as fast as possible, even though this may sometimes be a rather painful undertaking.

2 "I Would Rather Focus on Science …"?

Many colleagues – female as well as male – do not want to focus on equality, but claim to prefer to "concentrate on science itself." This is exactly the problem. The snag I focus on can easily be found where science and gender are inseparably intertwined. Although questions concerning women in the academy, questions of gender stereotypes and gender as one cross-cutting aspect of knowledge are not identical, they cannot be separated from one another.

In practice, only a remaining few academics and science politicians oppose equality openly; but the issue has been consistently marginalized or trivialized. British researcher Louise Morley (Morley 1999, 2003) has raised the question of whether micropolitics invade macropolitics, in this case up to the point of blockage. I argue that marginalization and trivialization occur exactly *because* the issue of gender plunges *in medias res*. Gender is so closely related to science and knowledge that things get rough the minute it enters the scene. When you raise the question of equality in science, reactions range from sensitivity, irritation, or boredom to circumvention, ironic arrogance or aggressiveness. The claim to consider equality as a hard criterion for employing new staff members or allocating resources is being denied by peers as external impertinence, as interference with academic freedom (see Baer 2006) and as a non-substantive disturbance of the striving for cognition. Thus, it is not an easy task, especially for those in leadership positions, to stand up for the cause of equality and ensure equality at all three relevant levels: in the institutions, in the culture of science, and in each and every head of academics. If we do not loosen this snag, however, nothing much will happen, and inequality will remain, to the disadvantage of the quality of science.

3 Science Requires Innovation – Also by Means of Diversity

Firstly, it is absolutely necessary to take the findings around effects of monocultures, hegenomic masculinity and false assumptions about gender-neutrality in science seriously. After all, the relationship between science and gender as well as between science and paradigmatic images of the scientist as middle-class and middle-aged heterosexual Western white male emerges in several dimensions and constitutes a complex issue.

As many other Northwestern countries, Germany has difficulties in the personnel sector, with almost gender-homogeneous academic elites, disproportionately few opportunities for women to get serious jobs in science, as well as a strong tendency to focus on the social background of candidates and peers instead of performance in recruitment procedures and assigning prestigious positions. For example, in Germany, scientists with migration backgrounds are quite rare, as are men without the mainstream lifestyle and biography. In addition, systematic efforts to ensure impartial personnel policies – on gender, social background, ways of living, age or ability – are the exception.

Diversity, as the EU and other actors tend to put it these days, is pretty much unknown to the German academic field. This is particularly problematic because some studies show that innovative results are to be expected when a diverse group of people reflect on a problem in a moderated way. If innovation is an indicator of quality in science, diversity is a need; however, that snag needs to come loose before we get there.

4 "This will Change over the Course of Time …"?

A typical reaction to calls for equality in science is the advice to wait patiently, but time will not work for us. It would be satisfying to trust the course of time; a widely spread argument claims that with a rising birth rate and with more female students, more women will be appointed, assigned, elected etc. Studies prove, however, that time is not a good partner in this respect. By waiting, change will not only come very slowly, but it may not come at all.

As Dr. Stancic, Deputy Director General in the EU Commission, pointed out at an Equal Opportunities Conference in Berlin in April 2007, the progression of careers in science is a gender-specific "leaky pipeline." It is striking that on particular levels and at certain points women are left behind, or more bluntly, drop out of the academy. Clearly, time is up and change is needed.

5 The Leaky Pipeline is Prejudice: the Gender Bias

Research on gender in science aptly documents that women do not quit their jobs because they unwilling to work in the scientific field. Nor do women usually quit for childcare. In Germany, the debate however often focuses exclusively on children, who are – based on a narrow-minded stereotyping presumption – handed over to women only. This does not get us far enough. Work-life compatibility and double-career measures are important factors for improving working conditions at universities or in research institutions. They would facilitate the decision of young women and men to strive both for a career in science and have a family.

But there is more at stake. The pipeline from which women drop out systematically, and others who do not fit the traditional mould don't get far either, suffers from prejudice, or as Peter Strohschneider, the chairman of the German Science Council emphasized at the Berlin conference, science as a system as well as women suffer from "exclusionary mechanisms" (also: Wissenschaftsrat 2007). More precisely: what steps do we take against the fact that talented women get less support and are less frequently promoted in their scientific work than men – starting with the choice of studies up to graduation and post graduate work? What steps do we take against systematic male preference and how do we make sure to fulfill the promise of meritocratic systems, and really honor achievement and performance? What steps do we take against the more overt forms of exclusion in the academy, like sexual harassment or sexism, as well as racist or homophobic harassment, when sexism is still treated like a trifling matter in many scientific cultures?

Here, it begins to hurt. The snag feels different and unpleasant now for the facts are as painful as the numbers are definite. After all, who wants to be told that they treat women and men unequally? No institution and no individual would invite that kind of criticism. Who wants to confront conscious or unconscious stereotype and bias? And who cannot immediately come up with examples of young women quitting their jobs because family was more important, or some other story of why it was really not the system which excluded someone but the individual who chose to leave?

Very often, research findings are ignored and replaced by randomly selected experiences. This cognitive resistance against the findings of unequal treatment of women and men and other forms of exclusion is especially outstanding in science. Science rests on the belief of objectivity so that prejudice can simply not be. In general, the issue at hand is discrimination, both regarding people and regarding content. But before this can be targeted, people need to be convinced of the cause.

6 Three Good Reasons

Today there are three major reasons to pursue equality in science, both regarding people and issues: *normative, economic* and *qualitative* reasons.

6.1 Fairness also Means "Part of the Fun"

For a long period of time, the *normative* reasons to pursue equality, or equal opportunities, or, as Stancic phrased it, human rights and democracy, were the main focus. For example, the request for unbiased admission to higher education and support for the scientific work of women at the beginning of the previous century has been framed as a requirement of justice. In 2006, Suzanne Fortier, President of the Natural Sciences and Engineering Research Council in Canada, pointed out at the OECD that simply everyone, including every woman, should have the opportunity to be "part of the fun" of the fascinating field of science.

Considering the access to science, it is important not only to think of the family obstacle already mentioned, of mothers and also of fathers. More generally, we need to think about all those confronted with prejudice. We also have to face aggravating time schedules, such as the obligation to be at work either very early or very late, the necessity of sending e-mails at night in order to make an impression, or the compulsion to attend lectures every evening for networking reasons and so on. These are rituals which disadvantage many, and do not support quality of work. Thus, more contemporary forms of science as a profession and more adequate indicators of competence are required in order to particularly eliminate the gender bias in matters of personnel and performance evaluation.

6.2 Demographic Change and Globalization: Science Requires Every Talent

Aside from equality, **economic survival** is an important issue today as well. This is the economic argument behind equality. The OECD and the EU agree that in the wake of serious demographic changes, qualified women are desperately needed today. To many, it is an alarming fact that China has been successful in integrating women for years in the technical sciences and is thus provided with many more talents than the competitors US or Europe. It is a shame – and also very expensive – that so many intelligent women "get lost."

This economic argument is tempting, since nobody needs to feel offended; it seems to be a win-win situation. Here, demographic change and globalization of the working world do have an impact on science as well. Only sometimes is there a hint of cynicism. As a colleague recently pointed out, nowadays just about everyone could become a professor, or – with a smile in my direction – a female professor. Everybody who is familiar with social history – and therefore knows about the fact that professions are gender-encoded, which is to say that there is a strong connection between the status and pay in a field and the presence of men or women – will know that fear of feminization inspires such ideas. The more women there are in science, the lower the income and the lower the prestige of the field; however, even such patterns of systemic discrimination may be subject to change.

Furthermore, everybody who does not want to be regarded as "human capital" struggles with this further economization or commodification of science, yet some are more easily persuaded by the economic argument than others. In any case, it is not wrong. A workforce profits from a larger pool of talent, and women are part of this, and thus will be needed in the future.

6.3 Prejudice ...??? Is it not Only Quality That Matters???

If we want European research to be a strong competitor in the marketplace of ideas and promote talents in an impartial way or bring them back from the U.S. and stop the often cited "brain drain," things become a little painful again: another snag to come loose. Does our problem not imply that especially female talents are currently confronted with prejudice? And does it not imply the accusation that decision-makers and "peers" are prejudiced? The cognitive refusal seems to indicate a lack of ability and will to confront the issue.

Generally, it is the belief in quality that pushes, or should push, research. Here is the third argument for fostering equality in science. The perception that quality alone matters and that this quality is measured in an impartial way prevails, and a sound equality policy should guarantee that this myth will become a reality. Right now the common belief that positions are given to people based on fair procedures, and that research funding especially is based on "mere scientific criteria." On the contrary, even journals like "Science" and "Nature," the lead organs of progress in research, publish proof of gender bias, or document that a publication by a male author is clearly better rated than one by a gender-wise non-identifiable person, and the latter is still better rated than one by a female author (Wenneras and Wold 1997; Lagendijk 2005; Barres 2006). Thus, it is high time to let go of the illusion that it is really only merit that counts. There is prejudice at work, and we had better confront it.

7 Bias in Science has a History

The snag which hinders progress towards equality in science now hurts almost unbearably. After all, the belief in the impartial objectivity and neutrality of science is inherent in the latter one. Questioning the fact that scientists are free of personal presumptions, in other words suggesting that they do not judge fairly but simply favor men over women, aims at the core of academic identity.

Academic thought has been based on an ideology of being non-gendered, and personally unmarked. By separating the private sphere and subjectivity – and thus aspects coded as female – from thought and rationality – aspects coded as male –, the category of gender has become a part of knowledge, yet has not been called one. Thus, "soft" perception does not belong to "hard" thinking, etc. In the 19th century it became necessary to strive for a different perspective of impartiality in science in order to be able to think only of a world of research. The researcher had become, as science historian Lorraine Daston has put it, the "*observer without character traits*." The social circumstances – which characterize science nonetheless – could thus extend their latent influence. Personal experience shapes perspective, and private norms and understandings inform research, as well as perception and attitudes encountered; however, many people still believe in the neutrality of science even today.

At this stage, the third argument for equality in science kicks in; we must free ourselves from the illusion that personal traits do not matter. As long as science blanks out gender as well as other exclusionary categories of "othering," of the processes to construct exclusion, science suffers from gender bias and systematically excludes, primarily, women. Thus, it is even more necessary to reflect on gender and diversity in favor of quality.

8 Without Gender there is no Quality

Research without reflection on gender, and thus on the particular significance of gender intersecting with other such relevant categories, simply causes a deficit. By now, several examples for this can be found in nearly all disciplines. Medicine risks severe errors in treatment when it paradigmatically orients itself to operating on male patients. Engineering sciences miss markets when they do not systematically reflect that women and men use and need technology variably in different circumstances (because there is no such thing as "women" and "men" in a common, non-distinguishable notion!). But also in the humanities and in social sciences, huge areas like the development of the welfare state, the problem of the "new wars" or of course questions of fairness are dealt with only partially when the dimension of gender remains on the outside. Therefore, an equality policy in science is a quality policy for every academic field.

9 Equality and Gender-Research are Contributions to Innovation and Excellence

A promotion of equality is not only a reaction to questions of fairness and necessary in an economical sense; in science, it is also a promotion of quality. Here, the snag comes into play again. Broaching this issue might not increase one's popularity, as it challenges the academic identity per se. The opening of science as a professional field beyond the mainstream, the change of scientific cultures and the reflection on the impact of gender on science are linked with each other very closely. By clarifying that and where exactly attitudes, presumptions and overall concepts, or formal and informal structures display multi-discriminatory effects, one risks offending individuals and the system with which they identify themselves and to which they basically owe their status, their reputation, and their power. So it may hurt to loosen this snag from the flesh of the academic substance.

Luckily, relief is assured. Namely, if a gender bias in science is eliminated, and thus gender plays a role that has to be systematically and critically considered, it will be part of the competition for the best employees as well as in the competition for the most valuable knowledge. Science has to be in motion, and the responsible state and private actors, as well as financial supporters, are able to push that motion. Yet to continue waiting, examining, and weighing is not the order of the day anymore. At some point, the snag will be removed and then we can really talk about quality and excellence.

Bibliography

Baer, Susanne, *Exzellenz, Verwaltungsreform, Gender – Mainstreaming, Bologna ... und weitere Erschütterungen der Universität*, in: Hügli, Anton, Küchenhoff, Joachim and Müller, Werner (eds.), *Die Universität der Zukunft. Eine Idee im Umbruch?*, Schwabe, Basel 2007, 139-154.

Baer, Susanne, *Gleichheit im Reich der Freiheit*, ?Quo vadis universitas? Universität Zürich (5), 2006, 1-9.

Barres, Ben, *Does Gender Matter?*, Nature (442), 2006, 133-136.

Daston, Lorraine, *Die wissenschaftliche Persona. Arbeit und Berufung*, in: Wobbe, Theresa (ed.), *Zwischen Vorderbühne und Hinterbühne. Beiträge zum Wandel der Geschlechterbeziehungen in der Wissenschaft vom 17. Jahrhundert bis zur Gegenwart*, Transcript, Bielefeld, 2003, 109-136.

European Commission, *Gender and Excellence in the Making*. Report of the Conference "Minimising gender bias in the definition and measurement of scientific excellence" Florence, 23-24 October 2003, Brussels 2004.

European Commission, *She Figures 2006. Women and Science. Statistics and Indicators*, Brussels, 2006.

Lagendijk, Ad, *Pushing for Power*, Nature (438), 2005, 429.

Morley, Louise, *Organising Feminisms: The Micropolitics of the Academy*, Macmillan, London 1999.

Morley, Louise, *Quality and Power in Higher Education,* Open University Press Books, Buckingham 2003.

Schiebinger, Londa, *Nature's Body: Gender in the Making of Modern Science.* Rutgers University Press, New Brunswick, new ed., 2004.

Wennerås, Christine and Wold, Agnes, *'Nepotism and Sexism in Peer Review'*, Nature (387), 1997, 341-343.

Wissenschaftsrat, *Empfehlungen zur Chancengleichheit von Wissenschaftlerinnen und Wissenschaftlern*, Bonn 2007, available online at: http://www.wissenschaftsrat.de/texte/8036-07.pdf (last checked 11 June 2008)

What About the Gender Gap? The Aspirations of Female High School Students to Study Physics

Tanja Tajmel and Zalkida Hadžibegović

1 Introduction

The underrepresentation of women in physics – the gender gap – is a fact in most of the so-called developed or high-income Western countries. The gender gap in physics is remarkably lower in the newly industrialized countries and in the former socialist countries. The discussion of whether the gender gap could be caused by the way math and physics classes were taught started in the 1970s and 1980s (Ormerod et al. 1979). The research efforts were triggered by studies which pointed out alarming differences between boys and girls in interest and school achievement in subjects like physics and mathematics (Hoffmann 1985; Enders-Dragässer and Fuchs 1989). Since then, recommendations have been developed on how to consider equally both boys and girls in the classroom.

Gender differences in math and science are still present, but have changed. This, among other points, is shown by the latest study of the Programme for International Student Assessment (PISA): In most countries the performance of boys is better in explaining phenomena scientifically, whereas the performance of girls is better in identifying scientific issues (OECD 2007). A recent study carried out in 10 US states revealed that girls and boys performed equally in math (Hyde et al. 2008). Nowadays young educated women in highly industrialized countries feel emancipated and free in choosing their careers, which raises the question of whether women will still be underrepresented in the next generation of researchers in physics or whether the gender gap in physics will soon be history.

To investigate this question we asked female high school students about their future aspirations. We focused on two countries: Germany as a high income country and Bosnia-Herzegovina as a former socialist country. We considered the migrant background of these women in order to investigate differences between women who emigrated from a low income (former socialist or newly industrialized) country to a high income country and women without a background of migration. The research was carried out within the framework of the PROMISE project (Tajmel and Starl 2005), an international project within the 6th Framework Program of the European Commission. The purpose of the project was to provide equal opportunities in science education and in the choice of science careers for female students and migrants. As girls and migrants are underrepresented in science, the project activities focused on these specific groups.

2 The Status Quo of Women in Physics

One central research objective of PROMISE was to enhance the knowledge of the numbers of females in physics and to compare the PROMISE-partner countries according to this parameter (Tajmel and Hadžibegović 2007). The data are based on the university-statistics of the respective partner countries. We found that the proportion of women in physics in Germany and Austria is lower than their proportion in society, whereas in contrast, the proportion of women in physics in Bosnia-Herzegovina and Turkey is equal or even slightly larger than the respective proportion in society. Thus, we state that women are *underrepresented* in physics in Austria and Germany, which both are *countries of residence* for migrants. *Underrepresented* means the proportion of a group in a certain field does not reflect the proportion of this group in society. In the following we focus on Germany as *the country of residence* and Bosnia-Herzegovina as *the country of origin*.

Table 1 shows the numbers and the proportion of women in physics at different academic levels at the physics department of Humboldt-University Berlin (source: Humboldt-Universität zu Berlin). This comparison reveals that there is a significant gap between the over-all proportion of female students (21%) and the proportion of female PhD-students (5.3%) and professors (4.2%).

	Total	**Women**	**Percentage of women**
Students (enrolled in 2004/2005)			
Physics diploma	115	27	23.5%
Physics teacher	38	9	23.7%
Diploma and teacher, all semesters	673	141	21.0%
PhD degrees 2004/2005	19	1	5.3%
Professors	24	1	4.2%

Table 1: The numbers and the percentage of women at the Physics Department, Humboldt University Berlin, academic year 2004/2005

Figure 1 illustrates the differences in numbers of female and male diploma students, teacher students, PhD degrees and professors at the Department of Physics at Humboldt-Universität zu Berlin in the academic year 2004/2005 (source: Humboldt-Universität zu Berlin). The majority of students are male and the gender gap on professor-level is very high.

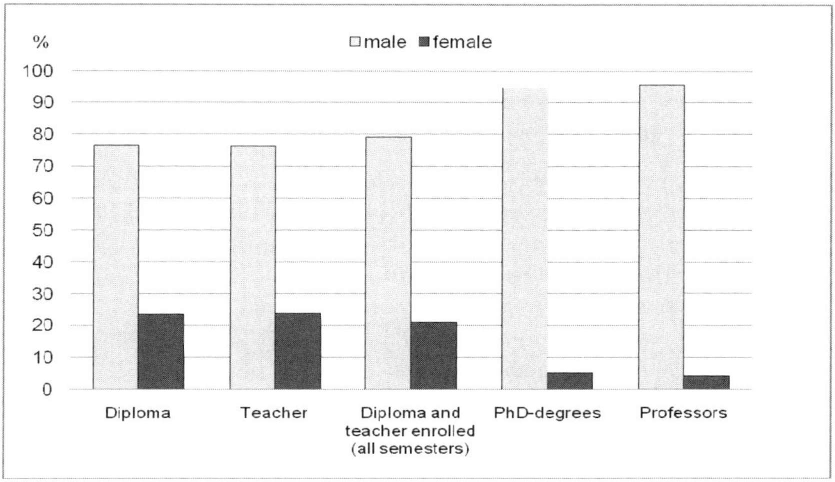

Figure 1: The numbers of female and male diploma- and teacher-students, PhD-degrees and professors at the Department of Physics, Humboldt-Universität zu Berlin, academic year 2004/2005.

Figure 2 illustrates the number of female and male students, who are enrolled at the department of physics at the University of Sarajevo. In each year of enrollment the majority of the students are female.

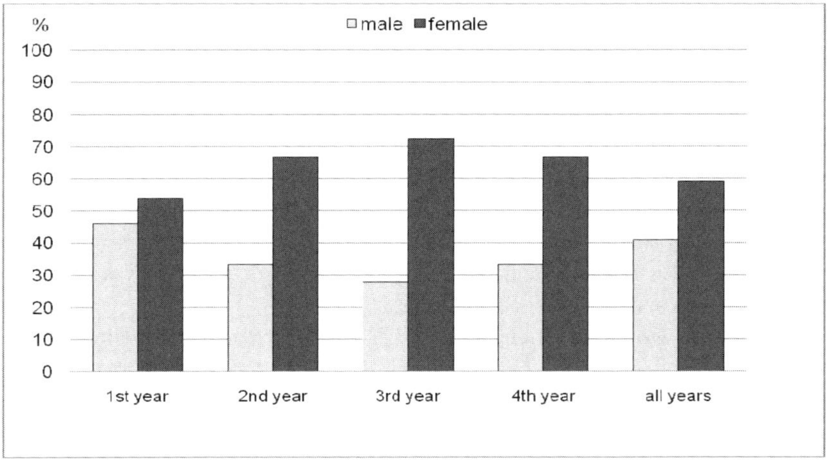

Figure 2: The numbers of female and male students at the University of Sarajevo in the academic year 2006/2007.

- Why is the proportion of female university students lower than their proportion in school?
- Why does the proportion decrease with the progress of an academic career?
- Why are there differences between the proportion of women in Bosnia-Herzegovina and in Germany?

A lot of research efforts have been directed to the field of *gender and physics education* (Ormerod et al. 1979; Ormerod 1981; Hoffmann 1985). Guidelines and suggestions have been developed on how to consider both girls and boys equally in the physics lessons (Herzog et al. 1998; Lorenzo, Crouch and Mazur 2006) and how to make science education more attractive by considering the identity development of girls and boys (Schreiner and Sjøberg 2007). Nowadays, young women seem to be emancipated, which raises another question:

- Will this situation of underrepresentation of women in physics change within the next generation?

In our research we focused on this question and performed a survey among female students of grade 10-13 in Bosnia-Herzegovina (N = 150) and Germany (N = 119).

Questions of this survey were:

- Which subjects do female students choose in school?
- What future aspirations do female students have?
- Who or what influences their decision?
- Are there differences between migrants and non-migrants?

3 Results

- Which subjects do female students choose in school?

The result of the investigation in Germany was that only 1 out of 119 female students stated an interest in studying physics. Remarkably, this student had a background of migration, whereas none of the interrogated non-migrant German students aspired to study physics. In total, science (physics, biology, chemistry) was chosen by 45.2% migrants and by 17.9% non-migrants. Physics was chosen by 11.9% migrants and by 3.6% non-migrants.

In contrast, we found evidence that in Bosnia-Herzegovina the already equal representation of women in science will remain, since for the majority of the students questioned, studying physics is an explicit option. More than 50% of the female Bosnian students choose science as major subject, including physics, biology and chemistry. Out of these three subjects physics was most frequently chosen by the students (21%) followed by biology (16%) and chemistry (13%).

- What future aspirations do female students have?

In the second part of the questionnaire the students were asked if they would like to study at a university and if so, which subject they would like to study. Then they were asked to give reasons for their choice. We were especially interested in whether the students feel that their parents support their choice. Table 2 summarizes the results of these questions. Again we distinguished between students who attended German schools, migrants and non-migrants.

- Who or what influences their decision?

In Germany the students indicated that *the interest in the subject* was the most important reason for their choice (43%), followed by *good results in the particular subject* (38%). In Bosnia-Herzegovina the most important reason was the *usefulness of the subject* for the future career (25%) followed by *the interest in the subject* (18%) and *the "good teacher"* (18%).

- Are there differences between migrants and non-migrants?

In the group of German female students we distinguished between migrants (students not born in Germany and/or both parents not born in Germany) and non-migrants. Moreover, also the students in Bosnia-Herzegovina exhibit a background of migration. They emigrated during and returned after the war. On average, each student spent 3.5 years abroad. Among the Bosnian students there was none who had a country of origin different from Bosnia-Herzegovina; they were repatriates, hence we did not categorize them as migrants. The majority of the migrant girls questioned in Germany were of Turkish origin.

If we compare migrants in Germany (most of them of Turkish origin), German non-migrants and Bosnian non-migrants, certain differences appear: migrants in Germany seem to be more motivated to enroll and study at a university than non-migrants, which is similar to non-migrants in Bosnia-Herzegovina. Migrants in Germany seem to get less approval from their parents for their choice to study than non-migrants in Germany. Parents of non-migrants in Bosnia-Herzegovina seem to approve the choices of their daughters similarly to non-migrant German parents.

Migrants and non-migrants in Germany are not aspiring to study physics, whereas for Bosnian students studying physics is an alternative. Table 2 gives an overview and a tendency of the answers to the questions.

	Germany	Bosnia-Herzegovina
Do you want to study?	YES Non-migrants: 71% Migrants: 91%	YES 100%
What do you want to study?	Pharmacy, medicine: 19% Languages: 15% Physics: rather NO	Sciences: 56% Physics: rather YES
What are the reasons for your choice?	Interest in the subject: 43% Good results: 38% Good teacher: 8%	Useful for future career: 25% Interest: 18% Good teacher: 18%
Do your parents approve of your choice?	YES Migrants: 56% Non-Migrants: 80%	YES 90%

Table 2: Overview of the answers to the questions.

4 Interpretation of the Data

The data show very clearly the following fact: in Germany, the interrogated female high school students do not aspire to study physics at all. It can be expected that the gender gap in physics will remain unchanged. Only 1 out of 119 female students could imagine studying physics, and this student had a background of migration. However, none of the interrogated non-migrant German students aspired to study physics. In Bosnia-Herzegovina, for more than the half of the questioned students studying physics was an option. It can thus be assumed that the representation of women in science will remain unchanged.

We assume the following reasons as possible explanations for this finding: in Bosnia-Herzegovina the situation can be seen as the heritage of the former Socialist Federal Republic of Yugoslavia (1945-1991). In this era strong foundations were created for the equality of women. In Bosnia-Herzegovina generations which were part of that era still live. These generations tend to teach their children that women can do just about any job that men can. The young women of today who are entering the university have mothers and female cousins in a wide range of professions and hence they readily choose similar professions. There are, therefore, role models for women in science. In contrast, in Germany these role models do not exist.

5 Conclusions

We assume that the underrepresentation of women in physics in Germany will not change unless a significant influence of female role models in physics emerges. To increase the number of role models already within the peer group of students, meetings of female high school students and university students have been planned. Further international cooperation at the student level in countries like Germany and Bosnia-Herzegovina can raise the awareness that female role models do exist in other countries. One specific example of support action is the so called Club Lise (Tajmel and Starl 2005, 41-42; see also Tajmel, Starl and Schön in this book). Club Lise is designed as a working group of female high school students interested in science together with university students, female PhD students and researchers. The Club Lise was established in Berlin, Sarajevo, Vienna and Istanbul as part of the project PROMISE with the objective of supporting young women in their choice of studying science and physics.

Bibliography

Enders-Dragässer, Uta and Fuchs, Claudia, *Interaktionen der Geschlechter*, Juventa, Weinheim, 1989.

Herzog, Walter, Gerber, Charlotte, Labbude, Peter, Mauderli, Donatina, Neuenschwander, Markus P. and Violi, Enrico, *Physik geht uns alle an. Ergebnisse aus der Nationalfondsstudie "Koedukation im Physikunterricht"*, Universität Bern, Bern, 1998.

Hoffmann, Lore, *Differences in the Subjective Conditions of Interests in Physics and Technology for Boys and Girls*, in: *Girls and Science and Technology. The third international GASAT conference. Supplementary contributions*, Chelsea College, London, 1985, 70-78.

Hyde, Janet S., Lindberg, Sara M., Linn, Marcia C., Ellis, Amy B., Williams and Caroline C., *Gender Similarities Characterize Math Performance*, in: Science, 321, 2008, 494-495.

Lorenzo, Mercedes, Crouch, Catherine H. and Mazur, Eric, *Reducing the Gender Gap in the Physics Classroom*, in: Am. J. Phys. 74, 2006, 118-122.

OECD, *PISA 2006 Science Competencies for Tomorrows World*, OECD Publishing, Paris, 2007.

Ormerod, M.B., *Factors Differentially Affecting the Science Subject Preferences Choices and Attitudes of Girls and Boys*, in: Kelly, Allison (ed.) *The Missing Half,* University Press, Manchester, 1981.

Ormerod, M.B., Bottemley, Jennifer M., Keys, Wendy P., Wood, Charles, *Girls and Physics Education*, in: Physics Education Vol.14, 1979, 271-277.

Schreiner, Camilla and Sjøberg, Svein, *Science Education and Youth's Identity Construction – Two Incompatible Projects?*, in: Corrigan, Deborah, Dillon, Justin and Gunstone, Richard (eds.), *The Re-emergence of Values in the Science Curriculum*, Sense Publishers, Rotterdam, 2007.

Tajmel, Tanja and Hadžibegović, Zalkida, *Would You Like to Study Physics? A Comparative Study on the Intentions of Female Students in Germany and Bosnia-Herzegovina to Study Science*. Paper presentation at the GIREP/EPEC-Conference, Opatija, 2007.

Tajmel, Tanja and Starl, Klaus, *PROMISE – Promotion of Migrants in Science Education*, European Training and Research Centre for Human Rights and Democracy (ETC Graz), Occasional paper No. 18, 2005, available online at: http://www.etc-graz.at/typo3/index.php?id=74 (last checked 15 August 2008).

Education in Turkey: In View of Children's Rights to Education and Equal Opportunity in Education

Münire Erden

1 Introduction

The aim of this article is to examine the Turkish Educational System in view of children's rights to education and equal opportunity in education. Some of the problems of the current educational system stem from the Ottoman Empire period. Indeed, 90% of the population was illiterate and lived as rural peasants when the Republic of Turkey was established in 1923. Although children's rights to education and equal opportunity in education were accepted as basic principles of the Turkish Educational System in 1973, governments had been trying to apply these principles since 1923. However, there are many serious problems in applying these principles, such as insufficient duration of compulsory education, low school enrollment rates, school abandonment and the education of girls. A rapidly increasing rate of population, im/migration, differences between regions, and the cultural and Islamic values of rural people are the basic causes of these problems. Recently, in order to overcome these problems, governmental and non-governmental organizations have worked in cooperation to find funding for big projects and campaigns for parent education, economical assistance for the families which need their children's labor power, and the increase in quality of education in the rural areas. The article focuses on the differences between rural and urban areas, and on gender inequality in Turkey. The problem is examined within a historical and social context.

2 Education in the Ottoman Empire Period

The Republic of Turkey was established on 29th October 1923, following the end of the war of independence. This relatively young republic was constructed on the economical and cultural heredity of the Ottoman Empire.

The history of the Ottoman Empire extends over more than six centuries. It was established in 1299 and it expanded its territory through military power between 1299 and 1693. The Empire also flourished economically and culturally during this period. An era of stagnation followed the growth era for the next 200 years. When the empire lost territory on all fronts, and administrative instability occurred due to the breakdown of the centralized government despite efforts of reform and reorganization, it declined and dissolution began. The economy of the Ottoman Empire depended on commerce, agriculture and tax incomes, most of which were collected from the foreign provinces. While a few port cities and cities on trade routes dealt with trade and most of the merchants were the non-Muslim minorities, much of the population lived in rural areas. When new trade routes were explored and the empire lost territory, tax incomes of the empire declined, taxation on agriculture was increased, which led to the impoverishment of the peasants.

The Ottoman Empire consisted of various communities with different religions and cultures. For this reason, a common educational system was not developed. Education for Muslims was controlled by the *ulema* and was directed along the lines of religion. There were two types of traditional schools for Muslims: *Sibyan* (infant) schools (primary education) and *madrasa* (secondary and higher education). Primary institutions were generally located either in or near the mosque of the community. They were often established by a *vaqf* (pious foundation). Expenditures of the schools, such as the teachers' salaries, were paid from the endowed income of the *vaqf.* Students merely memorized the *Koran* in these schools. There were no grades or levels. All children shared the same classroom or space under the supervision of a single teacher, called *Hojha.* Graduates of special programs at *madrasas* functioned as teachers of the *sibyan* schools.

Madrasas were generally located in a building complex that consisted of a mosque, hospital, public bath etc. The education lasted one to two years but could be extended if necessary. Programs of teaching or curricula seem to have been grouped under three faculties or specialties: (1) *Religion and Law,* (2) *Natural Sciences,* (3) *Instrumental* (or *auxiliary* for other) sciences. Thus, scientists, judges, and architects were trained together with religious leaders in these schools.

These schools accepted only male students. They provided high quality education up to 1600s, but after these years, due to serious curricular shortcomings (such as a lack of natural sciences) and anachronistic as well as obscurantist tendencies – looking back with longing rather than surging ahead – *madrasa* education seemed to be in a steady decline (Güvenç 2008).

In the stagnation period, some reforms were made in the military services and new secular schools were established for them. The other secular schools for civilians followed these schools in a few big cities during the 19th century. These modern schools accepted female students as well as male students and their activities were controlled by the state. In other words, the state took up the responsibility of education for the first time in 19th century. However, traditional schools also continued to exist under the control of religious institutions.

In sum, while the secularization of schools had begun in Europe with industrialization in the 17th century, this transformation was not realized in the Ottoman Empire. Thus, Turkey remained behind the developed European countries by approximately 200 to 300 years in this respect.

3 Reform Movements in Education at the Beginning of the Republic of Turkey

When the Republic of Turkey was established, approximately 90% of the population lived in rural areas and were illiterate and very poor. While a few of them worked on their own small lands, most of them had been working in slavery conditions for their landlords.

The founder of the republic and members of the governments believed that education was the most important key to the development of the country. In line with this view, firstly traditional and secular schools were integrated before they were all turned over to the Ministry of Education under a 1924 law. Thus, a secular educational system was established under the responsibility of the Ministry of National Education (MONE). Secondly, the Latin alphabet was accepted in 1928 and the first important and extensive non-formal education movement was initiated in order to teach reading and writing in the new alphabet to the public. "People's schools" were opened and attending to these schools became compulsory for the age group of 15 to 45 and 1.2 million individuals learned how to read and write in these schools between 1928 and 1942 (Başgöz and Wilson 1968).

The development of the Turkish national educational system, according to the number of enrollment by the type of school, is shown in Figure 1. According to Figure 1, the most important improvement was realized in the compulsory primary education during these years. The development in secondary and higher education, however, was still slow and insufficient.

Figure 1: Number of enrollment by the type of school and educational year.

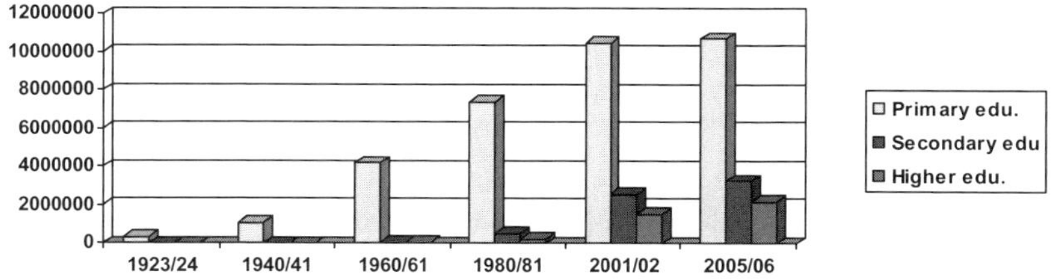

(1) Enrollment number of three year junior high schools is shown in the primary schools until 2001/2002 years. Source: Estimated from MONE Statistical Data 2007.

4 Current Turkish National Educational System

The current Turkish national educational system is divided into two main sections: formal and non-formal education. Pre-school education, primary education, secondary education and higher education are included in formal education. Non-formal education offers training to individuals who are outside the formal education system, in line with the general purposes and basic principles of National Education (MONE 2006-2007). The basic structure of the Turkish Educational System is shown in figure 2.

4.1 Pre-Primary Education

The first level of the Turkish educational system is pre-primary education. This level involves the education of children in the age group of 3 to 5 who have not reached the age of compulsory primary education. Pre-primary education, which is optional, aims at contributing to the physical, mental and emotional development of children. It helps them to acquire good habits and prepares them for basic education. Pre-school education institutions include independent kindergartens, nursery classes in primary schools and preparation classes in Turkey.

4.2 Primary Schools

Primary education involves the education and training of children in the age group of 6 to 14. It is compulsory for all male and female citizens and is free of charge in public schools. There are also private schools under state control. There is usually only one teacher for each class in the first five years of primary education. They provide children with basic knowledge and ensure their physical, mental and moral development in accordance with national objectives. The teachers are differentiated according to disciplines, such as mathematics, social sciences, natural sciences, music etc., in the upper three years of the school. The students are prepared for secondary schools in these years.

4.3 Secondary Education

Secondary education involves the education and training of students in the age group of 15 to 18. It is not compulsory and is free of charge in the public schools. Secondary education encompasses two categories of educational institutions, namely *general high schools* and *vocational and technical high schools* where a minimum of four years of schooling is provided after basic education.

General high schools are educational institutions that prepare students for institutions of higher education. They implement a four-year program over and above basic education, and the classes are comprised students in the 15-18 year age group. Vocational and technical high schools provide specialized instruction with the aim of training qualified personnel. The duration of instruction in these schools is also four years.

4.4 Higher Education

Higher education comprises the educational institutions at every stage based on secondary education with a term of at least two years. Higher education consists of *Universities, Institutes, Higher Schools, Vocational Higher Schools, Conservatories, Research and Application Centers*. The Higher Education Law, which went into effect in 1981, covers all higher education institutions and regulates their organization and functions. Institutions of higher education, under the supervision and control of the state, can also be established by private foundations in accordance with the procedures and principles set forth in the law, provided that these foundations are non-profit in nature. There is a tuition fee for higher education. However, successful students who lack financial means are provided with full support by private individuals and organizations, as well as by the state (Higher Education Council, Student Selection and Placement Center, 2006).

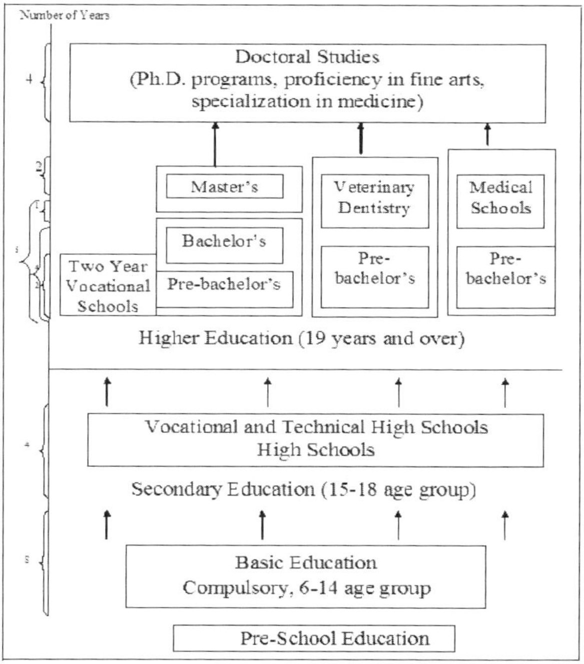

Figure 2: General Structure of the Turkish National Educational System

Source: Higher Education Council Student Selection and Placement Center (ÖSYM), *Selection and Placement of Students in Higher Education Institutions in Turkey*, Ankara, 2006.

4.5 Non-Formal Education

Non-formal education covers citizens who have never entered the formal educational system or are at any level of it or have left at that level. In Turkey, MONE and other ministries, non-governmental organizations organize free of charge non-formal training programs such as reading and writing, handy crafts, health and child care, especially for women who live in rural areas. However, these studies do not reach all people in need of these non-formal education facilities. Recently, vocational programs in line with the employers' needs have been opened by private educational institutions in big cities in order to meet the education needs of people.

5 Basic Principles of the Turkish National Educational System

The basic structure of the Turkish national educational system is outlined in the Basic Law on National Education (Law no. 1739) of 1973. The general purposes and basic principles of the system were also defined in this law. All of the educational institutions and their activities have to be organized in line with these principles.

Principles such as "The Reforms and Principles of Atatürk and the Nationalism of Atatürk" and "Democracy Education and Secularism" are based on the Constitution of Turkey. The aim of the "Scientific Approach to Education," "Planning," "Orientation," "Co-education," "School-Family Cooperation," "Continuity" and "Education everywhere" is to increase the quality of education. The "Needs of the Individual and Society" principle shows that needs of both individuals and society are equally important. "Generality and Equality," "Right to Education" and "Equal Opportunities" principles are basically in accordance with human rights and children's rights.

In the law, the generality and equality principle states that "education institutions are open to all citizens regardless of their sex, religion, language and race. No concessions shall be provided to any individual, family, group or class in education." A principle of the right to education entitles "every Turkish individual" to basic education. It states that "the citizens shall benefit from the education institutions following the primary education according to their abilities, talents and interests." Finally, the equal opportunities principle states that "equal opportunities shall be provided to every woman and man in education. Necessary assistance shall be provided through grants, scholarships, credits and other ways to successful students with weak economic conditions so that they can enjoy higher education. Special measures shall be taken in order to support children in need of protection and special education."

The educational system is obliged to obey these principles in practice. The generality and equality principle has been implemented without major problem. However, there are still some problems in the implementation of the right to education and equal opportunity in educational principles.

6. Concerns in Respect to the Right to Education

The problems of the Turkish National Educational System related to the right to education could be classified as the following.

6.1 Duration of Compulsory Education

When compared with developed countries, Turkey's eight years of compulsory education is insufficient. Although according to the first constitution of Turkey primary schools were compulsory and free of charge for the age group 7 to14, Turkish governments had accepted five years of compulsory education until 1997. After that, eight years of compulsory education were implemented by the new law. Currently, the government is trying to prolong compulsory education to 12 years, but the implementation of this seems difficult, especially in rural areas.

6.2 Enrollment Rates

Enrollment in all of the educational levels has not yet reached an acceptable rate and there are children who are still not in the educational system. The lowest enrollment rate in Turkey is in pre-primary, with only 13% (Eğitimsen 2008). Since Turkish governments began to focus on the development of primary schools, they have neglected pre-primary schools since the 1980s. However, these schools have not been demanded by parents, because traditionally women are usually housewives and it is believed that mothers can take care of their children at home better than the kindergarten. For that reason, sometimes grandmothers take on the responsibility of the childcare if the mother of the child works outside of the home. After the 1980s, especially educated parents comprehended the importance of pre-primary schools, and private kindergartens became widespread in big cities. Recently, MONE has begun to open nursery classes within primary education schools. The results of this were a relatively economical solution and increased enrollment rate in pre-primary education throughout over the country; however, the results are still insufficient.

The prior aim of the Turkish government was always to increase the enrollment rate in primary schools. The enrollment rate in the five years of compulsory education reached 89.4% in 1996. In the same year, the enrollment rate in three-year junior high schools was only 52.8%. Following the adaptation of the Basic Education Law (Law No. 4306) in August 1997, which mandated eight years of compulsory education, Turkey launched an unprecedented expansion of public primary schooling. The eight-year basic education program involved a broad range of actions that were financed to a large extent by government grants, but also by private enterprises and international development organizations also made significant contributions (MONE, 2005). Although to increase the span of compulsory education up to 8 years was a very difficult task both economically and traditionally in the rural areas, enrollment rate in primary school reached 89.77% in 2007 as a result of the tremendous effort (See table 1).

Despite this important development in compulsory education, approximately 10% of the children of primary school age are still not enrolled in the schools. Mostly, these are children with a weak economic background from rural areas and migrant children living in poor city areas.

Table 1: Schooling ratio by level of education and the educational year
A: Total / B: Males / C: Females (%)

Educational Year	Primary Education			Secondary Education			Higher Education		
	A	B	C	A	B	C	A	B	C
1997/98 (1)	84.74	90.25	78.97	37.87	41.39	34.16	10.25	11.28	9.17
1998/99 (1)	89.26	94.48	83.79	38.87	42.34	35.22	10.76	11.81	9.67
1999/00 (1)	93.54	98.41	88.45	40.38	44.05	36.52	11.62	12.68	10.52
2000/01 (1)	95.28	99.58	90.79	43.95	48.49	39.18	12.27	13.12	11.38
2001/02 (1)	92.40	96.20	88.45	48.11	53.01	42.97	12.98	13.75	12.17
2002/03 (1)	90.98	94.49	87.34	50.57	55.72	45.16	14.65	15.73	13.53
2003/04 (1)	90.21	93.41	86.89	53.37	58.08	48.43	15.31	16.62	13.93
2004/05 (1)	89.66	92.58	86.63	54.87	59.05	50.51	16.60	18.03	15.10
2005/06 (1)	89.77	92.29	87.16	56.63	61.13	51.95	18.85	20.22	17.41
2006/07 (1)	90.13	92.25	87.93	56.51	60.71	52.16	-	-	-

(2) Schooling ratios in the year 1997 and onwards were calculated by using the latest population projections according to results of General Population Census in 2000 year. Source: National Education Statistics, Formal Education 2006-2007

As shown in Table 1, schooling ratios for the secondary and higher education are also unsatisfactory. According to 2007 MONE statistics, enrollment rate in secondary school is 56.51%. These figures also show that the abandonment rate after primary school is very high in Turkey. However, although nearly all the students who graduated from secondary schools wish to attend universities, the capacity of the universities is not enough to meet the demands of the students. The enrollment rate at this educational level is only 18.85%.

6.3 School Drop-Out Rates

Further major concerns of the educational system are irregular attendance and the high drop-out rates in compulsory primary education. The drop out rate is about 37% for schools in rural areas. In addition, only 6% of secondary school-aged students attend secondary schools in rural areas. The drop-out rate in secondary school amounts to approximately 80-90% in rural areas.

6.4 Education of Girls

Girls are more disadvantaged than boys as far as enrollment rate and regular attendance at schools are concerned. As shown in Table 1, the enrollment rate for girls in all educational levels is lower than that for boys.

7 Reasons for these Problems

A rapidly increasing population, migration from rural to urban areas and differing religious and cultural values are the main reasons behind the enrollment problem in Turkey. Each of these problems is discussed briefly below.

7.1 Large Growth in Population

According to the earliest statistics, 13.5 million people lived in Turkey in 1927. Population increased at a rate of approximately 20-25% every 5 years and it reached about 70 million in 2007. When the distribution of children according to socio-economic status of families is examined, it shows that the families with low income and less education have more children than families with high income and a high education standard. For example, East and Southeast regions of Anatolia are the poorest parts of Turkey and the rate of population increase in this region was about 36% in the period from 1995 to 2000 (Statistics Institution of Turkey (SIT) 2008). As a result of rapid population increase, the need for new schools has increased. Thus, the construction of new school buildings is the one of the most important expenditures of the MONE budget.

Along with the rapid increase in population, unbalanced distribution of the population to regions is another problem. There are small villages with a population of 100-500 people located 3-10 kilometers away from each other in Eastern Anatolia. The transportation between them is sometimes very sporadic as a result of weather conditions. Although technological development has improved transportation in this region, governments have attempted to build a school for each village. Of course this is an important economic burden on the state.

7.2 Migration from Rural to Urban Areas

Prior to the 1950s, more than 80% of Turkish residents lived in rural areas. In the following years, migration started from rural to urban areas. According to SIT statistics, the proportion of the population living in urban areas was 32.6% in 2005. Migration led to new problems in urban areas; one of them is education. Migration increased the cities' population more than three times and has contributed to the increasing need for schools in big cities.

People often move to big cities to find a new job, though many have a difficult time finding a permanent job. Oftentimes this leads the immigrant to take on temporary jobs, such as selling small things on the streets or even begging. Children have also been used in these jobs. There are no reliable statistical data about child workers, but it is estimated that about 958,000 children aged between 6 and 17 work outside of the home (SIT 2008).

In addition, as a result of migration, the population of many rural areas has dramatically decreased, leading to school closures and the transformation of differentiated classrooms to multi-graded classes. The latter change renders all the governmental investments in the area redundant. A few students who live in these villages ride public transport to the relatively larger villages, or have been accepted to the boarding schools in their region. However, some families do not wish to separate from their children and they do not send their children, especially the girls, to the schools. Another problem is that the students, once enrolled at a school, may drop out.

7.3 Religious and Cultural Values Affecting Education

Turkey has a multi-cultural composition of population that was inherited from the Ottoman Empire. The sources of differentiation could be ethnic diversity and religious values. Some beliefs and values of religion lead to restrictions of girls' right to education. One of them is the headscarf, which is still under discussion among the people in Turkey. According to Muslim beliefs, girls cover their head with a scarf when they reach puberty. According to the Turkish constitution, however, school attendance with a headscarf is forbidden. For that reason, conservative families who live in urban and rural areas do not permit their girls to enroll in schools or withdraw them from the schools when they reach puberty. Recently most conservative families who believe in the importance of education tolerate this rule. Thus, the enrollment rate of girls has increased in urban areas.

Social values and pressure in rural areas are another factor that restricted the education of girls. Male members of the patriarchal families often do not value the education of women. They believe that women who attend schools do not obey them anymore. This belief is not actually related to religion, but reflects this as a rule of religion. Sometimes, there is social pressure on the families from their neighborhoods and communities. Thus, fathers restrict girls' right to education. For that reason, the motto of a campaign in support of girls' education was "*Daddy, send me to school.*"

One other factor is the early marriage of girls. When girls reach puberty, families prefer their early marriage and domestic roles over education. Sometimes, girls are made to get married so that the family can get a so-called bride prize. Sometimes girls also wish to get married at an early age because traditional and conservative families do not permit girls to flirt. Sometimes girls prefer early marriage to get away from family pressure. This tradition also increases the drop-out rate in rural areas.

Finally, parents keep girls at home so that they will care for younger family members and help with domestic work. For these reasons they can not attend school regularly and they cannot do their homework. This often leads girls to fail their classes.

Although scientific research about these problems is insufficient, the reason for the irregular attendance and drop-out rates at school is well known by the authorities. However, changing the beliefs of the families is very difficult.

The major reason for boys' irregular attendance and abandonment of school is economic. Boys are perceived as labor power by families with low income. In traditional extended families, the male child usually takes care of his aged parents and so boys are perceived as insurance for the parents (Kağıtçıbaşı 1980). For this reason, the elderly members give up all properties to the male members of the family and try to educate them in the family. Thus the sons of the small land owners work with their fathers starting at the age of 5-6 in rural areas. However, sons of small merchants work with fathers in small towns only after they graduate primary or secondary schools.

This traditional structure of families has been changing slowly in Turkey. Nowadays, the families have begun to perceive education as an important tool for increasing their children's status in society. The upper and middle class families have invested in the education of their children.

8 Problems about Equal Opportunity in Education

In order to obtain equal opportunity in education, all state schools except universities are free of charge and the same national curricula are applied throughout the country. In addition, course books, study books and teachers are selected by the MONE. The delivery of these books to the students is organized by the state.

Besides these, teacher training curricula of the educational faculties are similarly implemented under the control of the Council of Higher Education.

Teachers are selected for the state schools by means of a country-wide examination and they are randomly appointed to the schools by computer. Novice teachers are usually appointed to rural areas where they have to work for at least two years.

The aim of all these implementations is to ensure educational equality. Although the most important components of education, such as school curriculum, course books and curricula of the teacher training programs are similar all over the country, the quality and the results of education are different. The quality of schools depends on the cultural, social and regional properties. These properties can be summarized as the following:

1. Since the ratio of attendance for pre-primary schools is low and such schools are generally found in urban areas, the children in rural areas start primary school with a disadvantage. While the contributions of these schools are more important for children who grow up in uneducated and poor families, children of educated families with high income have the opportunity to attend these schools. For that reason, children who come from uneducated families are less successful than the educated ones and they can not attend secondary schools and universities.

2. Although the teacher training system is common and teachers are selected with an examination, novice teachers are generally appointed to the rural schools. For these teachers, adaptation to the rural area is not easy. For that reason, they do not work effectively in these schools. On the other hand, most of the male teachers join the army or are appointed to schools in more developed areas in one or two years. Students always change teachers and sometimes they do not even have teachers for short or long periods in rural areas. This discontinuity in education hinders student success.

3. Research has shown that the home environment and family support can greatly affect learning in school (Walberg, 1984). The income and education levels of families who live in rural areas in Turkey are very low. For that reason, the level of readiness of the children for schools in rural areas is also lower than that of children in big cities. In particular, in regions of Southeast and East Anatolia, families seem to disregard the importance of education. Families are not in a position to guide their children academically; on the contrary, they are especially unwilling to let their children go to schools. This attitude of the parents negatively affects students' academic success in school.

4. In small villages, due to such deficiencies as the small number of students, the insufficient number of available teachers and the impossibility of assigning a different teacher to each class, two or more grades are often put together in a single

classroom under the control of one teacher. Such classrooms in schools are called multi-graded classrooms. Instruction in multi-graded classrooms is more difficult than in independent classrooms. Teachers often cannot spare as much time for individual students because of the nature of the class. Students who graduated from these classes are usually doomed to failure after 5th grade and tend to drop out of school.

5. Since MONE gives priority to the construction of new school buildings, an insufficient portion of the budget is used for renovation and maintenance of the existing ones. However, maintenance expenditures of the schools are shared among the families in the richest parts of the cities. They also supply teaching materials (such as computer labs, libraries, reproduction of written materials etc.) for the school. Other schools located in rural areas and in the poorest regions of the cities are deprived of families' contribution. For that reason there are big differences among the state schools. These differences lead to inequality in education.

6. As a result of a rapidly growing population in cities, the numbers of students are very high for each school and it is necessary to double teaching shifts in these schools. While some of the students attend the school only in the morning, others attend in the afternoon. This implementation necessitates intensive lessons and short breaks between the lessons. Despite double teaching implementations, there are sometimes 70-100 students in a classroom. In contrast, there are 20-25 students in each class in private schools.

7. There are some special secondary schools, called *Science*, *Anatolia* and *Super secondary schools* in big cities. These schools are enriched with foreign language classes and more qualified teachers are appointed there. In addition, they provide good opportunities for the students. Thus, there is intense competition among the students to enter these schools. Students are selected for these schools by means of an examination. In order to pass this examination with high marks, families support their children with tutors or courses organized by the private sector. Thus, the children of poor families have little chance to do well on this examination and attend these schools. Besides these special schools, most of the high and middle class families send their children to private schools. These differentiations in the school system result in inequality in education.

9 Conclusion

Although a child's right to education and equal opportunity in education were only accepted as basic principles of the Turkish Educational System in 1973, governments had tried to apply these principles since 1923. In spite of the considerable and ongoing efforts of the state to overcome the educational problems by increasing enrollment rates and the duration of compulsory education, underway since the establishment of the republic, all this work seems to take a very long time as a result of the rapid increase of the population and the continuous migration into the urban areas from the rural ones. These quantitative problems could be solved financially. People have always made charitable contributions to education since the establishment of Turkey. This is a tradition which came from the Ottoman Empire. However, state, non-governmental organizations and charitable people could not change the situation very much until the implementation of eight-year compulsory education.

Using a combination of government and private contributions, MONE built 81,500 new primary education classrooms during the five year period between 1997 and 2002, increasing the number of classrooms by 30 percent. These investments have yielded a dramatic increase in educational coverage (MONE 2005). As a result of the success of this campaign, in 2003 MONE started a new campaign which is called "100% Education". In order to support this campaign, charitable contributions to education are 100% tax deductible. The funds obtained from these projects have gone to such expenditures as the construction of new schools, the renovation of old schools and the improvement of technological equipment in schools.

To increase the enrollment rate of girls in rural areas, MONE and UNICEF started a campaign called "Let girls go to school." About 222,800 girls have been enrolled in schools as a result of this campaign (MONE 2005). Another campaign is called "Snowdrop," and promoted the education of girls. This campaign was supported by The Ministry of State for Women and Family Affairs, the Association in Support of Contemporary Living and a telecommunication firm. In addition, there are some projects for pre-primary school-age children such as parents' education and mobile kindergartens.

As a result of these studies, the enrollment problem of Turkey is on the decline. However, improving the quality of education and overcoming inequality in education are still *the* important problems of the system. Nowadays, in order to improve the quality of education a new curriculum has been developed for primary schools. The curriculum emphasizes students' engagement and learning by discovery, despite the existence of severe problems of implementation in practice. The compensation for inequality in education still remains a great barrier.

Bibliography

Başgöz, İ. and Wilson, H.G., *Türkiye Cumhuriyet'inde Milli Eğitim ve Atatürk*, Dost Yayınları, Ankara, 1968.

Eğitimsen, available online at: http://www.egitimsen.org.tr/index.php?yazi=11 (last checked 11 June 2008).

Güvenç, B. *History of Turkish Education*, available online at: http://www.yok.gov.tr/webeng/histedu/histtredu.html (last checked 27 June 2008).

Higher Education Council Student Selection and Placement Center, *Selection and Placement of Students in Higher Education Institutions in Turkey*, Ankara, 2006, available online at: http://www.osym.gov.tr/belgegoster.aspx?f6e10f8892433cff7a2395174cfb32e15f640fc6104c033d (last checked 11 June 2008).

Kağıtçıbaşı, Ç., *Çocuğun Değeri: Türkiye'de Değerler ve Doğurganlık*, University Publications, Istanbul, 1980.

Ministry of National Education (MONE), *National Education Statistics Formal Education 2006-2007*, available online at: http://sgb.meb.gov.tr/istatistik/meb_istatistikleri_orgun_egitim_2006_2007.pdf (last checked 11 June 2008).

Statistic Institution of Turkey, available online at: http://www.tuik.gov.tr/PreTablo.do?tbid=26&tb_adi=Çocuk%20İşgücü%20İstatistikleri&ust_id=8 (last checked 11 June 2008).

Walberg, H.J., *Improving the Productivity of America's Schools*, in: Educational Leadership, XLII, (42, 8), 19-27. 1984.

3. The Response – Science Education in Diversity Classroom

Differences Between Students – Differences in Instruction? How to Make Physics Instruction Effective for All Students

Rita Wodzinski and Christoph T. Wodzinski

1 Introduction

Studies in science education have shown that instruction is particularly effective if it piques learners' interests, if it is based on students' prior knowledge and experiences, if it is adapted to their individual ability level, and if it provides room for successful and active learning (e.g. Duit 2003). However, these goals for instruction soon run into limiting factors when they are applied in real life classroom practice. How can we do justice to each student? How can we pay attention to each student? How can we take each student's interests and ability level into account? Varied methods of instruction open a path away from a "one size fits all"-style of instruction towards instruction that meets the needs and requirements of as many students as possible.

Experienced teachers implicitly use a wide range of different ways to address and support many students. They change their methods during lessons, look for various examples of every day applications of physics, for interested students they provide ideas how to work on topics of physics beyond classroom instruction or they offer additional tasks for those who need further support. These methods of varying instruction, however, are mostly chosen unconsciously. The aim of this article is therefore, to raise awareness of differentiation and to widen the range of possibilities and methods.

The fundamental basis for differentiated instruction is to recognize the differences between students. These differences are then taken as a starting point for teaching. It must be pointed out that these differences do not only refer to the actual learning preconditions for the respective topic, but also include facets of the personality of each student. In other words, differentiated instruction is based on the differences between students and also helps to rediscover students as individuals.

2 Internal versus Institutional Differentiation

The idea of differentiation has a long history. Nearly 200 years ago, the German philosopher and educator Johann Friedrich Herbart described the differences of minds as the biggest obstacle for education (Ahrbeck 1997, 739-769). In a similar sense, the authors of the PISA-study summarize, that "*catering for an increasingly diverse student body and narrowing the gaps in student performance represent formidable challenges for all countries*" (OECD 2003, 261).

Different countries have chosen different ways to deal with this problem of diversity. Some prefer a highly selective school system, where others favor a method of teaching that champions integration. In Germany and Austria, for example, students are already selected at the age of ten to attend one of four different types of schools. As PISA results have shown, there is a tendency for countries with selective school systems to perform less well, although this tendency is small and not significant. Another interesting result is that the researchers found out that "*countries in which students report a comparatively low level of individual support from their teachers are also those with a particularly high degree of institutional differentiation.*" (OECD 2003, 264)

The German discussion about differentiated instruction peaked in the 1970s due to a discussion about the introduction of non-selective comprehensive schools. At that time, differentiated instruction was sometimes seen as the best way to teach learning groups that were almost homogeneous. Since this time, differentiation at the secondary school level has not been discussed much, whereas in primary school differentiation has been developed further.

3 Differentiation in Physics Instruction

In many countries, efforts at differentiation concerning physics instruction have played a minor part up to now. In a traditional physics lesson, the teacher tries to control instruction in a central way. In addition to this, longer phases of practice which are usually a field for differentiation are not common in physics lessons. The main reason why more attention is paid to differentiated instruction nowadays can be seen in the strong connection between differentiated instruction and the aims of efficient classroom practice in general. In many countries, for example, improvements in science instruction are connected to a transition in teaching methods from traditional teaching to more student based methods and student-selected tasks. The rediscovered work of Vygotsky had an especially great impact on the discussion of differentiated instruction (Tomlinson and McTighe 2006).

According to Vygotsky, learning occurs when a task is a bit beyond the student's comfort level, and the student finds a support system to bridge the gap. This optimum degree of difficulty for learning is referred to as the students' zone of proximal development.

4 Differentiated Instruction and its Basic Aims

The aim of differentiated instruction is to support the individuality of each student. This means that, in the end, the goal is not to reduce, but to accept and to maintain, the variety among students. Differentiation is to be understood as a set of measures used to create supportive learning conditions for as many children as possible in a heterogeneous group. In this context, differentiation includes measures inside the classroom during instruction as well as beyond classroom instruction. Measures for internal differentiation during instruction may concern the entire class or smaller subgroups which, for instance, work on different learning tasks.

Differentiated instruction is sometimes seen as a way to accommodate especially challenged learners and/or gifted learners. Differentiation – as we describe it here is, in fact, addressed to all students.

4.1 Learning Independently

Differentiated instruction does not only mean that the teacher supports different groups of students with corresponding learning tasks. It also includes learners being enabled to look for and make their own use of suitable learning opportunities. Learning arrangements that allow students individual ways of learning are called self-differentiating. In particular, problems with various solutions are self-differentiating. But even if students choose their own ways of solving the problem, it remains the teacher's task to assess the range of possibilities and to adapt them to the group of learners.

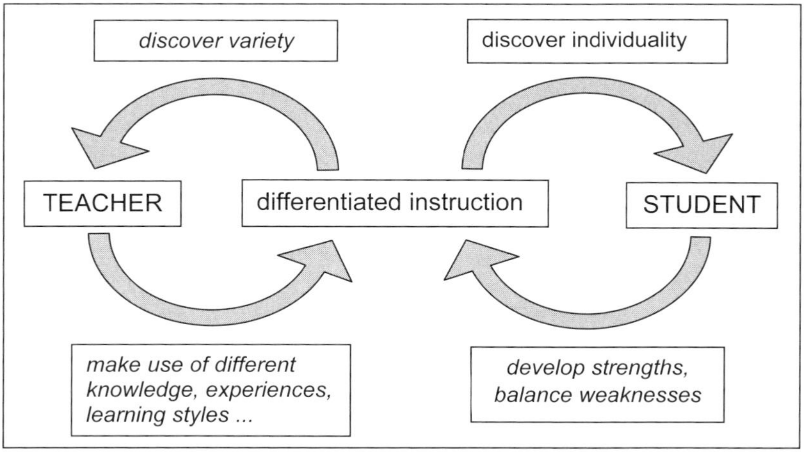

Figure 1: Aspects of differentiated instruction for teachers and students

According to the principle of lifelong learning students have to be enabled to control and develop learning processes increasingly on their own. A precondition is that students be able to assess their own needs, obstacles, and prerequisites of learning. To become aware of the students' individual prerequisites of learning is accordingly not only starting point for differentiated instruction on the side of the teacher but also the learning target for the student. It is one important step on the way to facilitating and to strengthening autonomy in learning.

Figure 1 emphasizes this aspect: Differentiated instruction can on the one hand be seen from the teacher's point of view as a way to improve teaching. On the other hand it can also be seen from the students' point of view as a way to discover and develop one's individuality.

4.2 Individual Learning

To teach in a differentiated way means to create learning opportunities so that everybody may learn successfully and with the most satisfaction possible. This may allow students to learn different content, to follow different processes and end up with different products of learning (Tomlinson and McTighe 2006). Consequently, we have to accept that students attain different goals in differentiated instruction. Differentiation in its extreme form (as realized in modern multimedia learning programs for example) leads to completely individualized instruction. But learning in school always includes the aim of achieving common goals inside a group of learners. For this purpose it is necessary to structure the learning environment carefully and to relate learning processes to one another.

5 Students' Differing Prerequisites

Changes in society during the last few years have led to an increasing heterogeneity in learning groups. The social structure of families, the attitude of students towards school and learning, and the organization of students' leisure time appear in a wider range than they did before. All these factors have an influence on learning in school and are to be taken into account when considering the effectiveness of pedagogical methods.

In order to describe the differences between students in the context of differentiation, often factors from the field of learning psychology are mentioned, such as

- prior experiences and prior knowledge,
- interest and motivation,
- readiness and ability to concentrate,
- preferences in learning and learning style,

- cognitive ability,
- …

But these aspects characterize students as learners from a very narrow viewpoint. They especially imply the danger of assessing students by searching for deficits referring to an "ideal student." Thinking of an actual group of learners, it is evident that individual needs and the individual background of students have additional influence on instruction. The listed variables above do not include those influences.

In the following we discuss some further aspects which play a part especially in learning physics and mark differences between learners.

5.1 Gender

Gender is also a decisive factor in learning differences. It is known that boys more often have experience with scientific and technical matters in their everyday life, that they are more interested in topics covered by physics lessons, and that they achieve better results than girls. Of course there are also many boys who are not interested in physics, just as girls are often very interested and highly successful students.

In the 1980s and 90s some studies were carried out concerning co-educative instruction of physics (primarily in classes of beginners) (Hoffmann 2002). Even if this idea of separating boys and girls in physics lessons is seldom discussed today, setting up gender homogenous groups is still a possible method of creating positive learning conditions, especially for girls. Moreover, studies show that instruction, adapted to the interests of girls, is of benefit to both girls *and* boys (Häussler and Hoffmann 2002).

5.2 Mathematical Abilities

In physics instruction, great differences can be noted in terms of mathematical abilities. Whereas some students especially like mathematical considerations, there are others, and they are not few, who have many difficulties in these cases. Consequently, the latter often reject physics. Something similar applies to experimenting: some students see their field of interest in experimenting and possess special skills in it, whereas others seek cognitive challenges in more theoretical issues.

5.3 Preferences in Learning

Furthermore, there are differences in regard to preferred learning methods. Some students like to work in groups or with a partner and are successful in their strategies, whereas others prefer to work alone. And while some learners profit the most from autonomous learning, others manage quite well with teacher dominated instruction.

In this context, affective factors play an important part. Studies show that teacher dominated instruction is very well suited for students with performance anxiety, whereas students who feel little or no anxiety prefer autonomous ways of learning (e.g. Cronbach and Snow 1977 or Hasebrook 1998).

5.4 Motivation

In addition, students of physics often possess different motivation for engagement in physics. Some of them are thinking of a job where knowledge of physics is important, while others already know that they will drop physics instruction as soon as possible.

Of course, students must fulfill certain minimal requirements at the end of a course. How deeply some students are involved and which main emphasis they choose, according to their interests beyond those minimal requirements, lies also in the hands of the students themselves. It is the teacher's task to enable students to learn. What is learned has to be decided to a significant degree by students themselves. The sooner it is possible to offer a variety in teaching suitable to as many students as possible, the sooner the students will use these offers productively.

6 How can Instruction be Oriented to the Preconditions of Students?

In classroom practice it is impossible to take into account all those features where differences exist between students.

As a first step, it is advisable to use a wide range of methods and media for instruction. In this way, each learner finds from time to time a learning environment optimal for his or her needs. In a second step, the adaptation of instruction to the actual conditions of students could be made more conscious and better focused. For this purpose, subgroups with similar preconditions could be set up, for instance with similar interests, similar experimental skills, similar mathematical abilities, etc. In order to fulfill the students' different conditions of learning, heterogeneous groups of learners can also be set up. For instance "better" students may function as tutors for those who are not as capable. Or students with extensive knowledge and prior experiences could let others participate in their experiences. Moreover, heterogeneous groups of learners offer possibilities for the individual to assess him- or herself in comparison to fellow students and to become aware of his or her own strengths and weaknesses more easily. In contrast, groups with similar ability level reduce the danger of expecting too much or too less of some students.

However, there is no general answer to the question of how groups of learners should be set up. Research results are not definite in this respect. Nevertheless, one should be concerned that the social structure of a group not be harmed in any fundamental way when it is set up in a homogeneous way.

However, the possibilities of differentiation are not exhausted just by setting up homogeneous or heterogeneous groups of learners. The possibilities range from measures of differentiation, which are mainly structured by the teacher, to lessons where students are provided with a high degree of autonomy and are expected to participate often.

7 How to Support Advanced Learners

For gifted and talented students, traditional instruction does not offer enough tasks for deep thinking and learning. As a consequence, students' talents are not fostered sufficiently and opportunities for individual development in cognitive and social fields are passed up. This can be followed by low motivation and sometimes severe behavioral problems.

Gifted and talented students need cognitively challenging problems. These can be given in class, but also tasks offered beyond classroom instruction. Some of these measures, for instance, are:

- to advise them to join programs for gifted students (beyond school),
- to form special study-groups for interested students in the school,
- to offer the opportunity to work as a tutor or to be supported by a tutor,
- taking part in science competitions.

7.1 Programs for Gifted Students

Such offers are explicitly addressed to gifted students who are especially talented in one or several fields. Many universities and some schools offer programs for gifted students.

7.2 Study-Groups

Study-groups offer the opportunity to discuss and work on a special topic in detail. Some schools are free to integrate study-groups in their regular program so that teachers are paid for this work. In many cases, setting up a study group requires a great personal commitment on the part of the teacher; however, the engagement of students solving problems that really interest them can be reward enough for the time and energy of the teacher.

7.3 Tutors

Fostering interested students by working as a tutor can easily be realized in study-groups or projects in school. Being a tutor offers the chance to improve and develop abilities (not only cognitive). In the same sense, "having a tutor" would be a good support for younger students.

7.4 Competitions

A good opportunity to support gifted students is to encourage them to take part in national or international competitions. To prepare the participation may as well be part of the work in a study-group or project at school.

8 How to Support Students with Learning Difficulties

It is a special challenge to foster students who are not as capable as others. Their difficulties may have different reasons. These may be difficulties with language (especially for learners who are not native speakers), difficulties in reading and writing, or behavioral problems. There are also affective problems such as performance anxiety or poor self image. Further difficulties are a slow pace of learning, lack of interest and motivation, as well as insufficient cognitive abilities. These problems can be met on three levels:

- by professional medical or psychological support,
- by appropriate training and,
- by differentiated instruction.

8.1 Professional Support

Disorders often have organic or psychological reasons; even performance anxiety is a psychologically determined problem. Appropriate instruction may only compensate these kinds of obstacles in learning to a slight extent. These students need professional medical or psychological support.

8.2 Appropriate Training

Starting in the 1980s, some training programs intended to deal with language problems or difficulties in reading and writing or meta-cognitive training were developed, for example the "Reciprocal Teaching" by Palinscar and Brown (1984) and the "training of meta-cognitive skills" by Lauth (1989). These two programs proved helpful in supporting less capable students. Both employ strategic training, which means that procedures are demonstrated and explained step by step. The support from the expert is successively reduced, but students are supported further on when they apply strategies autonomously and receive feedback on their progress. Results indicate that the use of meta-cognitive strategies in physics instruction can be supported even for less capable students within a specific training program.

8.3 Differentiated Instruction

Many students with learning difficulties differ from the others in their need for:

- more repetition for memorization,
- more time for structuring information, and
- more help for conceptual understanding (Zielinski 1995).

It is possible to help these students with different measures, as for instance (Zielinski 1995):

- providing additional time for learning,
- focusing on goals,
- controlling learning activities,
- assigning precise tasks and posing simple questions,
- providing immediately available support, and
- facilitating supportive contact between teacher and student.

From these rather general suggestions, the following recommendations may be derived for differentiated instruction that supports learning processes of students who are less capable or who are have difficulties with learning:

- ascertain prior knowledge and experiences carefully,
- put a main emphasis on imparting strategies of learning,
- make use of group learning in order to have time for the less capable students,
- let students with difficulties work together with highly efficient students,
- provide extra homework for the less capable students so they can work on their weaknesses,
- give positive feedback, even when only small successes are achieved, in order to encourage the less capable,
- consider – as far as possible – interests and needs from less capable students,
- refer less capable students to institutions for private coaching,
- if necessary develop an individual tutoring program together with psychologists.

Whether or not it is useful for students with severe educational handicaps to remain in class or to attend special classes has not been clearly answered by research yet. Nevertheless, we can assume at present that homogeneous groups of learners will provide more emotional relief and better social integration (Ahrbeck 1997, 759).

9 Requirements of Students and Teachers

Differentiated instruction requires students' total commitment and demands a certain degree of willingness to learn. Possibly, this kind of willingness has to be developed first. In principle, almost all measures of differentiation are based on the possibilities of allowing and enabling students to work to a great extent in an autonomous and cooperative way. In this context, it is important that learners develop basic learning techniques for autonomous study. Those have to be extended in class step by step.

Certainly, this kind of instruction, which offers students freedom for individual ways of learning, demands more time than traditional instruction. In the long run, this amount of time will be saved later on. Time is saved especially because students are enabled to learn autonomously and have developed a sense of self-responsibility. Besides, effectiveness of instruction depends highly on the fact that students are enabled to control their individual work in various ways.

This kind of instruction demands a lot from teachers as well – as was mentioned earlier. Instruction has to be planned and carried out with the students' individualities in mind. In this regard the role of the teacher changes: he or she is no longer mainly a transmitter of information, but also an organizer and adviser for learning. This has to be developed to a higher degree as instruction is more often planned to be open. Not only the students, but also the teachers have to achieve new competence, which needs time and effort, just like planning instruction in terms of content and methods. Nevertheless, differentiated instruction can be a relief because it can facilitate students' interests and willingness to learn and help to reduce classroom disturbances.

Bibliography

Ahrbeck, Bernd, Bleidick, Ulrich and Schuck, Karl, *Pädagogisch-psychologische Modelle der inneren und äußeren Differenzierung für lernbehinderte Schüler,* in: Weinert, Franz (ed.), Psychologie des Unterrichts und der Schule, Hogrefe, Bern, Toronto, Seattle, 1997, 739-769.

Cronbach, Lee J. and Snow, Richard E., *Aptitudes and Instructional Methods: A Handbook for Research on Interactions*, Irvington, New York, 1977.

Duit, Reinders, *Conceptual Change: a Powerful Framework for Improving Science Teaching and Learning,* in: International Journal of Science Education (6), Routledge, London, 2003, 671-688.

Hasebrook, Joachim, *Aptitude-Treatment-Interaction (ATI)*, in: Rost, D.H. (ed.), Handwörterbuch Pädagogische Psychologie, Beltz PVU, Weinheim, 1998, 10-13.

Häussler, Peter and Hoffman, Lore, *An Intervention Study to Enhance Girls' Interest, Self-Concept, and Achievement in Physics Classes*, in: Journal of Research in Science Teaching (39, 9), Wiley & Sons, Hoboken USA, 2002, 870-888.

Hoffman, Lore, *Promoting Girls' Interest and Achievement in Physics Classes for Beginners*, in: Learning and Instruction (12, 4), Elsevier, Amsterdam, 2002, 447-465.

Lauth, Gerhard, *Strategien der kognitiven Verhaltensmodifikation*, in: Goetze, Herbert and Neukäter, Heinz (eds.) *Handbuch der Sonderpädagogik* (6), Marhold, Berlin, 1989.

Organisation for Economic Co-Operation and Development (OECD) (ed.), *Learning for Tomorrows World – First Results from PISA 2003,* 2004; available online at: http://www.oecd.org/dataoecd/1/60/34002216.pdf (last checked 11 June 2008).

Palinscar, Annmarie S. and Brown, Ann L., *Reciprocal Teaching to Comprehension-Fostering and Monitoring Activities*, in: Cognition and Instruction (1), Lawrence Erlbaum Associates, London, 1984, 117-175.

Tomlinson, Carol Ann and McTighe, Jay, *Integrating Differentiated Instruction & Understanding by Design. Connecting Content and Kids*, Association for Supervision and Curriculum Development, Alexandria (USA), 2006.

Zielinski, Werner, *Lernschwierigkeiten, Verursachungsbedingungen – Diagnose – Behandlungsansätze*, Kohlhammer, Stuttgart, 1995.

German as a Second Language – Linguistic and Didactic Foundations

Heidi Rösch

German as a second language (GSL) in schools focuses on students with migratory backgrounds *and* difficulties with the German language, and therefore only on a part of the students with migratory backgrounds, whom I refer to as GFL (German as first language) students. Accordingly, GFL is not an educational concept for students with migratory backgrounds, but a concept for the advancement of German language competence with GFL students. In the PISA 2003 study of the "Situation of Children from Immigrant Families," there is a difference between the first and second generation; the first generation means people who emigrated from one country to another as children or youths, while second generation denotes children and youth with a migratory background whose parents immigrated to Germany, but who themselves were born in Germany and have spent their entire school career in Germany. Conspicuously, the students from the first generation in Germany and a few other countries show distinctly better school performance than students of the second generation, which, in Germany and New Zealand (but not in the same way in other countries), clearly correlates to the fact that the language of instruction is not spoken in the home. This brings researchers to demand an "*intensive language supplementation in the schools*" (OECD 2006, 4, translation Devon Donohue-Bergeler) for students with a migratory background who do not speak the language of instruction at home, and that means – without this being explicit – a promotion of the German language.

From the psycholinguistic perspective, one speaks of second language learners and places the focus on the level reached (beginner and advanced) and the type of acquisition. In general, GSL students do not acquire German within the framework of a bilingual first language acquisition (i.e. parallel to their other languages), but within the framework of a second language acquisition (i.e. with the introduction into pre-school or even starting in elementary school, and therefore later than their first language). The second language acquisition in German facilities oriented to this group often does not lead to the desired results, so that a group of "permanent GSL students" develops among youths of the second generation who only learn rudimentary German, although or perhaps because they go to German schools. With this, they belong to the group described above of second generation students with low educational success who do not speak the language of instruction at home and for whom – so it is to be assumed – the language of the home is, from a psycholinguistic perspective, the dominant language. Because it is also useful under the aspect of bilingualism to nurture the "weak language" especially, as seen from a psycholinguistic perspective, the language supplementation in the schools should concentrate on imparting an adequate competence in the language of instruction.

1 The General Conditions of Second Language Acquisition

Second language acquisition is determined by external and internal factors (see Klein 1999). On the one hand, external factors relate to the drive through social integration, the communicative needs, attitude towards the target language and the target language community as well as education in the family and school. On the other hand, external factors depend on access, the simplicity of input, the communicative possibilities and the linguistic surroundings. The lesser the drive and access factors are, the slower the second language acquisition progresses and the greater the likelihood of early stagnation. An examination of the external factors with these GSL students, who, despite attending a German school for years, barely make progress and therefore remain GSL students, supplies lasting reasons for this development. It is often shown that not only the extracurricular surroundings, but also the situation in the school has a share in the responsibility. Educational policies must therefore bear the responsibility for the improvement of, or compensation for external factors through targeted special educational measures – for example through a group constellation conducive to second language acquisition that makes it possible for students to experience social integration, or through the creation of communicative possibilities with students of the same age with German as a native language (GNL students) as well as through the promotion of a constructive attitude towards the target language and society of the majority.

Beyond this, the references to the external factors also supply suggestions for the GSL language supplementation: even under conditions unfavorable to second language acquisition (like in homogenous groups with the same native language), the access to the target language and the drive towards its acquisition should be raised. Under these conditions, it is counterproductive to allow the native language as a means of communication, to force the explanation of unknown words with the help of a dictionary or to fall back on the long-overcome grammar-translation method. When GSL students barely have contact to GNL students in and out of the school and practically live in surroundings with their native language, GSL instruction must provide a counterweight. The origin of students and their families can be incorporated through content in the instruction. For example, the instruction of Russian speaking immigrants could include the life, learning, vocational training etc. of their land of origin; the instruction of Turkish speaking students who live in Germany as the second or third generation could include the situation of their grandparents and parents or also the current situation in Turkey. The same applies for the inclusion of their current living situation as members of a minority group, as bilinguals, as second language learners in German schools, etc. This wealth of experiences should be included – in GSL instruction certainly in German, in order to compensate for the unfavorable external conditions for natural second language acquisition.

2 GSL and Bilingual Education

This approach is often defamed as a "ban of the original language;" it does not deal with a ban, however, but with positively forcing contact with the target language – namely within the frame of the GSL supplementation. Thus, it is not possible to derive statements about dealing with multilingualism of minority groups in schools and subject instruction nor is it appropriate to develop a (negative) response to bilingual concepts. The opposite is the case: bilingual concepts create the ideal framework for the GSL supplementation much more than monolingual German concepts. In this respect, GSL is not an anti-concept to bilingual education, but a concept that must be implemented in monolingual and bilingual models which are respectively subject to different conditions. In bilingual models, language and subject learning are separated from each other, at least in the beginning phase of second language acquisition. GSL remains an independent subject and the instruction in other subjects reacts additionally to the special language acquisition situation of the students. The monolingual regular school, however, must compensate for the language deficits (measured against monolingual students and the requirements of subject instruction targeted towards them) as quickly as possible to allow GSL students to participate in the subject-oriented learning process. Through this, a high level of time pressure and pressure to succeed is created for all those involved. This level of pressure is significantly greater than the level at "elite schools" such as the French Gymnasium or the National Europe Schools in Berlin. The pressure is increased when the situation of second language acquisition in the learner groups is so unfavorable because of a group constellation of up to 100% students with the same non-German language of origin, that a natural second language acquisition is widely hindered. Because educational policies allow such group constellations, although they follow the integration concept (in the sense of inter-ethnic co-education) without reacting to it with conceptual appropriateness, a bilingual model like that of the German International Schools should be added here. In this model, students without previous knowledge of the German language are instructed monolingually in German, although also here usually only the faculty speaks German, either as native speakers or the equivalent. These schools work much more successfully than schools with similar student populations in Germany. The reasons are, among other things: the educational level of the student families; the native language of the students is accepted as a language of communication and is at least instructed as a subject; the conceptual dealing with GSL that substantiates the bilingual approach; there is a preparatory phase in which the acquisition of the language of instruction has the highest priority, and language and subject learning are separated; there is usually also an accompanying phase that supports the acquisition of subject matter through a focus on language. Additionally, all subject instruction also undertakes tasks related to language instruction and, in ideal cases, achieves with this the combination of subject and language learning.

In the debate around educational policies about the schooling of GSL students, it appears to be useful to differentiate between bilingual, monolingual and second-language concepts in which the GSL supplement takes on the described specific role in each case.

3 Internal Factors of Second Language Acquisition

While the external factors determine the tempo of second language acquisition, the internal factors determine its type. Language assets, in addition to biological determinants, available knowledge from the native language, the foreign language instruction etc. play a central role. According to the Interlanguage Hypothesis (see Selinker 1992), second language acquisition is a creative, interactive, learner-controlled process in which the learners derive hypotheses about the language structure from heard language and experiment with them (so-called learner languages or in-between grammars). In the interaction process with speakers of the target language, they refine their interlanguage[1] and, with this, approach the target language. Second language acquisition follows set phases of acquisition that meanwhile have been empirically ascertained for different language areas:

The *acquisition of word order in sentences* is studied with the most detail at the present (see Haberzettl 2005) and proceeds in four phases according to Wilhelm Griesshaber (see 2005):

- Pre-phase: broken statements without finite verb or set-phrases (*anziehn, hause gehn*);

1 An interlanguage is an emerging linguistic system that has been developed by a learner of a second language (L2). It is idiosyncratically based on the learners' experiences with the L2. The learner creates an interlanguage using different learning strategies such as language transfer, overgeneralisation and simplification.

- Phase 1: finite verb in simple statements, sometimes incorrect in respect to number, person and time (*ich versteh*);
- Phase 2: finite und infinite verb parts are separated (*Der Junge hat gesagt*);
- Phase 3: inversion of verb and subject according to preceding deictic phrases (*hier, dort* etc.) and adverbs (*Dann brennt die*);
- Phase 4: finite verb is at the end in subordinate clauses (*... dass sie so nett ist*).

The acquisition of conjunctions begins with *warum* (why) often for *weil* (because) and *wann* (when) often for *wenn* (if). Later come *weil*, *wenn* and *dass* additionally. Subordinate clauses with w-adverbs and w-pronouns (*weswegen, weshalb, womit)* cause problems for a long time, as do the conjunctions *ob* und *als*. Also conspicuous are common interferences (i.e. transferences from the first language into the second) in the usage of question words and conjunctions (see Diehl et al. 2000).

The acquisition of pro-forms begins with deictic pronouns (for example personal pronouns) and goes on eventually to anaphoric pronouns that refer to previously introduced content (see Griesshaber 1999; Ahrenholz 2007).

The acquisition of morphology presents a lasting problem: with verbs, the regular forms and often-used irregular forms, for example of modal verbs, are acquired in the beginning (while GFL learners often create forms like *ich kanne, er musst*, GSL learners use the correct form very quickly). For a long time, an overgeneralization of the regular forms occurs before irregular forms are found (see Harnisch 1993; Jeuk 2003). Also the passive remains difficult and often leads to confusion, for example, when forms like *ich werde anrufen – ich werde angerufen* cannot be distinguished from one another (see Belke 2003, 188).

These findings have long-reaching consequences for the design of GSL supplementation.

4 Consequences for GSL Supplementation

Because second language acquisition is a cognitive process, the supplementation should also offer incentives for the cognitive penetration of the target language and experimentation with it. This means, according to the cognitive turning point (see Richter 2002; Börner 2004), that second language learners pick up the target language creatively and not imitatively. This cognitive process applies also to controlled language acquisition, to force it if need be, in that GSL learners and also the "permanent GSL students" are offered language material to decode and the process of building and testing hypotheses is made conscious and used for creating analogies.

Because second language acquisition, like every language acquisition, is an acquisition of structures, the supplementation should also place the acquisition of structures in the center. That does not mean the return to traditional grammar instruction or to the grammar-translation method, but the orientation to a concept of systematic language supplementation (see Belke 2003; Rösch 2003, 2005) that supports the synchronization of controlled and uncontrolled language acquisition. Since the study by Long (1983, cited in Baur 1986, 31), it has been known that every intervention that helps unstructured linguistic data from the situation of natural acquisition to crossover into structured knowledge impacts the second language learner in a positive way.

The progression should take into account the phases of natural acquisition and should also have the end result in sight, for this can turn out very differently. Relapses (especially with the transition from elementary school into secondary school) and fossilization on different levels have been observed. The importance of interaction with speakers of the target language, among other things, gives suggestions for correctional behavior: learners develop their interlanguage further when they hit upon contradictions or borders. If there is a lack of such experiences, the interlanguage solidifies, eventually intensifying the process of fossilization.

5 Organizational Forms and Target Groups of GSL Supplementation

The term GSL supplementation, or language supplementation for students with migratory backgrounds, is often used very imprecisely. Often concealed behind this term is (subject-related) supplementary instruction, less often language and/or subject instruction in the native language and least of all real GSL instruction. For GSL supplementation does not occur through the presence of GSL students, but by instruction that deals with GSL specific content, follows GSL specific intentions, uses GSL specific methods, includes GSL specific media and measures success related to GSL acquisition. GSL supplementation is language instruction that is either offered as a GSL course or as an instructional principle that is integrated into subject instruction. Neither approach represents an alternative, but both are to be thought of as complementary. The following organizational forms are useful for GSL courses:

- Preparatory GSL courses for GSL beginners put language learning in the foreground and widely exclude subject-related learning.
- Continuing GSL courses focus on subject-related language, pick up subject-related content and lead towards a synthesis of language and subject-related learning.

- Accompanying GSL offerings support the acquisition of subject-related content through the focusing on language means.
- Reactivating GSL courses for "permanent GSL students" backs up fundamental language competences connected with age-appropriate and school-relevant topics and are appropriate for preparation or accompaniment of transitional phases.

GSL courses are exclusively targeted towards GSL students and should be homogenously pieced together according to language level if possible in order to implement a language supplementation designed for the specific situation of second language acquisition. (If GNL students need language supplementation, they should also receive appropriate offerings.) Related to the languages of origin, the learner groups should be created heterogeneously if possible so that German becomes the "natural" language of communication in the group and so that one can place the acquisition or evolution of German language competence at the center of the instruction.

On the other hand, the subject instruction (and that accounts for the larger part of instruction) should be implemented in mixed groups and should consider both the situation of second language learning of the GSL students as well as the language problems of the GNL students. In subject instruction, implementing GSL as an instructional principle means that teaching subject-related language and dealing with subject-specific types of texts and communicative structures as a topic of learning in the subject instruction is implemented. Such an approach is also appropriate for GNL students; with an eye towards GSL students, it must be more fundamentally formed, i.e. simple language means must also be discussed, term-building processes must be accompanied and didactic touches must be offered to solidify structures for subject-related language.

6 Requirements for School Language

Students with migratory backgrounds who attend German schools and learn German as a second language are forced to use the language they are learning from the beginning as the language of instruction. Concretely, this means that they, as are children who are German native speakers, are expected to possess language competence beyond the level of colloquial language. In bilingualism research, there is a difference between BICS (Basic Interpersonal Communicative Skills) and CALP (Cognitive Academic Language Proficiency) based on Cummins (see 1997, 2000):

- BICS refers to situational language capabilities. This means that the meaning can be taken through the context, social and cultural experience, intonation or other non-verbal actions.

- CALP, on the other hand, requires a high language competence (above all grammatical knowledge); the taking of meaning occurs through pure language information.

While children who speak German as a native language (GNL) have the CALP level of syntax, logical forms and semantics at their disposal by the time they enter elementary school, many children with German as a second language (GSL) do not reach this level without targeted intervention, as dramatically illustrated in the previously mentioned examples.

The BICS level, on the other hand, can be reached, without help, within the first two years of the second language acquisition. Penner (see 2002) concludes from these results that the language supplementation should orient itself to the CALP level and that the native language supplementation should be separated from the necessity of supporting GSL children in German on the CALP level. New studies about language development of bilingual children and teenagers show that CALP abilities can be transferred not only from the first to the second language, but also vice versa and therefore in both directions.

The deciding factor appears to be that CALP competences are to be built at least in one language. If this happens in the second language, the requirements of the didactics are much higher than if this could happen in the first language. This specific challenge also marks a substantial difference from foreign language instruction, which does not have to worry about training the CALP level in the same way and above all is without this enormous time pressure and pressure to succeed.

The following practical examples from schools strikingly show the problematic situation:

6.1 Der Mähdrescher maht das Mehl (Second grade).

This sentence was formed by a native speaker of Turkish in the second grade in Berlin. The teacher had asked the children to write down what they remembered from the last class. The teacher brought this sentence with her to a training session in order to analyze the child's linguistic problem. The girl had apparently paid close attention and retained the introduction to the topic on the basis of the harvester (Mähdrescher), which she spelled correctly, and connected it to the also correctly written flour (Mehl) through the verb "maht". She formulated a complete sentence and conjugated the verb correctly. In any case, the verb "maht" creates questions: does she mean to mow, to grind, to do (mähen, mahlen, machen) or is she creating the word "mahen" as a combination between mow and grind (mähen and mahlen)? Through my questioning it became clear that the teacher placed special value on the teaching and retention of nouns pertaining to grains but did not particularly deal with the verbs. I advised her to take compound words in the future and lead back to the verbs and therefore the function of the devices, as well as to also describe the activity and function of the device with every further step on the way to bread and therefore make clear the connection between mill (Mühle) and grind (mahlen).

6.2 Ich baue das Regal mit der, äh dem Hammer zusammen. (Fifth grade)

In a German lesson on the topic of attributive additions, my intern in a fifth grade elementary school class in Berlin prepared a dice game in which, corresponding to number rolled, a time, place, manner or reason would be inserted into the sentence "Ich baue das Regal zusammen". A native speaker of Turkish produced the sentence above. My intern looked disturbed, but was pleased with the self-correction and eventual correct usage of the dative. I articulated to the boy my incomprehension of his choice of words and in this way realized that the boy had retained hammer as the general term for different tools and was not able to indicate what he meant: a screwdriver. I advised my intern to pursue and clarify such disturbances with the students in the future. The boy's reaction proved my point: he asked me if I was Turkish. In answer to my question of how he came to that conclusion, he said, "Because you're interested in such things." Apparently he was under the impression that German teachers are not very interested in his language development because they – like my intern – have not cultivated strategies with which to work constructively with linguistic breaches against the norm, instead of leaving them with the belief that hammer is a general term and stands for all sorts of tools. This well-intentioned "sparing pedagogy" hinders the learning process and in some cases supports an early fossilization of the second language acquisition.

6.3 Welche Aufgaben haben die verschiedenen Zahnarten? (Fifth grade)

A typical problem of GSL students named by high school teachers in Hamburg is that after reading the following text, they answer the question "What tasks to the different types of teeth have?" ("*Welche Aufgaben haben die verschiedenen Zahnarten?*") with "The long, sharp canine teeth are longer than the other teeth." ("*Die langen, spitzen Eckzähne überragen die übrigen Zähne.*")

Der Hund ist Fleischfresser (Fifth grade)
Während die Welpen heranwachsen, entwickelt sich ihr Gebiss vollständig. Sein Aufbau entspricht einem Fleischfressergebiss. Die langen, spitzen Eckzähne überragen die übrigen Zähne. Sie heißen Fangzähne, da sie bei der Jagd zum Ergreifen und Festhalten der Beute dienen. Die jeweils größten Backenzähne im Ober- und Unterkiefer besitzen scharfkantige Höcker und werden als Reißzähne bezeichnet. Sie arbeiten bei der Bewegung des Unterkiefers gegen den Oberkiefer wie eine Schere. Auf diese Weise können größere Fleischstücke zerkleinert werden. Die hinteren Backenzähne eignen sich auch zum Zermalmen nicht allzu grober Knochen. Mit den flachen Schneidezähnen werden Fleischreste von den Knochen abgeschabt.
(Natura 5/6. Klett 2006: 68-69)

The reading strategy of the students is easy to see through: they stop at the first sentence with teeth and copy it. The question of tasks is completely ignored, as well as the fact that it deals with different types of teeth. Therefore, the task must be worked up to in class. There must be a distinction made between two basic directions: the unburdening of the question, meaning that the question should be formed in smaller steps: What types of teeth are there? What tasks do they have? (Welche Zahnarten gibt es? Welche Aufgaben haben sie?) This approach to the question is defensive and is also found in approaches to simplify texts and make them GSL-appropriate. Texts used for instruction should, of course, be appropriate for students, and many textbooks need a revision in this aspect, but the goal cannot be the avoidance of all subject-related language. Therefore, we need offensive teaching strategies for instruction and must enable the students to learn to deal with such typical texts for their age, at least in the long term. For example, techniques for finding meanings through context should be taught. With this concrete example, one could work out the compound words dealing with teeth, a strategy that is transferable to other subject-related texts.

A further aspect is to support the students in becoming conscious of already available strategies and to learn to differentiate between effective and ineffective ones (like the one observed in biology class). In order to make this possible, effective strategies must be taught in class.

6.4 "Ich werde anrufen = ich werde angerufen" (Vocational School)

Stemming from the previously cited observation from Belke, we let teenagers determine who in each case is active ("etwas tut" – does something) in example sentences in active and passive (I am being asked – I will ask, I will operate – I am being operated upon, etc.; ich werde gefragt – ich werde fragen, ich werde operieren – ich werde operiert, etc.). The majority of the GSL-teenagers checked both, neither, or the incorrect one. They are apparently not capable of deciding who does something, and to whom something is done. If one takes into account that subject-related texts in school books often use the passive form, it is clear how difficult it must be for the students to understand the meaning if they cannot tell the difference.

Also, here the didactic consequence is that the passive should not just be dealt with in German instruction, but also in subject instruction whenever such forms arise in the textbooks. It does not therefore a question of less, but of more passive and general grammatical structures and their treatment in class. The classic transformation exercise (The teacher teaches the children. The children are being taught by the teacher; Der Lehrer unterrichtet die Kinder. – Die Kinder werden von dem Lehrer unterrichtet.) is in this case not very useful because the passive is used in this case when the active person should not be named or is unknown.

In summer language camps with minority teenagers, we asked the teenagers using passive sentences like "The tires are being changed" ("Die Reifen werden gewechselt"): Who does that? They come to the conclusion relatively quickly that one actually does not know who changes the tire. They then form sentences in which it is clear who acts: The trainee / A man / A person who has a car / My brother changes the tires. (Der Azubi / Ein Mann / Wer ein Auto hat / Mein Bruder wechselt die Reifen.) It is then practiced as an example in which one can discern that someone is active or the active person is not named. That leads to the verb form with being (werden) as a passive construction and is later related to the confusing future form. After this difference is clear, passive sentences with clues about the active person come naturally.

7 "Literalität" – Dealings with Writings and Writing

By the term "Literalität" (literary literacy), Groeben (see 2001) understands writing, written language structures and aspects that contribute to the development of these structures such as structured narration, a reflected language usage, the understanding of tables, reading of graphs and the discovery of the functions of writing. Studies of pre-school children from orally influenced cultures and families show that children bring with them competences in spoken language of the native language. Second language supplementation can build onto these competences by developing routines of reading and being read to with which children work out the functions of books, texts and writings in general, which supports literary tone as well as understanding and using a reflected and differentiated language (see Kuyumcu 2006, 42). Next to the encounter with books, setting up an office corner has been used to allow children to get to know how to deal with pens, notepads, hole punchers, etc.

At the time of school entry, children with migratory backgrounds possess, on average, somewhat weaker learning prerequisites than children without migratory backgrounds; in addition, their previous knowledge about learning to write is influenced by the native language, which means that they know letters and sounds from the native language, for example. At the end of the second grade, they do not fundamentally have more difficulties, yet there is an extreme distribution in terms of performance, which means there is clearly a larger allotment of rudimentary writing exercises for children with two languages (see Hüttis-Graff 2000, 105, 106). This could surely be worked on and overcome within the framework of a coordinated bilingual alphabetization. If and how this can succeed in the second language has not yet been academically studied. In any case, projects like Deutsch&PC (see Grießhaber 2007), which are systematically supplemented with small groups during the entire elementary school period, have led to more children with migratory backgrounds advancing to higher level secondary schools than the national average.

In the secondary level 1, GNL and GSL students show different, if not more, mistakes in the field of orthography; with GSL students, these mistakes lie in the field of grammar, especially morphology (see Fix 2002, 50). The text-writing competence is dependent on school experience (see Knapp 1997); teenagers with a short stay in Germany show a relatively good text and narrative competence that they presumably bring with them from the native language instruction from their country of origin, but show a low formulation competence in German. The reverse is the case with teenagers who have spent their entire school career in Germany. They have relatively good formulation abilities but low text and narrative competence. To the present, attempts at teaching these in the second language have apparently been unsuccessful. Therefore, the accent of the supplementation should be placed precisely here.

Similarities are found in other subjects. When the teenagers have acquired the foundations of mathematics, the natural sciences or the social sciences in their native country, they can use them in subject instruction in Germany and transfer them into the German language. In such classes, it is useful to work with glossaries in their native languages, to include knowledge acquired in the school of origin about written Meta-language and to "fill it in" with German language means. In order to hinder negative transfer in the formation of text types or in approach, it is useful to discuss explicitly the procedures that are customary in Germany.

Students who have spent their entire school career in Germany but could not develop an appropriate level of writing present a special challenge. They are found mainly, if not exclusively, in the lowest level secondary school or in corresponding courses at comprehensive schools. There is often stagnation or even obstruction related to the already acquired competences to be observed that one should counter by catching up on the non-acquired competences, reviewing the already learned competences and letting them evolve in the direction of the set goals.

8 Requirements of Subject-related Language

The first two examples relate to German instruction; yet also other subjects – as the biology text makes clear – have specific tasks in the supplementation of students with migratory backgrounds. A central aspect is the respective subject-related language, in other words, "*the entirety of all language means that are used in a field of communication limited by subject in order to guarantee understanding between people who are acting in this field*" (Hoffmann 1976, 170, translation Devon Donohue-Bergeler). This deals with a terminologically standardized subject-related vocabulary as well as the differentiated use of complex words like compound words or the formation of prefixes and suffixes. While subject-related terms are usually taught, a focus on complex words (in the text above words like carnassial teeth, fangs and canines – Reiß-, Fang- and Eckzähne) seldom takes place because GNL students can usually figure out the meaning themselves. A further attribute of subject-related language is the nominal style, impersonal constructions (passive, reflexive and infinitive constructions) and the so-called deverbalization, which means the displacement of information from the verbal to the nominal region. There are also specific text types (lab reports and event protocols, source texts, graphics, text and subject exercises, discussions, literary text analysis, etc.) that are taught in subject instruction and should be practiced. Formulas, different levels of symbols and rhetorical means that convey thought and communicative structures of the subject are difficult for all students and are therefore also usually taught. Here it is also the case that GSL students needed supplementation at the basic level.

An experiment at the Herbert Hoover School in Berlin shows the success of such an approach. A biology teacher who teaches three parallel classes prepared the class material linguistically with the help of his German teacher colleague and taught one class with a focus on language, while the others were taught in the regular manner. Linguistic tests at the beginning and end of the unit confirmed the success on the language level. Almost more telling, however, is that the students who were taught with a linguistic focus also did much better on the subject-related learning tests than the other students who were taught the same subject-related material.

9 Language of Mathematics and Natural Sciences

Words like *Addition*, *Halbgerade* or *Kurvendiskussion* signal mathematical content also to non-experts. In subject-related texts, nouns generally appear much more often than in prose texts (see Hoffmann 1985, 136). In mathematics, nouns signify mathematical objects (*Trapez, Gleichung, Relation, Funktion, Körper* etc.); they are created through nominalization (*Gleichung*) and attributes (*rechtwinkliges Dreieck*). Verbs are found less often in subject-related language compared to general language and signify actions in mathematics (*subtrahieren, differenzieren, zuordnen, punktspiegeln, potenzieren, integrieren* etc.), whereas the mathematical objects themselves act like subjects (*die Gerade schneidet den Kreis*), although the verbs do not show actions, but states of being or mathematical properties. In instructions, however, verbs stand for actions (for example *addiere);* modal verbs are often found (*man kann beweisen, wir wollen zeigen, man muss voraussetzen* etc.). Conjunctions take on an important function in mathematical statements and can easily lead to problems, for example when the subject is left out in the combination of two main sentences. Both of these statements are correct: *Es gibt Dreiecke mit einem rechten Winkel. Es gibt Dreiecke mit einem stumpfen Winkel.* Connecting the two sentences, which is useful in general language, here leads to the incorrect statement: *Es gibt Dreiecke mit einem rechten Winkel und mit einem stumpfen Winkel.* In contrast to general language, the language of mathematics is very precise and concerned with logic. Therefore the different meanings of the following sentence are clear to the mathematician, whereas the meanings in general language are fuzzier: *Wenn / Nur wenn / Genau dann wenn der Wecker klingelt, stehe ich auf.* The exercise texts are often formed passively or in a non-timely present.

10 Understanding Exercises from the GSL Perspective

In a teacher training session at a high school in Hamburg, the mathematics teachers brought up the required relevance to the "real world" in mathematics instruction. Students with a good understanding of mathematics, but who had demonstrated language problems fail with this type of exercise, whereas students with good language understanding are more successful with this exercise format. The following exercise on the topic of angle functions illustrates this: "*Die untergehende Sonne wirft immer längere Schatten. Erstelle mit Hilfe einer Zeichnung, eventuell mit einem Geometrieprogramm, eine Tabelle, die dir zur Sonnen'höhe' α die Schattenlänge s einer 10 m hohen Fichte angibt. Bestimme s durch Ausmessen für möglichst viele Winkel zwischen 0° und 90° in gleichen Abständen von 5°*" (MatheNetz 10).

The "real world" relevance in this exercise is the setting sun that creates shadows and the spruce that one should recognize as a tree. On the same page, there is a drawing that should support understanding – if the students recognize that it belongs to the exercise. It seems to me that the difficulty is increased for GSL students less because of the "real world" relevance, but because of the subject-related language. They presumably recognize the symbols α, s, m and ° and recognize also the terms table, (shadow) length and angle, which were dealt with in class. The first instruction is formed in the imperative case (*Erstelle*) and is surely also recognized as such, whereas the following nested sentence probably veils the actual instruction to be carried out and makes students wonder whether they have a geometry program or what that is. The same applies for the second instruction (*Bestimme*) that should be carried out through *Ausmessen* (another instruction hidden in a prepositional phrase).

The main task of linguistically-focused mathematics instruction concentrates on the signal words that transport calculating operations and reduces the "real world" relevance as much as possible. Related to the concrete exercise, spruces, other trees and the setting sun do not stand in the foreground; the angle function and with this the related exercise format do. As an introduction, I would consider with the students where angles appear, what an angle is in daily language and how this is different from an angle in mathematics, and what one can do with an angle in mathematics (draw, calculate, etc.), as well as the deciding reference values (for example side length in a triangle).

Using the drawing on which a spruce is seen, but not the sun, this is complemented in the sense of the first sentence, which means that the questions of how one should imagine a longer shadow and how the angle changes are clarified. The students consider how an exercise can look and compare their guess with the actual exercise. The sentences are reduced to the main substance, the actual task. Within the framework provided by the workbook *Mitsprache* (for the ninth and tenth grade), the following list is formulated that can also be used here:

- Read the instructions.
- Take it apart into partial steps. What is given? What is looked for? Find key words, relationships, connections.
- Look at the pictures with attention to detail. What information do they provide?
- Work with the information you found in the text and pictures and find the solution in this way.
- When you are finished: Read the instructions, your work and your solution again and decide if you are really finished.

11 GSL in Natural Science Instruction

The language of mathematics appears also in natural science subjects and therefore has a fundamental importance In addition, the language of natural science includes subject-specific formulas, terms, and specific sentence and text constructions that seldom appear in daily language, but appear often in all subject-related languages. Pictorial language (graphics, sketches, diagrams and other pictures that illustrate and explain scientific content) plays an important role in the natural sciences. Dealing with this symbolic and pictorial language is definitely also taught in the respective subject instruction, but often it is not sufficiently recognized that reading such symbols and pictures that should illustrate the complex processes in a simplified manner must also be learned before they can be used as an aid or way to consolidate information. Merzyn (see 1998, 1) observes critically that the less the students master the subject-related language, the more it hinders understanding on a pure language level. The natural science instruction overwhelms the students through a large number of subject-related terms that cannot be appropriately taught in the available time and hence cannot be learned. The overcrowding of terms – many of which are entirely negligible – misplaces the focus from the central idea of the class.

The language in a physics class is not the language of physics, but a language on the way to physics. It does not formulate in a substandard way, but is appropriate for students (see Leisen 1998, 9). This brings up an important principle of subject instruction, especially – but not exclusively – with an eye towards GSL students, cannot be stressed enough. Subject teachers should have the courage to consciously formulate appropriately for students while accompanying all students on their acquisition of the subject-related language. This includes supporting a constructive learning attitude towards the subject and the acquisition of the subject-related language, as well as teaching fundamental words, subject-specific word formation patterns, sentence schemes and argumentation structures without neglecting the problem-orientation of subject instruction. Writing should be worked on according to text types and the students should be taught the difference between the individual communicative techniques (define, describe, etc.).

The students' previous knowledge of the subject and subject-related language should be activated so that also GSL students can catch on to the main idea. An important method is to present content in a delayed manner. (Subject-related) vocabulary work is integrated, which means concretely that new terms (with article and plural) are introduced, suitable verbs (with the stem form for strong verbs) are taught with the appropriate prepositions, and subject-specific vocabulary is introduced in context, for example with the help of word fields.

Furthermore, the subject instruction should be configured in small steps. GSL students often do not have the confidence to continuously interrupt class in order to clarify vocabulary or formulation deficits. Therefore, partial results should also be tested, for example, in the form of additional supporting exercises and through the addition of topic-specific vocabulary lists.

In addition, there is the introduction and practice of subject-specific written communicative forms and text types, like writing a lab report in a natural science class or the conversion of an oral report into a written paper. Here, the work with example texts and other forms of generative writing has proved its worth.

Of course, natural science instruction will not do away with teaching subject-related terms, but it is worth considering that this is a lengthy process that should also be fulfilled as a process of term formation.

Because many GSL students show delays in term formation due to their specific language socialization in the German schools, there must be work done in term formation with subject-related terms with a look towards these students: in order to learn a new subject-related term, a broad representation of the term is important, as are positive and negative examples for the term and demarcation from neighboring subject-related and common terms. The learning of difficult terms carries on over the course of years and should therefore be appropriately accompanied.

The conscious use of daily language is useful in this because it is much more appropriate than subject-related language when accompanying the students in the acquisition process. The conscious orientation towards the daily language at the same time means a reduction of the subject-related language and means for the teachers that they

- use short sentence parts, active instead of passive forms,
- avoid nominalization and nesting,
- repeat sentence parts with important meaning and do without too much conciseness,
- reduce difficult subject-related terms and symbolization in the instructional text; but also form the text graphically.

The reduction of the subject-related language is also useful in order to test partial steps and give students the opportunity to form hypotheses about subject content in their familiar language. If one understands learning not only as instruction through teachers, but also as students' construction, thinking out loud (as the verbalization of hypotheses, expression of thoughts, etc.) is an important element, especially in natural science instruction and it supports the demand from Merzyn to use the language as "thoughts' cultivating organ" (translation Devon Donohue-Bergeler).

Bibliography

Ahrenholz, Bernt, *Verweise mit Demonstrativa im gesprochenen Deutsch*, de Gruyter, Berlin et al., 2007.

Baur, Rupprecht S., *Kann der Zweitspracherwerb ‚gesteuert' werden? – Perspektiven der Zweitsprachendidaktik*, in: Deutsch lernen, (11, 1), 1996, 31-49.

Belke, Gerlind, *Mehrsprachigkeit im Deutschunterricht*, Schneider, Baltmannsweiler, 2003.

Börner, Wolfgang and Vogel, Klaus (ed.), *Emotion und Kognition im Fremdsprachenunterricht*, Narr, Tübingen, 2004.

Cummins, Jim, *Bilingual Education*, in: Cummins, Jim (ed.): *Encyclopedia of Language and Education* (5), Kluwer, Dordrecht et al., 1997.

Cummins, Jim, *Language, Power, and Pedagogy: Bilingual Children in the Crossfire*, Multilingual Matters, Clevedon et al., 2000.

Diehl, Erika et al., *Grammatikunterricht: Alles für die Katz? Untersuchungen zum Zweitspracherwerb Deutsch*, Niemeyer, Tübingen, 2000.

Fix, Martin, *"Die Rechtschreibung ferbesern" – Zur Orthografischen Kompetenz in der Zweitsprache Deutsch*, in: Didaktik Deutsch (12, 7), 2002, 39-55.

Griesshaber, Wilhelm, *Sprachliche Prozeduren bei der Wiedergabe einer Hörspielszene*, in: Johanson, Lars and Rehbein, Jochen (eds.), *Türkisch und Deutsch im Vergleich*, Harrassowitz, Wiesbaden, 1999, 95-128.

Griesshaber, Wilhelm, *Profilanalyse*, 2005; available online at: http://spzwww.uni-muenster.de/~griesha/dpc/profile/ (last checked 11 June 2008).

Griesshaber, Wilhelm, *Zweitspracherwerbsprozesse als Grundlage der Zweitsprachförderung*, in: Ahrenholz, Bernt (ed.), *Deutsch als Zweitsprache. Voraussetzungen und Konzepte für die Förderung von Kindern und Jugendlichen mit Migrationshintergrund*, Fillibach, Freiburg, 2007, 31-48.

Groeben, Annemarie von der, *Literalität: Modewort oder alter Hut oder neue Aufgabe*, in: Pädagogik, (6), 2000, 6-9.

Haberzettl, Stefanie, *Der Erwerb der Verbstellungsregeln in der Zweitsprache Deutsch durch Kinder mit russischer und türkischer Muttersprache*, Niemeyer, Tübingen, 2005.

Harnisch, Ulrike, *Grammatische Progression – ein alter Hut? Zur Zweitsprachentwicklung türkischer Schulanfänger*, in: Deutsch lernen (18, 4), 1993, 313-334.

Hoffmann, L., *Kommunikationsmittel Fachsprache: eine Einführung*, Narr (Forum für Fachsprachen-Forschung), Tübingen, 1985.

Hüttis-Graff, Petra, *Rechtschreiblernen unter den Bedingungen von Mehrsprachigkeit. Plädoyer für die Schriftorientierung im Unterricht*, in: Valtin, Renate (ed.), *Rechtschreiblernen in den Klassen 1-6*, Grundschulverband, Frankfurt/M., 2000.

Jeuk, Stefan, *Erste Schritte in der Zweitsprache Deutsch. Eine empirische Untersuchung zum Zweitspracherwerb türkischer Migrantenkinder in Kindertageseinrichtungen*, Fillibach, Freiburg, 2003.

Klein, Wolfgang, *Zweitspracherwerb. Eine Einführung*, Athenäum, Frankfurt/M., 1999.

Knapp, Werner, *Schriftliches Erzählen in der Zweitsprache*, Niemeyer, Tübingen, 1997.

Kuyumcu, Reyhan, *"Jetzt male ich dir einen Brief." – Literalitätserfahrungen von (türkischen) Migrantenkindern im Vorschulalter*, in: Ahrenholz, Bernt (ed.), *Kinder mit Migrationshintergrund – Spracherwerb und Fördermöglichkeiten*, Fillibach, Freiburg, 2006, 34-45.

Leisen, Josef, *Förderung des Sprachlernens durch den Wechsel der Symbolisierungsformen im Physikunterricht*, in: Praxis der Naturwissenschaften – Physik (2, 47), 1998, 9-13.

Merzyn, Gottfried, *Sprache und naturwissenschaftlicher Unterricht. 10 Thesen*, in: Praxis der Naturwissenschaften – Physik (2, 47), 1998, 1.

OECD, *Wo haben Schüler mit Migrationshintergrund die größten Erfolgschancen? Eine vergleichende Analyse von Leistung und Engagement in PISA 2003. Kurzzusammenfassung*, 2006; available online at: http://www.pisa.oecd.org/dataoecd/2/57/36665235.pdf (last checked 11 June 2008).

Penner, Zvi, *Neue Wege der sprachlichen Förderung von Migrantenkindern in der Vorschule*, kon-lab, Berg, 2002.

Richter, Sigrun, *Die "kognitive Wende" in der Deutschdidaktik*, in: Hug, Michael and Richter, Sigrun (eds.): *Ergebnisse soziologischer und psychologischer Forschung. Impulse für den Deutschunterricht*, Schneider, Baltmannsweiler, 2002, 1-10.

Rösch, Heidi (ed.), *Deutsch als Zweitsprache. Sprachförderung in der Grundschule: Grundlagen – Übungsideen – Kopiervorlagen*, Schroedel, Hannover, 2003.

Rösch, Heidi (ed.), *Deutsch als Zweitsprache. Sprachförderung in der Sekundarstufe I: Grundlagen – Übungsideen – Kopiervorlagen*, Schroedel, Braunschweig, 2005.

Selinker, Larry, *Rediscovery Interlanguage*, Longman, London et al., 1992.

Ada Lovelace Mentoring – Engaging Girls and Women with Science and Technology

Sylvia Neuhäuser-Metternich and Sybille Krummacher

„True learning is guided by mentoring." – John Dewey, American philosopher of pragmatism, 1859-1952

Abstract

Girls and women continue to be dramatically underrepresented in the field of science and technology. Although many forces are at work, it is possible to pinpoint a few basic factors which keep a considerable portion of girls and women out of this area. However, attempts to increase their continued participation can only be successful if teachers at schools and universities and other significant persons in the economy learn how to interact with girls and women in science and technology more appropriately. Ada Lovelace Mentoring addresses both aspects: it is a very successful tool to attract girls and women as mentees to scientific and technical education and careers; at the same time it provides mentors with the chance to improve their gender competence.

1 Gender and Science – an Introduction

In recent years, many studies have highlighted an alarming decline in the interest in science, engineering and mathematics (SEM) among young people. Moreover, numerous countries in Europe have persistent difficulty in attracting women to SEM and leading them on to graduation. Unless more effective action is taken, Europe's long term capacity for innovation and the quality of its research will be at stake. Furthermore, the acquisition of skills that are becoming essential in all walks of life, in a society increasingly dependent on the use of knowledge and technological literacy (Dakers 2006), is also under increasing threat.

Technology, where science is put into action, is an area where the gender imbalance culminates. Girls and women are consistently and dramatically underrepresented in this area – both in education and in employment. Since 2004 their participation in technical training or engineering studies in Germany has actually been declining again. Thus, even today less than 20 per cent of German engineering degrees are granted to women.

Numerous projects, actions and campaigns that have been implemented in the last ten years at German universities, scientific societies, scientific cultural associations, enterprises, employers associations, and others have not been able to reverse this trend.

2 Mentoring for Girls and Women as Well as for Executives and Teachers – a Promising Effort

Mentoring has proved to be a very successful way to attract girls to scientific and technical studies and careers. However, to build up the necessary perseverance and self-confidence needed to survive in a still male dominated science-world requires more than the attempt to change the ideas and attitudes of girls and women. It is the gender competence of the school teachers and university professors as well as other significant persons that needs to be improved to assure an assertive environment in which the talents of girls and young women can grow to full strength.

Mentoring is a support concept where an experienced person, the mentor, meets with a less experienced person, the mentee, to establish an open and trusting relationship.

The mentor usually gives advice to the mentee on career issues and decisions like the choice of major fields of studies and practical work, exchanges experiences with her, gives useful tips, may help answer questions and find an internship engagement, or grant access to informal university or business networks and structures. Through all these interactions, the mentor can support the mentee in the development of her talents and her personality, reflect with her on experiences and provide feedback about her work. However, it is important that the mentee not see her mentor as just another teacher, but instead receive acknowledgement and positive feedback from the interaction with him or her. Her self-esteem can grow if she sees that her mentor is giving her credit and believes in her abilities to reach her goals.

Both mentor and mentee will learn about and from each other and develop social skills such as openness and respect towards others as well as the readiness to accept and provide feedback.

Mentoring has proved its efficacy in increasing the mentee's interest and attainment level while stimulating the mentor's motivation and understanding of gender issues. It is effective for all students, from the weakest to the most able, and is fully compatible with the ambition of excellence.

Due to the nature of its practices, mentoring is more likely to encourage relationships among the stakeholders of both formal and informal education. It also creates opportunities to involve scientists, researchers, engineers, universities, business enterprises, as well as local authorities such as community councils, associations, parents and other local resources.

3 The Ada Lovelace Mentoring-Network

Ada Lovelace Mentoring was introduced in Germany in 1997 as a pioneering concept of group mentoring. Its primary missions are to motivate young women to choose a career in SEM, as well as to build a network and strategic alliances between women and men active in the effort to improve the gender balance in science.

It is named after the English mathematician Ada Lovelace (1815-1852) in honor of her ground-breaking work in mathematical programming. Her instructions for the calculation of Bernoulli numbers on a calculating engine designed (but never implemented) by Charles Babbage is now considered the first computer program.

3.1 Female Students as Mentors

The Ada Lovelace Mentoring-scheme involves a whole spectrum of initiatives to encourage girls and strengthen their motivation towards SEM:

- Female students in science related fields get involved as mentors, they receive training in communication and moderation methods as well as supervision by a psychologist.
- These mentors visit girls in schools and act as role models by telling them about their own motivations to choose SEM at university, talking about their strategies for overcoming obstacles and generally providing first-hand insight into university life.
- Interested girls register as mentees and are invited to join the mentors at university courses, take part in their laboratory work or explore the Internet to encourage their online participation. Depending on the girls' interests, the student mentors organize workshops with special themes like Java-programming, which are highly frequented even by the school teachers.

These activities led to organizational changes and implementations of new kinds of initiatives, e.g.:

- In 2000, a chemistry-lab sponsored by the Robert-Bosch-Foundation was established at the University of Mainz: Ada-Lovelace-Mentors regularly do laboratory work with girls and boys in separate small groups together with their school teachers.
- Since 2001 the "Women's Project Laboratory" at the Dortmund University of Applied Sciences and Arts has offered opportunities for female engineering students and interested girls from regional schools to engage in exciting and

surprising hands-on experiments. These are regularly met with great enthusiasm and stimulate lively discussions between mentors and mentees.

3.2 Networking and Public Relations

In a next step, partnerships with local as well as global operating business and corporations like engineering associations were formed to address in particular the transition from school to work for both student mentors and mentees.

The target audience includes not only girls and women interested in science, but also parents, teaching staff at schools and universities, vocational guidance counselors, career advisers, employers, politicians and the media.

Thus, networking in the broadest sense was initiated to foster supportive relationships between male and female actors in the process, as well as the sharing of a wide range of experience and expertise.

This networking process also allowed for the development of further activities like inviting female scientists and engineers to be guest speakers or teachers in science classrooms, and especially maintaining contact with mentors and mentees beyond their university term and into the starting phase of their professional careers. From the interaction with female entrepreneurs in the network, the mentees quite often are encouraged to set up their own companies.

The Ada Lovelace Mentoring-Network has experienced rapid growth. With support from a European Union grant in 1999 the exchange of experience, good practice as well as systematic evaluation procedures was intensified and extended to include partners in Austria, Luxembourg and Switzerland.

The Ada Lovelace Mentoring activities have been presented at International meetings like the International Forum "Women in Engineering and Science" at the first World Engineer's Convention during EXPO 2000 in Hannover, at the 2nd Conference on Gender Equality in Higher Education at the ETH Zurich in 2000, and at the 10th GASAT-Conference at Copenhagen in 2001 together with the American partners AWIS and MentorNet. There have been co-operations with the organization "Women in Science and Engineering (WISE)" in Great Britain and with the "Association of Women in Science (AWIS)" in the United States.

3.3 Changing Scientific and Technical Culture

In July 2000, the Ada Lovelace Project and the Quality Assurance Project of the German Rectors' Conference (Hochschulrektorenkonferenz – HRK) together organized a conference on "Woman-Technology-Evaluation." In workshops and roundtable discussions participants analyzed the barriers for women in SEM and solutions for overcoming them. They agreed that modern science and engineering studies should no longer focus narrowly on technology, but view technical ideas and artifacts as essential parts of our common cultural heritage. To maintain high quality in studies of science and technology, curricula should no longer be limited to technical and mathematical competencies but should provide a holistic view on technology, relating it to effects on society, humans, and on the environment. Science and engineering education – as well as the professions – also have a responsibility to take into account the interests, needs, and values of women. Changing the contents, the teaching process and the culture of science and engineering education will not only improve the participation of women in science, but will make the field attractive to more men as well. Moreover, it will also serve the growing needs for diversity in industry.

3.4 Founding the Ada Lovelace Mentoring-Association

The concept of Ada Lovelace Mentoring soon proved to be very successful and became known far beyond the borders of Germany. In the framework of the growing network, many interested people engaged in Ada Lovelace Mentoring at their schools, universities, or companies.

This led to the foundation of the Ada Lovelace Mentoring-Association by several partners from universities, research institutions, employers associations, engineering councils and the private sector at the end of 2001 as a non-profit organization with tax-exempt status for charitable giving purposes. It is dedicated to initiating and strengthening mentoring strategies, networking with schools, universities, research institutions, employers associations, engineering councils and the industry, increasing the number of women in senior management, as well as in policy-making bodies. Beyond this, the Association is aiming at strengthening the process of gender mainstreaming, the approach of the European Commission to creating a gender inclusive labor market and integrating a gender perspective into every policy area as well as at transforming SEM curricula at schools and universities, the teaching process and the culture of SEM education.

Since the end of 2002, the Ada Lovelace Mentoring-Association has published "Ada-Mentoring – Journal for Mentoring and Gender Mainstreaming in Science and Technology," which addresses male and female professionals, students and teachers in science and technology as well as other stakeholders of both, formal and informal education.

Ada-Mentoring publishes original papers that report innovative ideas and programs related to the recruitment and retention of women in science and technology. Issues concerning women in science and technology are consolidated to address the entire professional and educational environment.

3.5 The Young Ladies' Network of Technology – YOLANTE

As one example of numerous mentoring initiatives that were established at universities and companies in the last 10 years, YOLANTE is presented here as a program through which many student mentors from the Ada Lovelace Mentoring participated as mentees.

In 2002 the Siemens AG, one of the founding members of the Ada Lovelace Mentoring-Association, initiated a mentoring program, the Young Ladies' Network of Technology – YOLANTE, aiming to inspire young women to join the promising world of technology and to encourage them to benefit from and shape various career and future opportunities in scientific and technological professions.

As of January 2008, YOLANTE has supported more than 400 young women from the very beginning of their technology-related or scientific studies. Participants are mentored by Siemens employees. Over an extended period of time, mentees have discussions with their mentors that aim to support them in their career and personal development.

The support granted by the mentor includes conveying knowledge, e.g. about diverse occupational fields, multifaceted information about the company and company structures, as well as orientation guidance for later career entry at Siemens and explanations of the rules of the game of business life, recommendations regarding university studies and establishing a network of contacts.

Mentees receive a traineeship or working student contract relevant to their studies and thus may gain practical experience through internships and student trainee activities. They get access to networks and interact with other female participants.

In this way their university studies are complemented by competence building and personality development.

4 Mentor's benefits

The Ada Lovelace Mentoring concept is built on the belief that effective mentoring benefits both the mentee and the mentor – and the evidence supports this notion. The mentees receive a lot of information, and those who are already interested in SEM are encouraged to choose a career in these fields.

But the benefits granted to the mentors seem to be at least as important:

4.1 Benefits for Student Mentors

The Ada Lovelace Mentoring-program supports self-confidence, leadership skills, and interest in the professional development of the student mentors. In addition, these students have the chance to make new friendships, build up their own network, and feel less isolated in their work environment as a result of the mentoring experience. They gain pride and satisfaction by mentoring, and the good relationship to other mentors can have a positive impact on their professional performance.

4.2 Benefits for Employee Mentors as Future Executives

If – as, for example, in the case of the YOLANTE mentoring program – Siemens employees act as mentors, these women and men learn a lot about young women and the reasons for their need of support. They experience that girls feel pressure to do everything and please everyone and are still discouraged from studying a scientific or technical discipline by various forces like:

- *pressure from peer groups* to choose the subjects that the majority of girls is studying to avoid exclusion from female networks;
- science teachers approaching girls with *teaching methods* that are not appealing or stimulating, and not taking into account that interests of girls are more diverse and not limited to the chosen major field of studies;
- being *objects of ironic remarks* as well as experiencing widespread prejudice and gender stereotypical behavior, e.g. amazement at their presence in the scientific or technical courses;
- being confronted with the *opinions and myths about the inadequacy of women* in the chosen scientific or technical field of studies.

If mentors are made aware of these factors which are often very subtly communicated, they can be more sensitive about them in future interactions with women, especially when they are in an executive position.

4.3 Benefits for Teachers as Mentors

In the framework of the Ada Lovelace Mentoring-Network, the perceptions of students, teachers, employment counselors and others concerned regarding science and technology have been assessed in a project funded by the EU "Medium-term Community action program on equal opportunities for men and women" from 1999 to 2000.

Key results indicate that gender biased opinions are prevailing when:

- men are seen as naturally gifted with logical thinking, and technical understanding is perceived as a male ability by half of the respondents of both genders;
- a considerable number of men is convinced of superior male cognitive abilities, whereas team building abilities and cooperative as well as communication skills are ascribed to women, above all by women themselves.

These very old prejudices and stereotypes have significant potential to undermine the interest of girls and women in science and technology.

Differences in the perceptions of both genders concerning teacher behavior in science and technology classes at school and at university may also lead to different attitudes towards science and technology and to discrediting the effectiveness of the performance of girls and women in these fields:

- A considerable number of girls feel that male teachers make more degrading remarks about them *in school* and discourage and ridicule them more often than boys.
- Women *at university* receive less credit for efficiency and feel discouraged because they receive more degrading remarks and feel ridiculed by male university teachers; they perceive male university teachers giving more respect to male students – a behavior that is also recognized by 16 per cent of male students; and they perceive male university teachers as giving more credit for efficiency to male students – a behavior that is also recognized by 33 per cent of male students.

Reality can be influenced by the expectations of others, as experiments on self-fulfilling-prophecy show. This influence can be beneficial or detrimental depending on which label an individual is assigned. The effects of teachers' attitudes, beliefs, and values on their expectations from students have been tested repeatedly. The Pygmalion effect or Rosenthal effect (Rosenthal and Jacobson 1992) more commonly known as the "teacher-expectancy effect" refers to situations in which students perform better than other students simply because they are expected to do so. In the case of female students in SEM, the teacher-expectancy effect leads them to internalize the expectations of not being interested or gifted. Teachers may unconsciously and unintentionally send signals about what they expect and thus behave in ways that encourage some students, e.g. male students in SEM, and discourage others, e.g. a considerable portion of female students in SEM.

These results quoted from the Ada Lovelace Mentoring-study on perceptions indicate that reputation building follows stereotyping to a great extent. On the other hand this means that teachers in the role of mentors for girls and women in SEM could become their advocates when they are made aware of the above mentioned discouraging factors:

In a first instance, teachers may change their own behavior towards girls and women in SEM when they recognize the negative impacts of the unreflecting teacher's behavior steered by stereotypes and myths that often lead girls to avoid scientific or technical careers. In the long run, continued exposure to gender issues through the participation in Ada Lovelace mentoring activities can lead to a better understanding on the part of the teacher for the need of active support to strengthen women's participation in science and technology.

5 Consequences and Suggestions

What are the consequences of viewing science and technology as a natural male ability? How can girls develop an interest for this area, especially the considerable proportion of girls in school who feel male teachers discourage and ridicule them, and make more degrading remarks toward them than toward boys? One consequence of these impressions may be that girls aged 14 to 19 years see themselves as talented and interested, yet estimate their talent and their interest as significantly lower than boys of this age do (Neuhäuser-Metternich and Krummacher 2007).

What happens to the motivation of those female students at university who feel discouraged and ridiculed and who are the target of degrading remarks by male university teachers, especially if, at the same time they perceive male university teachers giving more respect to male students?

For these girls and women, their experiences are initiating a journey away from reliance on their own efficiency in the area of SEM.

In Germany, the Higher Education Information System (HIS)[1] performs surveys of all students finishing school. Those who finished school in 2002 were asked about their specific interests and choice of educational area. The most relevant results in the context discussed here are the reasons for *not* choosing engineering. Groups of male and female subjects were formed according to their different competence profiles or self-images as one-sided technical/practical, technical-mathematical, or based on a diversity of abilities (Minks 2004):

- 63 per cent of girls describing their interests as one-sided technical/practical report *feeling not skilled enough* for an university education in engineering, compared to only 36 per cent of boys in this interest group;
- 45 per cent of girls with a technical-mathematical self image do *not feel skilled enough*, compared to only 24 per cent of boys;
- 55 per cent of girls with a diversity of abilities do *not feel skilled enough*, compared to only 40 per cent of boys.

The feeling of not being skilled or competent, even when technical interests are part of a person's self-image might have its origin and continued support in teacher

1 An organization supporting German institutions of higher education and their administrations within the area of higher education research through empirical studies.

behavior that does not give credit for efficacy in mathematics and physics as we have observed in our survey.

A considerable proportion of female students realizes that male university teachers in math and science give more credit for efficiency to male students than to female students. This experience might very well be one serious reason for women's lack of self-confidence and the courage to engage in SEM.

We are witnessing a real formative emergency when we see girls at school and young female students in university courses in SEM not receiving adequate credit to strengthen their self-confidence in an area generally dominated by males.

Women of all competence profiles will not regard engineering as a relevant option, and will not consider themselves capable of achieving a university degree in this field as long as the behavior of teachers and other significant persons in their lives does not change. Through their work as mentors for girls and women at school and university, teachers may learn about these correlations, reflect on their behavior and give more respect and credit to the achievements of girls and women in science and technology courses. If gender sensitivity develops and participation of women in science and technology grows, the culture of science itself will change and the results will improve.

Bibliography

Dakers, John R. (ed.), *Defining Technological Literacy. Towards an Epistemological Framework*, Palgrave MacMillan, New York and London, 2006.

European Commission: Joint Interim Report "Education and Training 2010".

European Union: Eurostat 2004, Implementation of "education & training 2010" work programme.

Minks, Karl Heinz, *Rituale und Zyklen im Ingenieurstudium und die Chance der Studienstrukturreform*, in: ADA-Mentoring (8), 2004, 9-11, available online at: www.ada-mentoring.de (last checked 11 June 2008).

Neuhäuser-Metternich, Sylvia, *The Ada-Lovelace-Project: Mentoring for Women into Science and Technology*, in: VDI (ed.), *Proceedings of the World Engineer's Convention. International Forum Women in Engineering and Science*, Hannover 19.-21.06.2000, VDI-Verlag, Düsseldorf, 2000, 87-92.

Neuhäuser-Metternich, Sylvia and Krummacher, Sybille, *Girls' and Boys' Perceptions of Science and of Science Teaching Practice, Understanding and Providing a Developmental Approach to Technology Education (UPDATE) Progress Report, Specific Support Action, Thematic Priority: Structuring the ERA / FP6-2005-Science-and-society-16, 2007,* online available at: http://www.ada-mentoring.de/redakteur/cms/upload/ADA_Research_snm_sk.pdf (last checked 18 June 2008).

Rosenthal, Robert and Jacobson, Lenore, *Pygmalion in the classroom*, Expanded edition. New York, Irvington, 1992.

For further information see: www.ada-mentoring.de and www.siemens.de/yolante

Social Constructivism and Social Constructivist Curricula in Turkey to Meet the Needs of Young People Learning Science: Overview in the Light of the PROMISE Project

Seval Fer

1 Introduction

In this chapter of the book, the author attempts to identify the secondary school curriculum, including science courses developed and put into practice by the Ministry of National Education (MONE) in accordance with the principles of social constructivism in the countryside since the school year 2004/2005. "Social Constructivist Learning" (SCL) consists of practices, norms and beliefs that shed light on the questions of what knowing is and how an individual knows. Knowledge is seen as socially and culturally constituted. In this framework, contrary to learning theories with single correct answers, aspects and perspectives, multiple perspectives and thoughts in constructivist epistemology might have answers in science education in regard to the linguistic and cultural diversity of classes. In this context, the experiments and problems of the new curricula are shared by explaining the "Social Constructivist Learning Environment" (SCLE) as an alternative to meet the different needs of young people. It also signifies the importance of SCLEs in today's corporate world, where the gender dimension, linguistic and cultural diversity, methodological problems, and intercultural misunderstandings of migrants that are often not considered in general education are taken into consideration in science classes. Moreover, the author correlates the SCL with the overall objective of the "Promotion of Migrants in Science Education" (PROMISE) project in order to promote migrants in science education. Finally, the author concludes by suggesting ways to make the SCLEs successful in intercultural science classes based on constructivist epistemology.

These suggestions would be useful for educational authorities such as teachers and educational scientists.

2 Constructivism and Social Constructivist Learning Environment

In psychology, there are different theories on learning that explain the learning process. There are three leading theories that fall under two paradigms. As seen in figure 1, the first and older two theories are the behaviorist and cognitive theories, which fall under the realist paradigm. In these theories, each individual attains the same, realistic, complete and true understanding pertaining to the world. In this context, the behaviorist theory focuses on the overt behaviors that can be observed and measured; the cognitive theory focuses on the mental process underlying the learning process. On the other hand, the constructivist theory, which falls under the unrealistic paradigm, states that there is an external world in which individuals can acquire experience. In this world, meaning is given by individuals to the world. Whereas in the realistic paradigm learners are passive recipients, in constructivist epistemology – in the unrealistic paradigm – learners actively explore new information before constructing meaning, knowledge and knowing from the new information by linking it to previous experience and knowledge.

According to Davis and Sumara (2002), different kinds of constructivism, such as radical, cognitive, situated, social, cultural, socio-cultural and critical, are encountered in literature. Richardson (2003) mentions 18 kinds of constructivism that comprise methodological, radical, didactic and dialectic forms in literature.

As seen in figure 1, the most common of these are cognitive, radical and social constructivism. Social constructivism is related to Vygotsky's ideas and is based on the idea that all knowledge is constructed socially, and is in the social-centered group of constructivism. As a matter of fact, while Piaget (see 1955) tries to examine the process of acquiring knowledge, Glasersfeld (see 1995; 1996) examines the relation between knowledge and reality, and puts more emphasis on individual elements in the process of constructing knowledge. However, both Piaget and Glasersfeld explain the learning process by means of individual experiences in daily life, and what is understood from those experiences. Thus, there are two varieties in the individual centered group of constructivism.

Common criticism of cognitive and radical constructive tendencies addresses their focus on individual elements, saying that this does not take into consideration the social dimensions of learning, especially the relationship between learners, knowledge and teachers. (Doolittle and Camp 1999; Fosnot 1996; Richardson 1997). However, it does not seem possible to understand the cognitive structures of individuals without observing them in the social context. In this context, social constructivism is thought to eliminate the deficiencies of cognitive and radical constructivism. In this chapter of the book, SCLE is examined because it is based on sounder foundations, because it supports educational practices and is accepted in theoretical and research literature, and because it is suitable for the aim of this chapter of the book. At this point, it will be beneficial to explain Vygotsky's ideas first, and then move on to an explanation of SCLE, since his ideas of social functions of learning not only had an impact the formulation of SCL but they also presented guidance for organizing learning processes and environment.

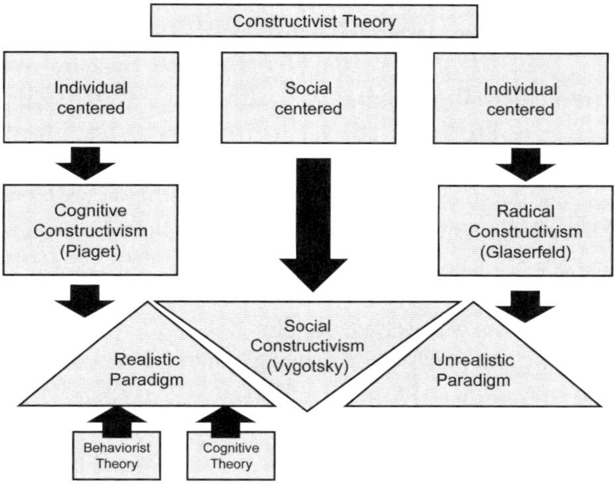

Figure1: Tendencies of Constructivism and the Epistemology

Two important concepts for Vygotsky are thought and language. It is important to note that, according to Vygotsky (1962), language has a part not only in thought development but also in the development of consciousness as a whole. Vygotsky (1930) explains his idea: "*The acquisition of language can provide a paradigm for the entire problem of the relation between learning and development.*" According to Vygotsky (1929), while a child grows up, she does not only add cultural phenomena and events to her experiences, but also understands habits and forms of cultural behavior and forms as a cultural method. Individuals acquire the way of learning by using language and thought in their culture and society. On the other hand, the major theme of Vygotsky's theoretical framework is that of the zone of proximal development. Vygotsky (1930) explains the zone of proximal development as "*the distance between the actual developmental level as determined by independent problem solving and the level of potential development as determined through problem solving under adult guidance or in collaboration with more capable peers.*" In this framework, Vygotsky submits practical suggestions to educators indirectly by the zone-of-proximal-development explanations. To put it simply, through interactive communication in collaborative learning environments, learners develop their thinking through language. At the same time, learners also develop their language through thinking. Thus, an essential feature of SCLE is that it creates the zone for proximal development process.

SCL is also influenced by Dewey who expressed his ideas before Vygotsky. Dewey's famous expression: "*learning by doing*" constitutes an active learning method that is used in social constructivist learning. According to Dewey (1915), learning is reflection upon what the learner has experienced. This understanding of the learner changes her view of – and action in – the world and the world is changed by new understanding of the learner. It is also necessary for learners to interact with one another in real social situations in order to understand life and the world itself.

SCL sheds light on the questions of what knowing is and how an individual knows by explaining knowledge as being socially and culturally constructed (Fosnot 1996). The construction of meaning does not occur personally, on the contrary, it is a result of mutual communication between individuals (Jonassen, Howland, Moore and Marra 2003; Jonassen and Rohrer-Murphy 1999). In this frame, knowledge is built by society after individuals come to an agreement about cultural applications and about reality (Doolittle and Camp 1999). The SCL process occurs in a learner through the use of existing basic cognitive processes, such as experiences, beliefs, knowledge, skills and mental models in order to organize the learning process in a social and cultural environment. This process requires continuous mental variation, making connections between current knowledge-knowing and learning experiences. Which meaning is accepted by the learner and how the new meaning is harmonized in the mental models of the learner is decided by the learner herself, and interactions with others help in this process via a social and cultural context. This understanding encourages learners to discover concepts, relations and knowledge by constructing them in a social concept. Contrary to popular belief, SCL does not deny that reality exists outside the person; however, it denies the fact that there is a single way to reach to that reality or world. The reasoning behind this idea is the belief that, because students have different backgrounds, experience and knowledge, as well as personal differences, every person reaches meanings or whatever they reach by using a different way to the same content or concept. So, it will not be wrong to state that SCL suggests that the relationship between the learner and knowledge cannot be finite and absolute; it can be improved or changed (Fer and Cirik 2007).

In a SCL design, learners and teachers participate in the design process as a characteristic of design. Moreover, the design process has a complex, non-linear structure that sometimes can lead to chaos (Wilson 1997a, 1997b; Wilson, Teslow and Osman 1995) around big ideas with multiple goals (Gagnon and Collay 2001).

The active learning method is the key principle of SCL design, in which learners construct knowledge by means of physical and mental activities and by actively engaging with learning activities (Gibbons 2003; Jones and Southern 2003). These activities might be problem solving, doing projects, having real-life experiences, story-writing, developing newspapers, searching, researching, doing experiments, developing puzzles, playing games, as well as story-telling, role playing, skepticism, analysis, and synthesis (Kalem and Fer 2003). SCL also focuses on the sharing of individual meaning; and the knowledge constructed by cooperation with peers (Gagnon and Collay 2001). Thus, another important method used in a SCL design is collaborative learning. The common point of this method is that group members are responsible for both their learning and the learning of group members; the success of the group is rewarded. For group-work to be truly collaborative, there should be some special features among the students in a group, such as different backgrounds and individualities including sex, social status, socio-economic status, and academic success, as well as some characteristics like peer-collaboration and cooperation, good communication and interaction, social skills, faithfulness, equal opportunity, group-rewards, both in individual and in group assessments (Avcı and Fer 2004).

Other activities are applied in a SCL design that encourage making sense of the subject matter, exposure to multiple sources of information, and opportunities for students to demonstrate their understanding in diverse ways, such as problem-based learning, inquiry activities, and dialogues with peers and teachers (Windschitl 1999). Activities are facilitated by shared studies and research. During this process, learners discover different solutions (Alesandri and Larson 2002). Encouraged to think and research, they construct the meaning actively and learn it through discovery (Gould, 1996). Learners also construct their experiences through discussion, or with collaborative groups in problem-solving activities (Tobin and Tippins 1993). Problems are related to the life of the learners and their interests. Moreover, project-based studies with cooperation make the learners evaluate their knowledge in a social context and allow them to construct the meaning and knowledge easily (Vermette, Foote, Bird, Mesibov, Haris-Eving, and Battaglia 2001).

One of the important duties of teachers in a SCLE is to assess the students' learning (Tobin and Tippins 1993). Outcomes of SCL activities are unique and varied, and learning is a reflection of assessment. Thus, learners play an active, effective and critical role in assessment, and come to understand the meaning of what they have experienced via an assessment process (Alesandri and Larson 2002). The authentic assessment approach is suitable for SCL. In this framework, learning and assessment processes should be linked together. Thus, learners continue to learn throughout the assessment process. Authentic assessment includes peer-assessment and self-assessment. In self-assessment processes, learners evaluate their own personal development levels of learning according to the criteria they determine with their teachers. On the other hand, in the peer-assessment process, learners evaluate each other based on their perspectives in terms of agreement on learning levels, values, quality and criteria (Fer and Cirik 2007). According to the research (i.e.

Chen and Lou 2004; Topping, Smith, Swanson and Eliot 2000), feedback obtained from peers is more effective than feedback obtained from teachers in learning.

SCL focuses on what learners do, and not what teachers do. The teacher undertakes a facilitative role for learners to acquire knowledge (Jaramillo 1996; Vermette, et al. 2001). In learning, learner-teacher and learner-learner interactions are the basic mechanisms. The teacher works with learners: she explains, informs, inquires, asks questions, corrects and directs the learners to make explanations. When the learner later solves a problem alone, he uses the cooperative learning principles independently that he learned before (Vygotsky 1934/1978/1987; cited in Green and Gredler 2002).

Although there is a much greater advantage to using a SCLE, as explained before, it also has some limitations that can be summarized as follows: (1) a learner needs much more time for the construction process since time is used in a flexible way. This is necessary for learners to develop their understanding and perception processes, and to participate in necessary activities, (2) both educators and learners need to make too many preparations (Farris 1996), (3) to apply constructivism in a traditional environment and classroom is very difficult, (4) to apply constructivism with a teacher who is educated in a traditional environment is very difficult (Fer and Cirik 2007).

The research (e.g. Abd-El-Khalick 2001; Akar and Yıldırım 2004; Banet and Ayuso 2003; Clark and James 2004; Cobern, Gibson and Underwood 1999; Glasson and Lalik 1993; Hand, Treagust and Vance 1997; Henderson and Mirafzal 1999; Matthew and Norma 2002; Maypole and Davies 2001; Tsai 2000) concerned with constructivism has focused on secondary and university education and has presented positive results in regard to effects on the learning process, as well as learners' and teachers' views and perceptions. In this framework, contrary to learning theories with single correct answers, aspects and perspectives, it is seen that SCLE might have solutions in science education in order to take into consideration the linguistic and cultural diversity of classes. Moreover, organizing learning environments for science courses, according to the epistemological principles of SCL might be one of the alternatives in today's corporate world where issues like gender, linguistic and cultural diversities, methodological problems, and intercultural misunderstandings of learners must be taken into greater consideration.

3 Curricula in Turkey Based on the Principles of Social Constructivism

MONE has initiated a reform action by a grant from the European Union. In this context, the basic (1-8 grades) school curricula including "Science and Technology curriculum for 4-8 grades" were developed and put into practice by MONE throughout the entire country starting in the school year 2004/2005. In line with the basic educational curricula, secondary education (9-12 grades) curricula including "Physics, Chemistry, Biology curriculum for 9-12 grades" have been also started to be developed, and some of them, put into practice by MONE in the countryside in the 2006/2007 school year, are still being implemented. The new curriculum development process is based on constructivism, although constructivism explains learning and instruction as mentioned in the previous section, and not the curricular framework. In this context, it might be useful to share concepts, experiments and problems of the new curriculum process.

In the new curricular process, national and international experts (from Finland, the United Kingdom, Germany, the Netherlands, and Denmark) worked together in teams. The key issue was the elimination of gender disparities in primary and secondary education by 2015 (SBEP 2005). Through curricular reforms, it has been built both on Turkish tradition and global trends by putting an emphasis on the nature of SCLE.

The purpose of the new curricula is to bring up students as effective and active members of society in terms of meeting their individual needs by integrating school and outside school environments. The new curricula are intended to create the opportunity and environment for learners to understand themselves, the society and the world they live in, and to contribute to them. The main idea behind these curricula is summarized as follows: (1) to align curricula with basic and secondary education curricula in the European Union countries, (2) to integrate secondary school curricular content and structure with basic education curricula, (3) to ensure a balance of gender issues in education, (4) to increase equality of opportunity by designing a more flexible curriculum, (5) to increase relevance of instruction to economy and democracy, (6) to establish multi-level skill-concept-learning strategy relations in the curricular content, (7) to establish a consensus on a general framework for skill domains as core skills for all students, including Turkish language and literature, social studies, science, and information and communications technologies (Karip 2005). The guidance of the new curricula (SBEP 2005) is summarized in table 1.

Table 1. The Guidance of the New Curricula	
Aims	Develop the knowledge and skills that are necessary for life. Enable learners to develop moral, ethical, social and cultural issues within their own customs and traditions, and to recognize their country, the European Union, and their location in the world. Enable learners to develop themselves as people who know their duties in society and who are in harmony with their environment. Respect differences between learners in personal characteristics, learning styles, and learning potentials. Empower learners to make democracy their lifestyle and develop respect for human rights. Learn to use information technologies efficiently and productively in order to reach an objective.
Content	Pay attention to topics important for society like health, environment, nature, etc. Provide contexts and environments where students may improve their creativity, innovativeness, entrepreneurship, leadership characteristics, problem-solving, scientific thinking and critical thinking skills. Create integrated fields of learning, making learners aware of structures and relationships between elements. Content and activities are contextualized and connected to in the students' environments, life styles, and economic activities. Learning cannot only happen in school. Create and refer to a wealth of informational sources like newspapers, magazines, books, students' parents and other people who are experts in their subject domains.
Task Design	Learner and learning centered. Stimulate learners' research desire and natural curiosity. Create transfer contexts and tasks by the knowledge and skills learned. Encourage students to cooperate to see and understand the views, different interpretations and solutions of other students. Design tasks and activities that integrate, create and use knowledge and concepts, as well as allow transfer in new contexts. Design tasks, particularly group tasks, like a report, a newspaper article, etc., with a reflection or evaluation of what has been acquired, how this acquisition was reached and whether or not there are alternative ways. Define skill practice in at least three steps (acting out, training, application).
Teacher Strategies	Apply basic strategies such as direct instruction, self-instruction, asking questions, helping by asking questions, coaching.
Testing	Create assessment as an inseparable part of teaching and learning. Test both learning output and learning process via authentic assessment.

The process of the curriculum development model for both basic and secondary curriculum is presented in figure 2.

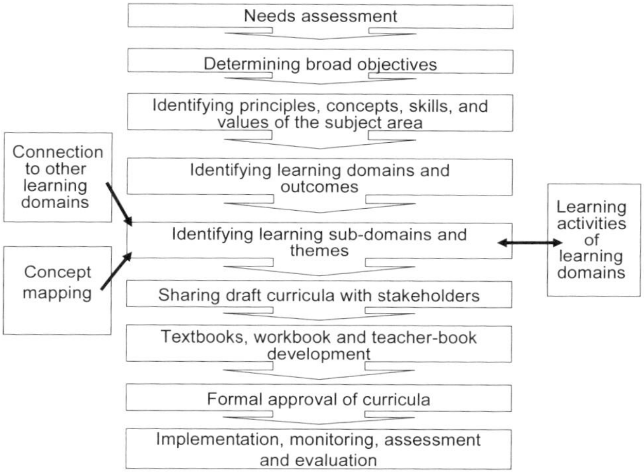

Figure 2: The Curriculum Development Model in Turkey

As seen in figure 2, the process of the curriculum development model for both basic and secondary education starts and ends with evaluating the needs of the individual and society. Through this model, a significant change has been introduced into the approach to curriculum development, from a subject-centered towards a learner-centered approach, from a behaviorist towards a social constructivist theory (MEB-TTKB 2005). "*The New Curriculum provides integration of subjects and tasks thus avoiding overlaps between programs and creating efficiency*" (SBEP 2007, 5).

In concert with the newly developed curricula, development of educational materials packages has been in progress according to principles of SCL and based on international standards in pedagogy and didactics which consist of student textbooks and student workbooks, teacher books, test materials, and audiovisual (languages only) and informational technology material (SBEP 2005; 2007, 4).

In terms of the secondary science curricula including "*Physics, Chemistry, Biology curriculum,*" the new curricula brought changes that are in line with SCLE, as well as with other countries such as the United States, the United Kingdom, Singapore, Finland, Holland and Israel. However, for the 9th grades, the core curriculum is the same for both general and vocational education, and then differentiation in each field throughout the 10th to 12th grades at the secondary level comes only after the basic subjects of the 9th grades are mastered (Karip 2005).

In terms of content, the science curricula including the "*Physics, Chemistry, Biology curriculum*" (MEB-TTKB 2007a,b,c) have been prepared by considering the integrity between the basic and secondary school curricula according to the development level of the students for each grade. The content is organized around learning domains which include concepts, principles, and theories of science, with an emphasis on conceptual knowledge, and with a real life context-based approach in order to relate content to everyday life, as well as to develop a positive attitude towards science for students. This aims to develop scientific concepts as well as scientific perception. Another aim is to adopt the idea of associating science within itself as well as with other subjects and disciplines with an interdisciplinary approach, which is mainly based on SCL. Besides content, there are also changes in the skill domain that consists of five skills, such as problem solving, information and communication skills, as well as changes in science-technology-society-environment outcomes, scientific research and scientific process skills, also attitudes and values, which are connected with a spiral approach for each learning domain in order to develop core competencies for students across the curriculum.

The most prominent change in the newly developed curricula seems to be the way the content is delivered via the learning and instructional process, which are based on SCL. In this frame, individual differences are taken into account not only by means of differing expectations from the students, but also by employing different methods or strategies through learning styles, tasks and activities with the effective participation of the students during the learning and instructional process. Moreover, learning domains are enriched with activities including realistic and authentic tasks. Through active learning, students are not only physically, but also mentally active in the learning process, and through collaborative learning, they can share and debate their solutions and approaches. Furthermore, the curriculum places more emphasis on a learning environment where the students learn within a collaborative group through problem solving, researching, and discovering. The main aim of these kinds of activities is for students to realize that science does not only consist of rules and memorization, but that it is an entertaining, meaningful and logical discipline. Moreover, the activities carried out during the instructional and learning process are meant to improve the understanding of the learning domains and concepts of science. All of these attempts aim to enhance students' active participation in learning science. The curriculum is also open for technology usage. In this context, the teacher has to require taking new roles such as questioning, organizing, coaching, and guiding while reducing the traditional roles such as telling, dictating, and teaching.

Another significant change in the curricula is the approach taken towards the assessment of learning that is in line with SCL; that is, more emphasis is given to process evaluation than product evaluation, with self-assessment and peer-assessment techniques via authentic assessment existing alongside traditional assessment. That is, instead of using only tests and exams, such tools as portfolios, projects, task performances, and group work are used in the assessment of a student's learning.

The strengths of the newly developed science curricula including the physics, chemistry and biology curriculum are as follows: (1) ensuring that the learning needs of all students are met through equitable access through learning and life skills competencies, (2) opportunities in skills and competence development via exploring, discovering, and sharing, (3) learning concepts connected to real life, (4) creating learners with open, exploring minds, and self-confidence, (5) creating active and motivated learners, and (6) using not just traditional testing and marking, but also authentic assessment via supporting and coaching (SBEP 2005). However, some problems exist with the science curricula such as: (1) the curriculum has been evaluated and revised with very limited feedback from pilot schools and other stakeholders, (2) it seems that all interest in curricular changes is focused on the change itself, rather than how the change will be distributed, (3) although pedagogical content is developed based on the principles of SCL, it seems that there is more emphasis put on content than necessary, (4) the teachers will play a major role in the implementation of the new curricula and it will not be easy for them to adapt to the new roles. However, the most noteworthy point in the discussions surrounding the implementation of new curricula is the fact that there has been little attention given to teacher training in line with the new curricula, (5) it is not usual to find and use technological and multi-instructional materials for science teaching in a typical classroom, since many teachers may not be used to incorporating the use of these materials into science teaching; however, they are now required to use them in their classrooms, (6) materials such as textbooks, student textbooks, workbooks and teachers' books in line with the new curricula will play a major role in the implementation of the new curricula. However, they have not yet been published for all levels and courses of science education at the secondary school level.

The existing literature reveals that there is little research at the basic school level, and no research at the secondary school level concerning the implementation of new curricula. For example, Toptas (2006) found that science teachers in primary schools were regarded as having insufficient sources, lacking any instructional medium, and having insufficient time for instruction and evaluation. Furthermore, there is an insufficient number of activities used in implementing the new curricula. Similarly, teachers had problems with assessment methods in practice. Moreover, Temiz's (2005) research revealed that 4th grade science teachers had problems with assessment methods in practice. Additonally, Baykul (2005) stated that students' higher order thinking might improve with the new curricula but there are problems with learning activities and assessment in science curricula. Güzel and Alkan's (2005) research also showed that although primary school students had positive opinions about the application of the SCLE utilized in the new curriculum, they could not establish relations with science, the real world and the school.

As a result, although the curricular changes are called a reform, it is too early to treat them as such, for it is not known if the curricular changes will produce the intended results. Therefore, there is a strong need for joint research with universities to evaluate the effect of the curricula. However, as Avenstrup (2004, 8f.) states: "*Longitudinal studies in Denmark have revealed that greater social fluidity as a result of changing cultural capital through education was found to be more limited than hoped, even in a relatively equitable social democratic society.*" Still, the new curricular experiences in Turkey might represent one of the alternatives for creating the opportunity and environments for learners to understand themselves, the society and the world they live in, and to contribute to them, as well as to bring up young students as effective and active members of society in terms of meeting their individual needs by integrating in-school and extracurricular environments for science courses.

4 Social Constructivist Learning Environment with the PROMISE Objectives

Common methods of science education do not consider a change of society within linguistic and cultural diversity. Migrants often suffer from general education systems due to the lack of consideration of their linguistic and cultural background. In addition to linguistic and cultural communication problems, intercultural misunderstandings, differences in countries of origin and countries of residence are considered to hamper the successful integration of migrants. This often results in migrant pupils who do not feel addressed adequately in science education. Moreover, as there are communication problems between migrants and teachers, the teachers do not know the reasons for the bad performance of the migrants, that is, whether there are language-problems or problems in the comprehension of science. The consequence is that there is no specific support for migrants, as teachers do not know what kind of support is needed (Tajmel and Starl 2005). For a detailed description of the barrier analysis and the solution oriented PROMISE approach see Tajmel, Starl and Schön in this book (chapter 2).

The general aim of the PROMISE project was to promote "migrants in science education and in choosing science careers by developing new concepts and the best practices in science education in consideration of the linguistic and cultural diversity of classes in cooperation between countries of origin and countries of residence" (Tajmel and Starl 2005, 5). The project was finished with successful outcomes. However, SCLEs as well as Turkish curricular experiences based on the principles of social constructivism might represent one of the alternatives for continuing the pursuit of the project objectives of PROMISE as a contribution to the sustainability of the project outcomes to promote migrants in science education. The suggestions in conjunction with this subject are explained in the next section.

5 Conclusion and Suggestions

As can be seen from the previous sections, the SCLE might provide opportunities and help to promote further advisory assistance in order to pursue the goals of the PROMISE project. The correlation between the overall objective of the project and a SCLE might be utilized in order to extend the project's outcomes into a long term solution to promote migrants in science education. SCLE may also be able to present insight to teachers and educational scientists since it positively influences the communication between teachers and migrant students and among students, as well as among the people of the countries of origin and countries of residence. This may also lead to an improved experience of integration for young people with a background of migration, which in turn will have a positive effect on the number of migrants choosing science careers. With the consideration of the cultural and linguistic background of migrants, the pupils would feel more addressed as individuals. This could also result in an improved experience of integration for migrants with a general impact on society.

A SCLE will differ considerably from a traditional one in terms of the teaching and learning process, the classroom environment and the roles of teachers and learners. This difference is due to the emphasis on learning rather than teaching. Although constructivism focuses on the provision of information relating to the learning process and knowing itself, it also provides suggestions for the teaching environment. In view of these suggestions a SCLE Model for a constructive learning is designed and shown in figure 3.

As seen in figure 3, SCLE is comprised of four dimensions: Learner analysis, determination context, construction of meaning and evaluation. It should be kept in mind that all the activities under these dimensions should not be structured or organized by others; they should be formed and applied with the students.

In order to make SCLE successful in intercultural and multilingual classes, it is necessary that the teachers themselves be aware of their own construction of science. In this framework, it is noteworthy that the problem of harmonization of teacher training to this new approach has been taken into account. The possibilities of resistance due to educators' existing mental frameworks have also been taken into account; thus, with the help of previous experience, and without abandoning the principles of constructivism, advisory efforts have been under way.

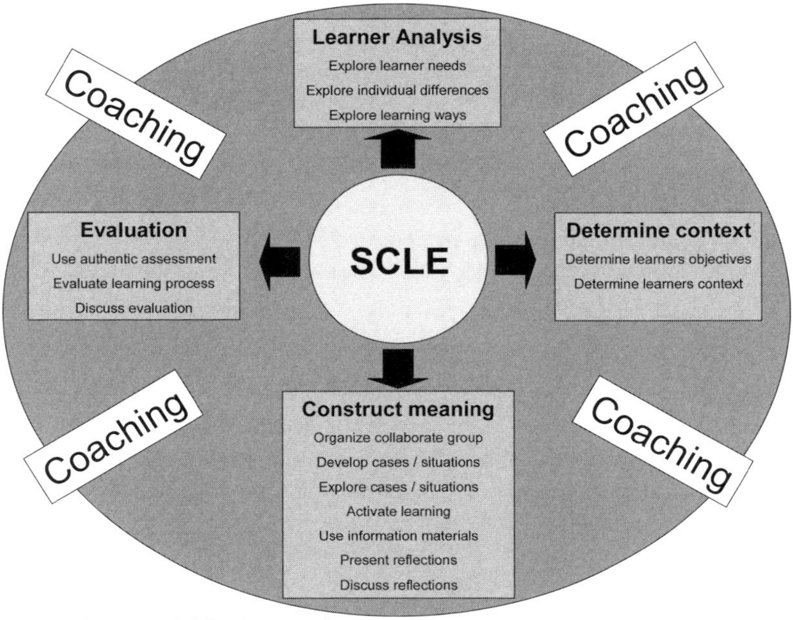

Figure 3: A SCLE Model for Constructive Learning

Finally, in light of SCLE, social constructivist curricula and the PROMISE project, the suggestions are summarized below in order to make the SCLE successful in intercultural and multilingual science classes with cultural and linguistic diversity. These are of particular interest to educational authorities, teachers and educational scientists: (1) to focus strongly on adapting courses and providing support so that all students have the opportunity to succeed in science education (2) to harmonize the international differences in a SCLE in order to optimize the integration of migrants in school and social life, leading to better integration of migrants as a general impact on society and the increase in the probability that the next generation of migrants living in Europe, as well as migrants returning to their countries of origin, will choose science careers (3) to set up the harmonization of activities, methods and tools in science education such that the gender dimension and the linguistic and cultural diversity of classes are taken into consideration, as well as to overcome linguistic and cultural differences and barriers in science education by utilizing SCLE (4) to provide insight for teachers and educational scientists in teaching linguistically and culturally diverse classes by considering gender mainstreaming in science classes via SCLE (5) to develop and institutionalize a comprehensive, long-term training program for teachers in classes of cultural and linguistic diversity, both in countries of origin and countries of residence, in order to support successful linguistic and intercultural communication between teachers and students, as well as to develop different learning and teaching concepts, methods and tools in science teaching (6) to pursue and institutionalize the cooperation of officials, universities, schools and experts between countries of origin and countries of residence after the PROMISE project in order to understand the linguistic and cultural diversity in learning science, as well as in questions of science education for the international harmonization of methods and educational standards, concepts, methods and tools in science education (7) to have a basis for communication between school authorities, teachers in the countries of origin and countries of residence, and the migrant community by utilizing the new curricular experiences in Turkey (8) to collect and document teachers' experiences and their best practices for teaching in classes of cultural and linguistic diversity in an effort to establish a dialogue between countries of origin and countries of residence (9) to conduct joint research to evaluate outcomes of the different science education methods in countries of origin and countries of residence, as well as linguistic and cultural barriers in science education, in order to raise the interest of migrants in science. This can be achieved by developing and proving the best practices for science education on the basis of the research and the experiences to (10) follow up and improve the science curriculum into a sustainable science learning situation that supports the life-long learning needs of students and the social and economic well-being of students.

In conclusion, in order to organize learning environments for science courses, SCLE might be utilized as one of the alternatives in today's corporate world where issues like gender, linguistic and cultural diversities, methodological problems, and intercultural misunderstandings of learners are taken into greater consideration. SCLE also helps to support and enhance the originality and subjectivity of individuals, and their own unique preferences, as well as their cultural and linguistic properties.

Bibliography

Abd-El-Khalick, Fouad, *Embedding Nature of Science Instruction in Preservice Elementary Science Courses: Abandoning Scientism, but ...*, in: Journal of Science Teacher Education (12, 3), 2001, 215-233.

Akar, Hanife and Yildirim, Ali, *Olusturmaci Ogretim Etkinliklerinin Sinif Yonetimi Dersinde Kullanilmasi: Bir Eylem Arastirmasi* [Using Constructive Teaching Activities in Class Management Lesson: An Action Research], Egitimde Iyi Ornekler Konferansi, 2004; available online at: http://www.erg.sabanciuniv.edu/iok2004 (last checked: 11 June 2008).

Alesandrini, Kathryn and Larson, Linda, *Teachers Bridge to Constructivism*, in: The Clearing House: Educational Research, Controversy, and Practices (75, 3), 2002, 118-122, available online at: ProQuest database: http://proquest.umi.com/pqdweb?index=0&sid=2&srchmode=2&vinst=PROD&fmt=2&startpage=-1&clientid=46825&vname=PQD&RQT=309&did=109945377&scaling=FULL&ts=1214560801&vtype=PQD&rqt=309&TS=1214562342&clientId=46825 (last checked 19 September 2004).

Avci, Suleyman and Fer, Seval, *The Effects of Jigsaw II Techniques in a Cooperative Learning Environment on Students: a Case Study at Kartal Vocational Training Center*, in: Education and Science (29, 134), 2004, 61-74.

Avenstrup, Roger, *The Challenge of Curriculum Reform and Implementation: Some Implications of a Constructivist Approach*, 2004, available online at: http://tedp.meb.gov.tr/doc/Pubs/4a2%20SBEP%20website%20content%20download%20implementing%20the%20New%20Curriculum.pdf (last checked 11 June 2008).

Banet, Enrique H. and Ayuso, Gabriel E., *Teaching of Biological Inheritance and Evolution of Living Beings in Secondary School*, in: International Journal of Science Education (25, 3), 2003, 373-407.

Baykul,Yasar, *2004-2005 Yillarinda Cikarilan Matematik Programi Uzerine Dusunceler*. [Ideas on 2004-2005 Mathematics Curriculum], Egitimde Yansimalar VII: Yeni Ilkogretim Programlarini Degerlendirme Sempozyumu, 14-16 Kasim 2005 Erciyes Universitesi, Kayseri, Turkey, 2005, 231-238.

Chen, Yining and Lou, Hao, *Students' Perceptions of Peer Evaluation: an Expectancy Perspective*, in: Journal of Education for Business (79, 5), 2004, 275-283, available online at: EBSCOhost database: http://web.ebscohost.com/ehost/resultsadvanced?vid=7&hid=116&sid=98dac085-072b-4c98-bd89-5ce0ff859871%40sessionmgr109 (last checked 17 June 2008).

Clark, Ian F. and James, Patrick. R., *Using Concept Maps to Plan an Introductory Structural Geology Course*, in: Journal of Geoscience Education (52, 3), 2004, 224-230, available online at: http://findarticles.com/p/articles/mi_qa4089/is_200405/ai_n9399646/pg_9 (last checked 11 June 2008).

Cobern, William W., Gibson, Adrienne T. and Underwood, Scott A., *Conceptualizations of Nature: an Interpretive Study of 16 Ninth Graders' Everyday Thinking*, in: Journal of Research in Science Teaching (36, 5), 1999, 541-564.

Davis, Brent and Sumara, Dennis, *Constructivist Discourses and the Field of Education: Problems and Possibilities*, in: Educational Theory (52, 4), 2002, 409-428, available online at: http://www.ualberta.ca/~bdavis/DavisSumaraEdTheory.pdf (last checked 11 June 2008).

Dewey, John, *Democracy and Education: an Introduction to the Philosophy of Education*, McMillan Company, New York, 1915.

Doolittle, Peter, E. and Camp, William G., *Constructivism: the Vocational and Technical Education Perspective*, in: Journal of Vocational and Technical Education (16, 1), 1999, 23-46, available online at: http://scholar.lib.vt.edu/ejournals/JVTE/v16n1/doolittle.html (last checked 11 June 2008).

Farris, Pamela J., *Teaching bearing the torch*. Madison: Brown Benchmark Publishers, 1996.

Fer, Seval and Cirik, Ilker, *Yapilandirmaci Ogrenme: Kuramdan Uygulamaya*. [Constructivist learning: From Theory to Implication], Istanbul, Morpa Yayinlari, 2007.

Fosnot, Catherine T., *Constructivism: a Psychological Theory of Learning*, in: Fosnot, Catherine T. (ed.), *Constructivism: Theory, Perspectives and Practice*, Teachers College Press, New York, 1996, 8-33.

Gagnon, George W. and Collay, Michelle, *Designing for Learning: Six Elements in Constructivist Classrooms*, Corwin Press, California, 2001.

Gibbons, Beatrice A., *Supporting Elementary Science Education for English Learners: a Constructivist Evaluation Instrument*, in: Journal of Educational Research (96, 6), 2003, 371-380, available online at: http://findarticles.com/p/articles/mi_hb3507/is_200307/ai_n8304467 (last checked 26 June 2008).

Glasersfeld, Ernst v., *Radical Constructivism: a Way of Knowing and Learning*, The Falmer Press, Washington, 1995.

Glasersfeld, Ernst v., *Introduction: Aspects of Constructivism*, in: Fosnot, Catherine T. (ed.), *Constructivism: Theory, Perspectives and Practice*, Teachers College Press, New York, 1996, 3-7.

Glasson, George E. and Lalik, Rosary V., *Reinterpreting the Learning Cycle From a Social Constructivist Perspective: A Qualitative Study Of Teachers' Beliefs and Practices,* in: Journal of Research in Science Teaching, (30, 2), 1993,187-207, available online at: Wiley InterScience database: http://www3.interscience.wiley.com/journal/112752900/abstract?CRETRY=1&SRETRY=0 (last checked 24 June 2008).

Gould, June S., *A Constructivist Perspective on Teaching and Learning in the Language Arts*, in: Fosnot, Catherine T. (ed.), Constructivism: Theory, Perspectives and Practice, Teachers College Press, New York, 1996, 92-102.

Green, S.K. and Gredler, Margaret E., *A Review and Analysis of Constructivism for School-based Practice*, in: School Psychology Review (31, 1), 2002, 53-70, available online at: EBSCOhost database: http://web.ebscohost.com/ehost/resultsadvanced?vid=5&hid=104&sid=b5e59108-b75b-4a78-8906-ddf8031ed183%40sessionmgr107 (last checked 26 June 2008).

Guzel, Esra B. and Alkan, Huseyin, *Evaluating Pilot Study of Reconstructed Turkish Elementary School Curriculum*, in: Educational Sciences: Theory & Practice (5, 2), 2005, 410-420.

Hand, Brian, Treagust, David F. and Vance, Keith, *Student Perceptions of the Social Constructivist classroom*, in: Science Education (81), 1997, 561-577, available online at ProQuest database:
http://proquest.umi.com/pqdweb?index=0&did=16995738&SrchMode=2&sid=2&Fmt=2&VInst=PROD&VType=PQD&RQT=309&VName=PQD&TS=1214569610&clientId=46825 (last checked 17 June 2008).

Henderson, LaRhee L. & Mirafzal, Gholam A., *A First-Class-Meeting Exercise for General Chemistry: Introduction to Chemistry Through an Experimental Tour*, in: Journal of Chemical Education (76, 9), 1999, 1221-1223, available online at: ProQuest database:
http://proquest.umi.com/pqdweb?index=0&did=44227726&SrchMode=2&sid=12&Fmt=2&VInst=PROD&VType=PQD&RQT=309&VName=PQD&TS=1214562245&clientId=46825 (last checked 17 June 2008).

Jaramillo, James A., *Vygotsky's Sociocultural Theory and Contributions to the Development of Constructivist Curricula*, in: Education (117, 1), 1996, 133-140, available online at:
http://findarticles.com/p/articles/mi_qa3673/is_199610/ai_n8734319 (last checked 26 June 2008).

Jonassen, David H., Howland, Jane L., Moore, Joi L. and Marra, Rose M., *Learning to Solve Problems with Technology: a Constructivist Perspective*, New Jersey, Merrill Prentice Hall, 2003.

Jonassen, David H. and Rohrer-Murphy, Lucia, *Activity Theory as a Framework for Designing Constructivist Learning Environments*, in: Educational Technology, Research and Development (47, 1), 1999, p. 61-79, available online at:
http://www.springerlink.com/content/p32303k135654844/ (last checked 11 June 2008).

Jones, Eric D. and Southern, Thomas W., *Balancing Perspectives on Mathematics Instruction*, in: Focus on Exceptional Children (35, 9), 2003, p. 1-16, available online at:
http://findarticles.com/p/articles/mi_qa3813/is_200305/ai_n9255554/pg_26
(last checked 11 June 2008).

Kalem, Salih and Fer, Seval, *The Effects of Active Learning Model on the Learning, Teaching and Communication Process of Students*, in: Educational Sciences Theory & Practice (3, 2), 2003, 433-461.

Karip, Emin, *Secondary Education Curriculum Reform in Turkey, Curriculum Reform to Improve Educational Outcomes and Future Opportunities for All Students*, Videoconference to Shanghai Poverty Conference, February 2, 2005, available online at:
http://info.worldbank.org/etools/docs/library/122743/700_emin_karip.ppt
(last checked 11 June 2008).

Matthew, Hughes and Norma, Daykin, *Towards Constructivism: Investigating Students' Perceptions and Learning as a Result of Using an Online Environment, Innovations*, in: Education & Teaching International (39, 3), 2002, 217-224.

Maypole, Joanne and Davies, Timoty G., *Students' Perceptions of Constructivist Learning in a Community College American History 11 Survey Course*, in: Community College

Review (29, 2), 2001, 54-79, available online at SAGE database: http://crw.sagepub.com/cgi/content/abstract/29/2/54 (last checked 19 June 2008).

MEB-TKKB, (Milli Egitim Bakanligi-Talim ve Terbiye Kurumu Baskanligi), *Ilkogretim 1–5. Sinif Programlari Tanitim El Kitabi* [Ministry of National Education-Board of Education, *A Guide to Primary School Curriculum for 1-5th Grades*], Ankara, MEB Basimevi, 2005.

MEB-TKKB, (Milli Egitim Bakanligi-Talim ve Terbiye Kurumu Baskanligi), *Ortaogretim Fizik Dersi 9. Sinif Ogretim Programi* [Ministry of National Education-Board of Education, *Curriculum for 9th Grades Physics*], Milli Egitim Yayinevi, Ankara, 2007a.

MEB-TKKB, Milli Egitim Bakanligi-Talim ve Terbiye Kurumu Baskanligi), *Ortaogretim 9. Sinif Kimya Dersi Ogretim Programi* [Ministry of National Education-Board of Education, *Curriculum for 9th Grades Chemistry*], Milli Egitim Yayinevi, Ankara, 2007b.

MEB-TKKB, Milli Egitim Bakanligi-Talim ve Terbiye Kurumu Baskanligi), *Ortaogretim 9. Sinif Biyoloji Dersi Ogretim Programi* [Ministry of National Education-Board of Education, *Curriculum for 9th Grades Biology*], Milli Egitim Yayinevi, Ankara, 2007c.

Piaget, Jean, *The Construction of Reality in the Child*, Cook, Margaret (transl.), 1955, available online at: http://www.marxists.org/reference/subject/philosophy/works/fr/piaget2.htm (last checked 11 June 2008).

Richardson, Virginia, *Constructivist Teaching and Teacher Education: Theory and Practice*, in: Richardson, Virginia (ed.), *Constructivist Teacher Education: Building a World of New Understandings*, The Falmer Press, London, 1997, 3-14.

Richardson, Virginia, *Constructivist Pedagogy*, in: Teachers College Record (105, 9), 2003, 1623-1640, available online at: EBSCOhost database: http://tg6zm3ts4h.search.serialssolutions.com/directLink?&atitle=Constructivist%20Peda-gogy&author=Virginia%20Richardson&issn=01614681&title=Teachers%20College%20Record&volume=105&issue=9&date=20031201&spage=1623&id=doi:&sid=ProQ_ss&genre=article&lang=en (last checked 17 June 2008).

SBEP (Support to Basic Education Programme), (2005), available online at: http://tedp.meb.gov.tr/main.php?ID=01-01 (last checked 11 June 2008).

SBEP (Support to Basic Education Programme), *Draft Guidelines and Framework for Educational Materials (GFEM) Report*, 2007.

Tajmel, Tanja and Starl, Klaus, *PROMISE – Promotion of Migrants in Science Education*, European Training and Research Centre for Human Rights and Democracy (ETC Graz), Occasional paper No. 18, 2005, available online at: http://www.etc-graz.at/typo3/index.php?id=74 (last checked 15 August 2008).

Temiz, Nida, *Ilkogretim 4. Sinif Matematik Dersi Yeni Ogretim Programinin Yansimalari*, [Reflections of New 4th Grade Mathematics Curriculum], XIV. Ulusal Egitim Bilimleri Kongresi, Pamukkale Universitesi Egitim Fakultesi 28-30 Eylul 2005, Denizli, Turkey, 2005.

Tobin, Kenneth and Tippins, Deborah, *Constructivism as a Referent for Teaching and Learning*, in: Tobin, Kenneth (ed.), *Constructivism: the Practice of Constructivism in science education*, Lawrence Erlbaum Associates Publishers, New Jersey, 1993, 3-21.

Topping, Keith J., Smith, Elaine F., Swanson, Ian and Elliot, Audrey, *Formative Peer Assessment of Academic Writing Between Postgraduate Students*, Assessment and Evaluation in Higher Education (25, 2), 2000, 149-167, available online at: Informaworld database:
http://www.informaworld.com/smpp/title%7Econtent=t713402663 (last checked 27 June 2008).

Toptas, Veli, *Ilkogretim Matematik Dersi (1-5) Ogretim Programinin Uygulanmasinda Sinif Ogretmenlerinin Karsilastiklari Sorunlarla Ilgili Gorusleri.* [Ideas of Classroom Teachers About Application of Elementary Mathematics Curriculum (1-5th grades)], Ulusal Sinif Ogretmenligi Kongresi, Bildiri Kitabi, Volume 1, Ankara, Kok Yayincilik, 2006, 277-285.

Tsai, Chin-Chung, *Relationships Between Student Scientific Epistemological Beliefs and Perceptions of Constructivist Learning Environments*, in: Educational Research (42, 2), 2000, 193-205, available online at:
http://www.blackwell-synergy.com/doi/abs/10.1111/j.1467-8535.2004.00442.x (last checked 11 June 2008).

Vermette, Paul, Foote, Chandra, Bird, Cliff, Mesibov, Don, Haris-Eving, Sharon and Battaglia, Cathy, *Understanding Constructivism(s): a Primer for Parents and School*, in: Board Members Education (122, 1), 2001, 87-93, available online at: http://findarticles.com/p/articles/mi_qa3673/is_200110/ai_n8999926 (last checked 11 June 2008).

Vygotsky, Lev, *The Problem of the Cultural Development of the Child*, 1929, available online at:
http://www.marxists.org/archive/vygotsky/works/1929/cultural_development.htm (last checked 11 June 2008).

Vygotsky, Lev, *Mind and Society*, 1930, available online at:
http://www.marxists.org/archive/vygotsky/works/mind/chap6.htm (last checked 19 June 2008).

Vygotsky, Lev, *Thought and Language (Thinking and Speaking)*, 1962, available online at: http://www.marxists.org/archive/vygotsky/works/words/ch04.htm (last checked 19 June 2008).

Wilson, Brent G., *Reflections on Constructivism and Instructional Design*, 1997a, available online at: http://carbon.cudenver.edu/~bwilson/construct.html (last checked 19 June 2008).

Wilson, Brent G., *The Postmodern Paradigm*, in: Dills, Charles R. and Romiszowski, Alexander J. (eds.), *Instructional Development Paradigms*, Englewood Cliffs NJ, Educational Technology, 1997b, available online at:
http://carbon.cudenver.edu/~bwilson/postmodern.html (last checked 19 June 2008).

Windschitl, Mark, *The Challenges of Sustaining a Constructivist Classroom Culture*, Phi Delta Kappan, (80, 10), 1999, 751-755, available online at ProQuest database: http://proquest.umi.com/pqdweb?index=1&did=42309548&SrchMode=1&sid=1&Fmt=2&VInst=PROD&VType=PQD&RQT=309&VName=PQD&TS=1214570959&clientId=46825 (last checked 19 June 2008).

Does Migration Background Matter? Preparing Teachers for Cultural and Linguistic Diversity in the Science Classroom

Tanja Tajmel

1 Introduction

The cultural and linguistic diversity of students requires certain competencies of their teachers, such as culture- and language-sensitive pedagogical skills, awareness of cultural aspects of the subject as well as knowledge of particularities of the teaching language and about possible difficulties for second language learners. The linguistic heterogeneity in physics classes makes the integration of language teaching increasingly important. Science teachers are rarely trained in these competencies. Most of them have chosen mathematics or computer science as a second subject, but not languages. Many of those teachers were last confronted with language learning when they were attending school as students themselves. Understandably, these teachers do not feel competent to identify linguistic problems of second language learners or to include language promoting measures in their lessons. Likewise, most science teachers were not trained in cultural aspects of the natural sciences and, thus, do not reflect on these aspects. Additionally, teachers unconsciously construct ethnic differences and attributions, through which a certain "view" on migrants is created. The attitude of the teachers' expectation might already constitute a barrier for successful science learning.

The first step in preparing teachers for linguistic and cultural diversity is to initiate a process of reflection. Teachers are sensitized to the language and the linguistic demands that are required in science lessons and reflect on their views on migrants. The next step is the quality development of science classes, the professional development of science teachers and the development of appropriate teaching material for implementation in school. The evaluation of the science classes is again integrated into the development process.

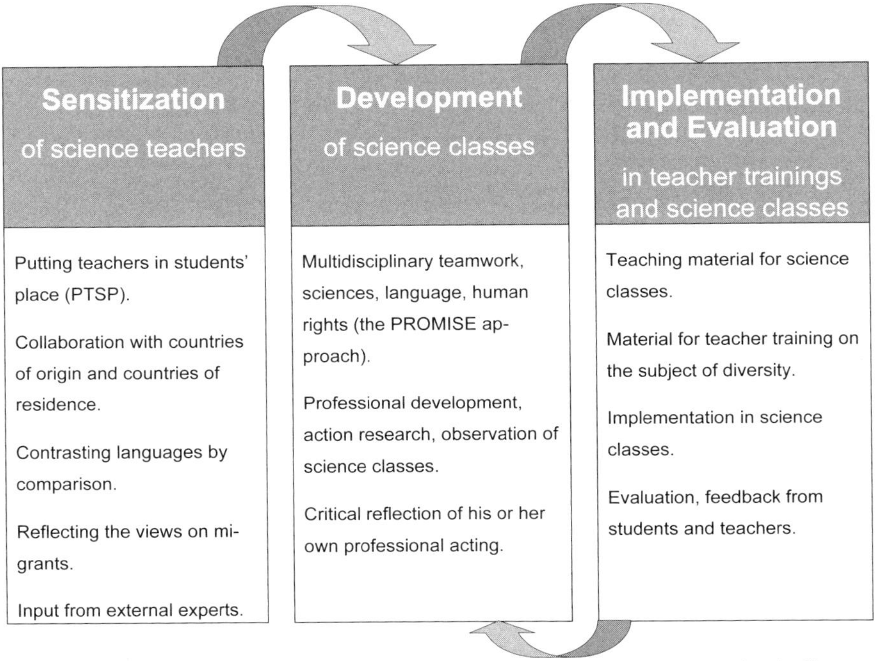

Sensitization
of science teachers
Putting teachers in students' place (PTSP).
Collaboration with countries of origin and countries of residence.
Contrasting languages by comparison.
Reflecting the views on migrants.
Input from external experts.
Development
of science classes
Multidisciplinary teamwork, sciences, language, human rights (the PROMISE approach).
Professional development, action research, observation of science classes.
Critical reflection of his or her own professional acting.
Implementation and Evaluation
in teacher trainings and science classes
Teaching material for science classes.
Material for teacher training on the subject of diversity.
Implementation in science classes.
Evaluation, feedback from students and teachers.

Figure 1: The three phases of the quality development process in science education in diverse classrooms.

2 Teachers' Views on Migrants

Science teachers were asked what they consider to be a barrier for successful science education for migrants. The teachers named "language barriers" in the sense of the lack of language skills on the part of the migrants and "barriers due to the socio-economic background of the students." This shows that the barriers are predominantly seen on the part of the migrants and less on the part of the teacher or the science classes.

Teachers who explicitly speak out on the socio-economic background of the "migrant" students allocate these students to a certain social rank, mostly to the workers' milieu. It is believed that students of this social rank are not supported in their education by their families. Though it is stated by teachers that this was also the case with non-migrant students, the latter are perceived as a heterogeneous social group whereas migrant students are perceived as a homogeneous group, which on the whole is allocated to a lower social rank (Weber 2003). The perspective of the teachers can thus be called "deficit-oriented" instead of "resources-oriented." Examples of common statements of a deficit-oriented perspective are listed below:

> *"Migrants have insufficient linguistic competencies."*
> *"The parents, particularly the mothers, are uneducated."*
> *"Education is less important in migrant families."*
> *"Migrants have a low socio-economic background."*
> *"Migrant families have low income."*
> *"Migrant families cannot afford investments like private lessons."*

The teachers' perception of the homogeneity of the group of migrant students can be seen as a construction of ethnic differences (Weber 2003). With this perception comes the generalization of the students' *second language* simply as *language,* which disregards the students' *first language*. The belief that "migrants have insufficient linguistic competencies" suggests that they do not have linguistic competencies at all and it does not take into consideration the first language competencies of students with a migrant background. Consequently, the lack of the linguistic competencies is often interrelated to a lack of cognitive competencies. Cognitive competencies can indeed interrelate to linguistic competencies, but, of course, in regard to the native or first language of a child and not in regard to a second or foreign language. Nobody would consider him- or herself generally as linguistically incompetent due to his or her poor language skills in any foreign language. Yet this is attributed to students with migrant background. Thus, the realization of equal opportunities in science education requires first of all a raising of awareness, reflection and sensitization of science teachers, science teacher trainers and science education researchers.

3 Sensitization and Awareness Raising

The sensitization process needs input. In our context the input of disciplines like languages, human rights, gender and diversity research, migration research or intercultural education and also the experience of getting to know teachers from different countries, countries of origin and countries of residence, help to create new perspectives on the situation, to reflect on the constructions of ethnic differences and to get a resources-oriented instead of a deficit-oriented view of migrants.

3.1 Putting Teachers in Students' Place (PTSP) – "Prinzip Seitenwechsel"

PTSP is a method of sensitizing teachers to the linguistic requirement of a certain classroom situation. Here, the method is applied to the observation of a physical experiment.

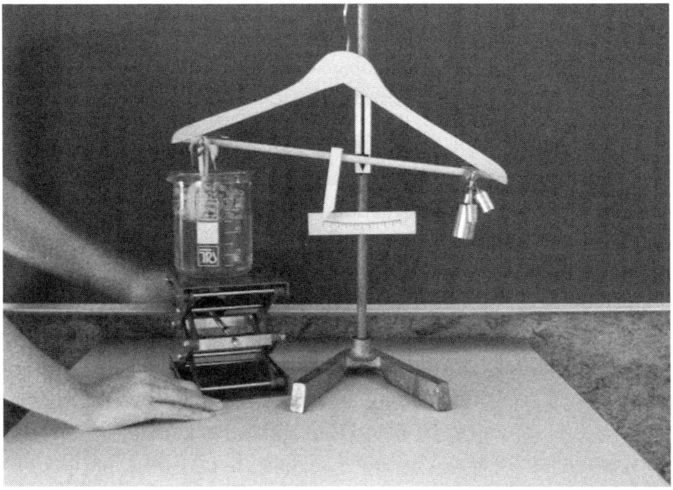

Figure 2: Demonstration of an experiment. In this experiment a coat hanger is used as beam scale. The scale beam is brought in balance by a stone (on the left side) and weights (on the right side). When the stone is steeped in the water the scale beam is no longer in balance and the beam scale becomes inclined.

The demonstration and observation of an experiment is an essential element of the physics classroom. To put the observation into words necessitates specific language skills even when no technical terminology is required. Teachers try to make the task easier by asking the students to describe the observation "in their own words." At first glance, the task seems to meet all the different linguistic competencies of all students as every student has his or her "own words" and every "own word" is allowed. But, unknowingly the teacher expects certain linguistic skills and a certain duration of time which the student will need to express the observation. Correspondingly, if a student does not have the required faculty of expression, the task – to a certain extent – will not be fulfilled. The teacher assumes different reasons for the insufficient performance, but probably not linguistic reasons. Taking into account the fact that second language learners need more time for expression, and that the required "own words" are actually words in a second language and not in their first language, and thus, presumably will differ from the "own words" of a native speaker, it can be expected that these students won't fulfill the task to the teacher's satisfaction.

To sensitize teachers to this specific problem, teachers themselves are put in the position of students by a teacher trainer and thereby change their perspective ("Prinzip Seitenwechsel"). The trainer conducts a physical experiment. The teachers are asked to observe the experiment, to describe the observation in 2-3 sentences and to write them down. The teachers are asked not to use their native language but a second or foreign language.

⇨ Observe the experiment.
⇨ Describe your observation.
⇨ Do not use your first language, use a foreign language.
⇨ Write your description down.

Box 1: The request of the teacher trainer by putting teachers in students' position.

Most of the teachers are surprised at how difficult it is to put the observation into words in a foreign language. Interestingly, this difficulty is also reported by foreign language teachers. The teachers reported having personally experienced "the feeling" of the situation of a student whose first language differs from the language of the science classroom. As the teachers experience the linguistic barriers on their own, the understanding of the situation and the motivation to change the situation is different compared with the understanding without changing the perspective from the teachers to the students' one.

In the next step the teachers name the specific problems they meet in this situation as well as the support which they consider helpful in fulfilling the task. The reported problems and the requested support are categorized and listed in Table 1.

The supportive measures were considered helpful and can be taken as a basis for the development of linguistic supportive resources for the observation of experiments in science classes.

I experienced the following PROBLEMS:		The following SUPPORT would help me to fulfill the task:
I need more **time**.	→	To give more time.
I got stuck for the right **words** (verbs, nouns).	→	To give vocabularies, to name the objects. To provide a dictionary.
I did not find the correct **phrase**.	→	To give a kind of cloze. To give parts of sentences.
I was unsure about the correct **collocation/preposition**.	→	To give collocations/prepositions.

Table 1: The teachers defined the problems they experienced and named supportive measures which would be helpful to fulfill the task.

3.2 Contrasting the Languages

Although many of the migrant students in Austrian and German schools are of Turkish origin, most of the teachers don't know about the linguistic differences between German and Turkish. Actually, many so called "language problems" of migrants can be deduced from these differences. The contrasting of the languages makes teachers aware of these differences. Table 2 contrasts the English, German and Turkish languages.

	English	German	Turkish
Articles	+	+	-
Gender	+	+	-
Verb prefix	+	+	-
Prepositions	+	+	-
Irregular verbs	+	+	-
Irregular plural nouns	+	+	-

Table 2: Linguistic characteristics and differences between the English, German and Turkish languages.

4 Professional Development of Science Teachers towards Diversity

Professional development requires structures and frameworks to give teachers the opportunity to become knowledge creators instead of information receivers. Teacher-networks and partnerships between universities and schools are regarded as adequate structures for this purpose. To improve the quality of science teaching, in the 1990s various projects on interdisciplinary instruction and interdisciplinary networking were carried out, such as the Anglo-American STS (Science-Technology-Society) – and STSE (including environment) – approach (Aikenhead 1994, Tal, Dori, Keiny and Zoller 2001), the German project PING (Praxis Integrierte Naturwissenschaftliche Grundbildung) (Lauterbach 1992), and the Austrian project IMST (Innovations in Mathematics and Science Teaching) (Krainer et al. 2002). The represented disciplines have been mostly mathematics, physics, chemistry, biology, and computer science.

4.1 Interdisciplinary Cooperation of Natural Sciences and Languages – The PROMISE Approach

The professional development for science teachers in culturally and linguistically diverse schools improves specific skills and knowledge relevant for instructing second language learners which are not sufficiently established at the present. These teachers need to gain a profound knowledge of language-learning processes and about the specific problems of second language learners, as well as how they are different from those of foreign language learners. Consequently, there is one further discipline which we propose to be necessarily included in the interdisciplinary teamwork in order to improve the quality of science education in culturally and linguistically diverse classes: the languages.

The PROMISE approach (Tajmel and Starl 2005; Tajmel, Starl and Schön in this book, chapter 2), is based on the interdisciplinary cooperation of sciences and language as well as social sciences and human rights in order to address issues of gender- and diversity mainstreaming. Thus, the PROMISE-Teams consist of science teachers, language teachers, science education researchers and researchers in second language acquisition. The PROMISE-Team is designed as an interdisciplinary *cooperative* collaboration, free of hierarchy, where each member is an expert in his or her field. It is important that each member adopt a resources-oriented position, willing to reflect critically on his professional actions with regard to diversity and to the key task of the team: to develop and modify science lessons and science teaching methods in order to make them accessible and acceptable to migrants. The formal leader of the PROMISE-Team merely organizes and coordinates tasks. For scientific and content-based input, external experts are regularly invited.

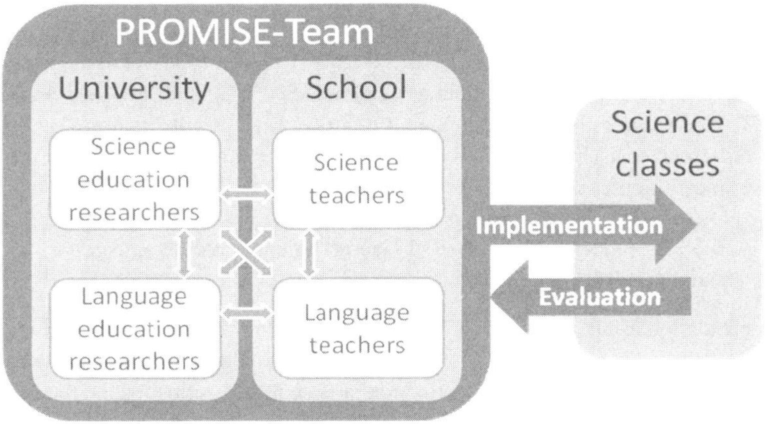

Figure 3: Concept of the PROMISE-Team development process, here with a focus on the collaboration of the disciplines of *natural sciences* and *language*.

4.2 Action Research and Diversity Sensitive Research Tools

Action research is a process of problem solving, which is led by individuals who are working with others on a team. The aim is to improve the method of problem solving by a reflective circle of planning, actions and fact-finding about the result (Lewin 1946). In science education action research has been used as a method of increasing the quality of teaching and learning in teacher training and professional development (Altrichter, Posch and Somekh 1993), in the research on science learning, and in curriculum development. Research tools are the interview, questionnaires, and video observation of lessons, among others.

Within the PROMISE-Team development process, action research was used to identify good practices and to develop science lessons, which in parts have been videotaped and discussed within the team. In this regard it became evident that diversity does not only have to be considered in teaching material like worksheets and textbooks, the linguistic diversity must also be considered also in the research tools like questionnaires and interview guidelines. A student probably does not give an answer or the wrong answer when filling in a questionnaire because he or she does not understand the question. Thus, linguistically sensitive questionnaires include the possibility of stating that the question was not understood. The language used in the questionnaire should also be appropriate for second language learners.

QUESTION	Strongly certain	Certain	Slightly	Not at all	I did not understand the question.
Would you like to become a scientist?	□	□	□	□	□
....	□	□	□	□	□

Figure 3: Example of a questionnaire which considers the potential problems of second language learners.

5 Improving the Quality of Science Classes by Considering the Language

Second language learners face different kinds of linguistic barriers when attending science classes. We understand the expression "linguistic barrier" to be a barrier caused by insufficient consideration of linguistic abilities, which might impede the success of migrants in education in the natural sciences to such an extent that they do not achieve a proper natural science education. These barriers hamper the teaching and learning processes on different levels. Reducing the barriers means improving the quality of science education (Tajmel 2009a).

Thus, two challenges to teachers can be distinguished (Tajmel and Schön 2008):

- The first challenge is to have a *language-sensitive pedagogy*. When a teacher cares that subject matter be understood in a subject-specified and linguistic way, when different linguistic abilities are carefully taken into consideration, then you can call the education *language-sensitive*. This is shown, for example, by assignments and texts that are linguistically appropriate for second language learners.
- The second challenge is the *promotion of language* in the science classroom. The integration of methods like German as Second Language (GSL) (Rösch in this book, chapter 3), English as Second Language (ESL) (Mohan 1986), Deutschsprachiger Fachunterricht (DFU) (Leisen 1999), Scaffolding (Gibbons 2002) and Rich Scripting (McWilliam 1998) in the science classroom systematically supports students both in learning content and language.

5.1 The Language in Science Lessons

In order to set appropriate measures two questions arise: *to what extent is language a part of natural science education?* This question directly leads to the next: *what specific language skills should a student have in the natural science class in order to be successful?* The problem is concerned with qualitative and quantitative aspects: quantitative, because the size of the students' vocabulary, i.e., the number of known words, is important for the understanding of whole texts. Qualitative, because in order to be successful in education, a specific linguistic register, namely the "Bildungssprache" (Gogolin 2006, Gogolin in this book, chapter 2) or the "Cognitive Academic Language Proficiency (CALP)" (Cummins 1979) as well as a proper general command of language and a specialized knowledge is required.

In physics classes, like in every other subject, different linguistic varieties are applied (Tajmel 2009b). Here are two examples:

Text example 1: two students measure the temperature of water.

S2: Wait ... look.
S1: Let me ...
S2: Yes, it is nine.
S1: Nine point ...
S2: Look there.
S1: The hot ... show the hot one.

Text example 2: text of a physic textbook.

> "Because of the homogeneity of the universe, no exchange across the border of the volume under consideration can affect the thermodynamic balances. Every representative part of the universe can be envisaged as a thermodynamically isolated and homogeneous system. It can consist of different components that are not necessarily in reciprocal thermodynamic equilibrium, but are mixed homogeneously in the large." (Liebscher 2005)

The two texts differ in their conceptuality: The first text is *conceptually oral* whereas the second text is *conceptually written* (Koch and Oesterreicher 1985). The production of a conceptually oral text requires "Basic Interpersonal Communicative Skills (BICS)" (Cummins 1979). Children acquire BICS in the pre-school and school-external environment including family, peer group, and friends. The production and comprehension of the second text requires Cognitive Academic Language Proficiency. CALP has to be learned as if it were a completely new language and the mastery of CALP represents a major factor for educational achievements. Most children are confronted with CALP for the first time in school, and it is the language a child learns in school when he or she starts writing and reading. Thus, the science teachers' task is to prepare didactically not only the scientific content but also the transition from BICS to CALPS in the framework of his or her subject in order to make the texts comprehensible and in doing so, to make the content accessible to the students.

5.2 Examples of Teaching Material

PHYSICS	***LANGUAGE***
Estimate how much the volume of the pictured subjects is. Give your estimate in millilitres (ml) und cubic centimetres (cm^3).	the estimate to estimate, I estimate The volume **amounts to**.... The body **has** a volume **of** .... One *ml* **is** one cm^3. Two *ml* **are** two cm^3.
A glass of tea 	**Answer:** The tea-glass _____ a volume **of** nearly _________ ml. *You can also say:* The volume of the tea-glass **amounts to** __________ cm^3.
A perfume 	The volume of the perfume bottle _____ ________ ml. The perfume bottle _______ a volume ____ ________ cm^3.
A bottle of mineral water und a cup 	The volume of the water bottle ...... ___________________________________ ___________________________________ ___________________________________ The cup ..... ___________________________________ ___________________________________ ___________________________________

Figure 4: A students' worksheet from the science classes developed by the PROMISE-Team.

Calling teaching material linguistically sensitive implies that it is linguistically modified and simplified in order to support migrant students in understanding the content. Exercises to vocabularies and sentence structures which are typical for a certain topic are implemented and promote the improvement of the students' language skills.

One of the classes developed by the PROMISE-Teams is on "Floating and Sinking" (Tajmel et al. 2007). Figure 4 gives an example of the students' worksheets. The worksheets have two parts: One part for physics, one part for language. The physical part is basically the instruction you find in ordinary lessons without promotion of language. The language part gives explicit linguistic support by providing new vocabularies, adequate prepositions (… the body *has* a volume *of* …), collocations (*to read the meter*) and relevant sentence structures (passive forms like *The body is made of wood.*). New words are explained by the teacher. He or she gives also examples for their contextual use. When working with the worksheet, the students use the new vocabularies in the context of the experiment.

6 Summary and Outcomes

Linguistic and cultural diversity in the science classroom requires linguistic and cultural sensitivity on the part of the teachers. After two years of intensive PROMISE-Teamwork in Germany, Austria, Bosnia-Herzegovina and Turkey, the impact of the teamwork on the teachers' awareness of language and diversity was evaluated by questionnaires and interviews. 75% of the teachers stated that PROMISE has raised their awareness of discrimination in science classes, 82% stated that PROMISE increased their awareness of specific problems of migrants and 73% of the teachers stated that they pay more attention to language now. The teachers reported that the discussion of the science lessons within the PROMISE-Team and with teachers from other countries had an important impact on the reflection and professional development process.

Putting teachers in the students' place has turned out to be an effective method of initializing the process of sensitization and awareness-raising for the linguistic barriers in science classes. It has turned out that interdisciplinary cooperative teams consisting of language and science teachers provide an adequate framework for quality-development processes like the teachers' professional development, the reflection on the teachers' professional actions and the development of linguistically supportive material for teaching and teacher-training. This contribution now closes with the statement from a teacher who was asked about his experience as a member of the PROMISE-Team:

"I have learned that science and language learning have a lot in common: by doing science you have to ask questions, you have to collect data, you have to communicate, you have to solve problems, and you have to make decisions, etc. All those activities are used for developing communication and language learning skills too!"

> The materials for science lessons and teacher training, which are mentioned in this contribution – worksheets on diverse topics, videos of science classes, a video for putting teachers in the students' place – is available on the CD-ROM which comes with this book.

Bibliography

Aikenhead, Glen S., *What is STS Science Teaching?*, in: Solomon, Joan and Aikenhead, Glen S. (eds.), *STS Education: International Perspectives on Reform*, John Wiley & Sons, Toronto, New York, 1994.

Altrichter, Herbert, Posch, Peter and Somekh, Bridget, *Teachers Investigate Their Own Work: An Introduction to the Methods of Action Research*, Routledge, New York, 1993.

Cummins, Jim, *Cognitive/Academic Language Proficiency, Linguistic Interdependence, the Optimum Age Question and Some Other Matters*, Working Papers on Bilingualism, No. 19, 1979, 121-129.

Gibbons, Pauline, *Scaffolding Language Scaffolding Learning: Teaching Second Language Learners in the Mainstream Classroom*, Heinemann, Portsmouth, 2002.

Gogolin, Ingrid, *Bilingualität und die Bildungssprache der Schule*, in: Mecheril, Paul and Quehl, Thomas (eds.), *Die Macht der Sprachen. Englische Perspektiven auf die mehrsprachige Schule*, Waxmann, Münster, 2006.

Koch, Peter and Oesterreicher, Wulf, *Sprache der Nähe – Sprache der Distanz. Mündlichkeit und Schriftlichkeit im Spannungsfeld von Sprachtheorie und Sprachgebrauch*, in: Romanistisches Jahrbuch 36, 1985, 15-43.

Krainer, Konrad, Dörfler, Willibald, Jungwirth, Helga, Kühnelt, Helmut, Rauch, Franz und Stern, Thomas (eds.), *Lernen im Aufbruch: Mathematik und Naturwissenschaften. Pilotprojekt IMST²*, Studienverlag, Innsbruck, 2002.

Lauterbach, Roland, *Praxis Integrierter Naturwissenschaftlicher Grundbildung (PING)*, in: Häußler, Peter (ed.), *Physikunterricht und Menschenbildung*, Institut für Pädagogik der Naturwissenschaften (IPN), Kiel, 1992.

Leisen, Josef (ed.), *Methoden-Handbuch Deutschsprachiger Fachunterricht (DFU)*, Varus-Verlag, Bonn, 1999.

Lewin, Kurt, *Action Research and Minority Problems*, in: Journal of Social Issues (2, 4), 1946, 34-46.

Liebscher, Dierck-Ekkehard, *Cosmology*, in: *Springer Tracts in Modern Physics*, Volume 210, Springer, Berlin/Heidelberg, 2005.

McWilliam, Norah, *What's in a Word? Vocabulary Development in Multilingual Classrooms*, Trentham Books, Stoke on Trent (UK), 1998.

Mohan, Bernard, *Language and Content*, Addison-Wesley, Reading (Mass.), 1986.

Tal, Revital T., Dori, Yehudit J., Keiny, Shoshana, Zoller, Uri, *Assessing Conceptual Change of Teachers Involved in STES Education and Curriculum Development – the STEMS Projekt Approach*, in: International Journal of Science Education (23, 3), 2001, 247-262.

Tajmel, Tanja and Starl, Klaus, *PROMISE – Promotion of Migrants in Science Education*, European Training and Research Centre for Human Rights and Democracy (ETC Graz), Occasional paper No. 18, 2005, available online at: http://www.etc-graz.at/typo3/index.php?id=74 (last checked 15 August 2008).

Tajmel, Tanja, Holtschke, Jörg, Neuwirth, Johannes and Rösch Heidi, *Projekt PROMISE. Sprachförderung im Physikunterricht. Schwimmen – Sinken. Sekundarstufe 1.* Berlin 2007. On the CD-ROM that comes with the book.

Tajmel, Tanja and Schön, Lutz-Helmut, *Internationale Zusammenarbeit zur Förderung von Migrantinnen und Migranten in den Naturwissenschaften – das Projekt PROMISE*, in: Nordmeier, Volkhard and Grötzebauch, Helmut (eds.), *Didaktik der Physik. Beiträge zur Frühjahrstagung der DPG – Berlin 2008*, in preparation.

Tajmel, Tanja, *Unterrichtsentwicklung im Kontext sprachlich-kultureller Heterogenität am Beispiel naturwissenschaftlichen Unterrichts*, in: Fürstenau, Sara and Gomolla, Mechthild (eds.), Migration und schulischer Wandel: Unterrichtsqualität, VS Verlag, Wiesbaden, 2009 (in print).

Tajmel, Tanja, *Bildungssprache im Fach Physik*, in: Gogolin, Ingrid, Michel, Ute and Reich, Hans (eds.), *Herausforderung Bildungssprache*, FörMig Edition, Waxmann, Münster, 2009, in preparation.

Weber, Martina, *Heterogenität im Schulalltag. Konstruktion ethnischer und geschlechtlicher Unterschiede*, Leske + Budrich, Opladen, 2003.

4. The Outlook – Conclusion and Recommendations

Towards Science Education Unlimited – Conclusion and Recommendations

Klaus Starl and Tanja Tajmel

Very briefly we attempt to summarize the statements of the various contributions by formulating recommendations towards all stakeholders involved in science education. As stakeholders we consider decision-makers at all levels, universities, school authorities and school administration, teacher training institutions, teachers, students and their parents, educational scientists, employers' associations and trade unions and all other actors concerned in the one or other way.

The right to education should be taken seriously. In order to promote careers it is an appropriate approach to implement a human rights based education system. It considers a right to science education and therefore supports economic goals as well. As a first step it is recommended to ratify important conventions protecting the right to education. We are convinced that exclusion does not pay.

Obstacles to the enjoyment of the right to education in general and the right to science education in particular should be removed on every occurring occasion. It is furthermore recommended to implement and promote participation of all societal groups in education. We are convinced that paternalist approaches are not sustainable and are at risk to neglect gender and minority perspectives.

Education needs gender – and cultural mainstreaming strategies for the sake of enjoyment of individual rights, particularly the right to be different, but also in order to improve societal results of education. It is important to implement gender- and cultural mainstreaming at all levels of education, from kindergarten to university, as well as from primary school teachers to ministerial administration.

In order to know about compliance with educational standards, to evaluate education policy and its implementation and in order to react appropriately on needs of adjustments, *monitoring and research is recommended.* We are convinced that fact-based policy planning is the appropriate way to achieve equal opportunities in education. Comparative studies on the performance of migrants in science education and scientific careers are needed in order to find out what are the potential barriers and causes for different performance and what are the framework conditions leading to different outcomes. It would be of particular interest to compare pairs of residence/origin-countries with different migration pattern and different political settings, e.g. immigrants to EU member states from third countries; immigrants from EU member states to third countries (Switzerland, Norway); movements between EU member states; different language constellations; different teacher education systems; different institutional school system settings and so on.

In order to fully comply with the requirements of availability, acceptability and adaptability of the right to science education *appropriate efforts in teacher training* should be made. Attempts in harmonization and exchange should be considered and implemented when appropriate.

Implementation of equal opportunities requires necessarily *role models*. The *heterogeneity of the society* should be represented on every level of education and careers. The underrepresentation of a certain group is an alert-signal. School, university, administration, the education system in general, as well as access to the respective labor market need a seriously implemented equality strategy which is compliant with the EU equality directives. The laws and policies related to citizenship, naturalization, and access to the labor market for foreigners should be amended in the light of the improvement of the education system and the access to scientific careers for all instead of exclusionary and protectionist labor market policy. Qualifications need to be mutually recognized.

Text books need to be revised regularly in order to fulfill requirements of changing societies and changing educational requirements.

Language education has to be systematically implemented in every school subject. To enable each individual to successful participation in society, second language acquisition and the acquisition of certain language registers ("Bildungssprache") should be an inherent part of teaching in school.

5. The Practice – Teaching and Teacher Training Material

The Practice – Material for Teaching and Teacher Training (CD-ROM)

Tanja Tajmel and Klaus Starl

The CD-ROM that comes with this book contains material for science lessons and for teacher training. The material consists of videos, worksheets, lesson concepts, teaching units and presentations. It was developed by the PROMISE-Teams and the Clubs Lise of Berlin, Vienna, Istanbul and Sarajevo according to the PROMISE-Workplan (Tajmel and Starl 2005, 29-45) and follows gender and diversity mainstreaming criteria.

1 Workplan – Conception of the Work of the Partners

Project Partner	European Training Centre	Humboldt-Universität zu Berlin	University of Vienna	University of Sarajevo	Yildiz Technical University	Deutsche Gesamt-metall
Focus	Migration, Human Rights and Education	Language in Science Classrooms	Observation of Science Lessons	Club Lise and Astronomy	Role Plays, Alternative Teaching Methods	Support, Networking
	⇩	⇩	⇩	⇩	⇩	⇩
Product	Assessment, gender and diversity mainstreaming	Science lessons with linguistic promotion	Video-scenes of science lessons	Astronomy workshop	Women in science, biographies, role models	Conferences, Publications

2 Material for Science Lessons

- The PROMISE-Lessons "Floating – Sinking" represent a complete teaching unit of 6-8 lessons with worksheets on sinking and floating. In these lessons an explicit focus is placed on language promotion, as well in the lessons "Electric Bell" and "Newton Opticks".

- The "Parachute" lessons, the "Astronomy Workshop" and the "Hands-On Experiments" describe low-cost experiments with a focus on practical and creative work.

3 Material for Teacher Trainings

- The videos V1 and V2 demonstrate the method of *putting teachers in the students' place* or *Prinzip Seitenwechsel* for the purpose of sensitizing teachers to linguistic barriers in science lessons. Teachers themselves are put in the position of students by a teacher trainer and so experience the students' perspective ("Prinzip Seitenwechsel"). The trainer conducts a physical experiment. The teachers are asked to observe the experiment and to put their observation into words. The teachers are asked not to use their native language, but rather a second or foreign language.
- The videos V2-V6 show scenes of science lessons, grades 6-10, in German. The videos were part of the professional development process of the PROMISE-Team members. The background information to the videos consists of short descriptions of the lessons' concepts, information about the school and the teachers' self-reflections. Each video has been transcribed in English and German.

4 Club Lise Material

- The interview with the Turkish physicist Ayşe Erzan was part the work of Club Lise Istanbul on female role models in the natural sciences and was presented together with a power point presentation about female scientists. The power point presentation is a separate file. The interview is in Turkish with English subtitles. The transcription of the interview is in English.
- The Club Lise Show was written and staged by female high school students from grades 10-13, who were members of Club Lise Berlin. The students collaborated in pairs. Each pair has chosen a scientific topic and designed an experiment on this topic. The experiment was part of a 10 minute sketch. The sketches were premiered at the 2nd International Club Lise Meeting 2007 in Sarajevo and have been performed since then on several occasions. The file shows the power point presentation and photos of the Club Lise Show.

5 CD-ROM Operating Instructions

In order to start the CD-ROM and display the video- and PDF-files, an internet-compatible computer with a CD-ROM drive is required. Further, an installed current version of Adobe Reader and an internet browser (Internet Explorer, Firefox, Opera, Safari, or similar) are needed.

The videos are in Flash-format. They are embedded in the html-software installed on the CD-ROM. The CD-ROM should start automatically. The CD-ROM-browser then opens the content page and you can select and open the menu items by clicking on the menu button.

In case the video-files do not open, the current plug-ins for playing the videos might not be installed. In this case please connect your computer with the web and follow the download instructions of the browser.

The Authors

Susanne Baer is professor of Public Law and Gender Studies at the Faculty of Law and Centre for Trans-disciplinary Gender Studies at the Humboldt University of Berlin, director of the GenderKompetenzZentrum, member of the EU Expert Group on Women in Research Decision Making, visiting professor at CEU Budapest; works on comparative constitutionalism, law against discrimination, and socio-cultural legal studies at the Humboldt University, Berlin, Germany.

Veronika Bauer is currently working as a human rights lawyer at the European Training and Research Centre for Human Rights and Democracy at Graz (ETC). She holds an LL.M and a Master Degree in Human Rights and Democratisation and has worked in the areas of anti-discrimination law, internet law and human rights law.

Münire Erden is professor in the Educational Sciences Department in the field of Curriculum and Instruction at the Yildiz Technical University in Istanbul, Turkey. She has published eight books and several articles and has worked on national UNICEF projects in Turkey concerning the improvement of curriculum and instruction. Current research interests of the author are active teaching methods and individual differences.

Seval Fer is associate professor in the Educational Sciences Department in the field of Curriculum and Instruction at the Yildiz Technical University in Istanbul, Turkey. She has published four books, contributed chapters to two books, and published several articles; she has also worked on national and international projects for the Ministry of Education in Turkey concerning curriculum and instruction. Current research interests are social constructivist instructional design, learning and thinking styles.

Stephanie Gilardi held an internship at the ETC Graz while teaching English through an exchange program administered by the Fulbright Commission/Austrian Ministry of Education in 2007-2008. She is an honors graduate of Wellesley College in the class of 2007.

Ingrid Gogolin is professor of Educational Research at the Institute for International Comparative and Intercultural Education at the Hamburg University and president of the European Educational Research Association (EERA). She is scientific advisor for several bilingual school experiments, scientific advisor and spokeswoman for the model program FÖRMIG – Support for Immigrant Minority Children and Youth (www.blk-foermig.uni-hamburg.de) and coordinator of the EERQI – European Educational Research Quality Indicators project (www.eerqi.eu).

Zalkida Hadžibegović, educated in Physics (History and Philosophy of Physics and Astronomy) is assistant professor in the Department of Physics at the University of Sarajevo.

She is a mentor and trainer for talented and gifted high school students and their pedagogical leader for the International Physics Olympiad on behalf of the Bosnian Physical Society. Her research focuses on the history of science and physics education, especially on active learning science.

Barbara Herzog-Punzenberger, trained in social anthropology and political science, is currently focusing her research on migration, settlement and education. For more than a decade she has tried to understand the consequences of societal processes, structures and institutions for immigrants and their descendants, as well as for members of linguistic and other minorities. During the last few years she has been working in the context of the international consortium TIES (www.tiesproject.eu) specializing in a country comparative view on the descendants of immigrants from ex-Yugoslavia and Turkey.

Sybille Krummacher is a scientific staff member at the Research Centre Jülich, Germany, at the staff unit for Corporate Development and External Relations. Born in Frankfurt/Main, Germany; attended highschool in Frankfurt/Germany and was an exchange student in the USA; B.Sc. from American University of Beirut/Lebanon, diploma and Ph.D. from the University of Freiburg/Germany; more than 20 years of basic research in physics in international and interdisciplinary surroundings; study and research periods in France, the USA and Lebanon; active in the promotion of women in science and gender issues; member of the board of the Ada Lovelace Mentoring-Association.

Sarah Kumar is researcher at the European Training and Research Centre for Human Rights and Democracy in Graz. She has collaborated in two UNESCO commissioned studies on the right to education of vulnerable groups and on discrimination in education. She is currently finishing her thesis in international law at the Karl-Franzens-University of Graz.

Sylvia Neuhäuser-Metternich is professor of social competencies, mentoring and gender mainstreaming at the Dortmund University of Applied Sciences and Arts, Department of Information Technology and Electrical Engineering; chair of Ada Lovelace Mentoring-Association, an organization dedicated to motivating young women to choose a career in SEM as well as building a network and strategic alliances with women and men. Educated and trained in psychology at the University of Mainz, Ph.D. at the University of Giessen; author of books on communication in the workforce.

Heidi Rösch is professor of German literature at the University of Education in Karlsruhe, until 2007 she worked at the Technical University of Berlin (http://www.ph-karlsruhe.de/cms/index.php?id=roesch). Her focal points are: German as a second language, intercultural literature and intercultural communication in educational contexts.

Lutz-Helmut Schön is professor of physics education at the Department of Physics at the Humboldt-University of Berlin. He is scientific advisor of several teacher-training and curriculum-development programs and has published several textbooks. The author is founder and head of the "UNILAB-Schülerlabor" in Berlin and was, together with Tanja Tajmel, scientific organizer of the PROMISE project.

Svein Sjøberg is professor of science education at the Oslo University, Norway. His current research interests are social, cultural and ethical aspects of science education, science education and development, and gender and science education in developing countries. He has many international commitments and has won several international awards. He was member of the Advisory Group for the Science and Society action plan of the 6th Framework Programme of the EU. Since 2002 he is organizer of ROSE (The Relevance of Science Education), a comparative project on pupils' interests, attitudes, perceptions etc. and of importance to science teaching and learning. Information and articles at http://folk.uio.no/sveinsj/.

Klaus Starl is senior researcher and executive secretary at the European Training and Research Centre for Human Rights and Democracy in Graz (ETC Graz). He specialises in the fields of non-discrimination, the right to education and local level policy for the implementation of human rights. Klaus Starl cooperates on these issues intensively with UNESCO and the EU. He was coordinating the project PROMISE within the FP 6 of the EU.

Tanja Tajmel, trained in physics education and philosophy, is lecturer for GSL (German as Second Language) in Science Teacher Pre-service Studies in the Department of German Literature at the Humboldt-University of Berlin. She is a trainer of in-service science teachers in schools with cultural and linguistic diversity. Her research focuses on gender and diversity issues in physics education, especially on the integration of language learning methods in physics classes. The author was designer of the PROMISE-Team and the Club Lise and was, together with Lutz-Helmut Schön, scientific administrator of the FP6 project PROMISE.

Christoph T. Wodzinski worked in the field of learning psychology and professional teacher development in physics education at the Leibniz-Institute for Science Education (IPN) in Kiel, Germany.

Rita Wodzinski is professor of physics in primary and secondary education at the University of Kassel in Kassel, Germany.

Disclaimer

promise

promotion of migrants in science education

PROMISE – Promotion of Migrants in Science Education – was a Specific Support Action within the FP6 of the European Commission, Science and Society, Restructuring the European Research Area. The project was a cooperation of 6 partners in Austria, Germany, Bosnia-Herzegovina and Turkey. PROMISE was developed in 2004/05 by Tanja Tajmel, Humboldt Universität zu Berlin, and Klaus Starl, ETC Graz.

From October 2005 until September 2007 the project was implemented by the ETC Graz as the co-ordinating organisation, the Humboldt Universität zu Berlin, Didactics of Physics, as the scientific project leading organisation and University of Vienna, University of Sarajevo, the Yildiz Technical University in Istanbul and the Gesamtverband der deutschen Arbeitgeberverbände der Metall- und Elektroindustrie.

PROMISE was funded by the European Commission, DG Research and co-funded by the Humboldt Universität zu Berlin and the Gesamtmetall Arbeitgeberverband Initiative THINKING.

Judith Bennett, John Holman, Robin Millar and David Waddington (Eds.)

Making a difference

Evaluation as a tool for improving science education

2005, 222 p., pb., 34,00 €
ISBN 3-8309-1508-X

This book is divided in three sections. *Setting the Scene* provides an overview of some of the key issues that have engaged educational researchers and potential "users" of educational research, as regards the evaluation of educational practices.
In the second section of the book, *Examples of curriculum development and evaluation*, we draw on ten examples of science curriculum innovation to illustrate different approaches to evaluation. In each chapter, the authors describe the nature of the innovation and the data that have been collected to evaluate it. They describe what has been learned from these data, and what other workers in science education might learn from them.
In the final section, *Evaluating innovation in science education: Some reflections*, common features in the approaches used to evaluate the programmes are identified.

Peter Nentwig, David Waddington (Eds.)

Making it relevant

Context based learning of science

2005, 360 p., pb., 34,00 €
ISBN 3-8309-1507-1

"Teaching in context" has become an accepted way of teaching science in both primary and secondary schools. The conference organised by IPN and the University of York Science Education Group, *Context-based science curricula*, drew on the experience of over 40 science educators and 10 projects.
Part A of the book consists of two papers on situated learning and on implementation of new curricula. Part B contains descriptions of five major curricula in different countries and evaluation results. Part C gives descriptions of three projects that are of smaller scale and their materials are used as interventions in other more conventional curricula. Part D consists of the summary of some of the findings that came out of the chapters in the earlier parts and looks at the future.

David Waddington, Peter Nentwig, Sascha Schanze (Eds.)

Making it comparable

Standards in science education

2007, 440 p., pb., 38,00 €
ISBN 978-3-8309-1901-8

One of the most significant developments in school education in recent years has been the development and introduction of standards, a subject of considerable controversy. This book is the result of a symposium that was arranged by two leading science education groups, one at IPN (Leibniz Institute for Science Education at the University of Kiel) in Germany and the other at the University of York, UK. The seminar brought together experts from 15 countries. The controversies surrounding standards remain. However, this book gives a succinct and authoritative overall account of the advantages and disadvantages of their introduction taken from the experiences of many countries.

Silke Mikelskis-Seifert, Ute Ringelband, Maja Brückmann (Eds.)

Four Decades of Research in Science Education – from Curriculum Development to Quality Improvement

2008, 272 p., pb., 29,90 €
ISBN 978-3-8309-2018-2

This volume gives an overview of research in science education with the focus on physics education from 1970 to the present. Different approaches to improve physics instruction in schools will be discussed. The first part of this book is dedicated to the curriculum research work and its further development. The second part deals with questions concerning students' understanding and interest as well as research on conceptual change, constructivism, analogies used in physics education and the model of educational reconstruction. In the third part, we will change to the teachers' perspective. In the last decade, teachers' professional development has been seen as one of the most important factors of quality development in schools. Selected aspects of the following programmes will be presented: a Videotape Classroom Study in Germany, the IMST programme (Innovations in Mathematics and Science Teaching) in Austria, the project "Physics in Context", and the programme SINUS (programme for increasing the efficiency of teaching mathematics and the sciences).